Best walks in the South-West

By the same author for Constable

A guide to the Cambrian Way
A guide to the Cleveland Way
A guide to the Cotswold Way
Holding the heights
Best walks in North Wales
Best walks in Southern Wales

Best walks in the South-West

Richard Sale

Constable London

First published in Great Britain 1992
by Constable and Company Limited
3 The Lanchesters
162 Fulham Palace Road
London W6 9ER
Copyright © 1992 Richard Sale
The right of Richard Sale to be identified
as the author of this work has been asserted by him
in accordance with the
Copyright, Designs and Patents Act 1988
ISBN 0 09 470620 4
Set in Times 9 pt by
CentraCet, Cambridge
Printed in Great Britain by
Butler and Tanner Limited, Frome

A CIP catalogue record for this book
is available from the British Library

Contents

Illustrations and maps   7
Acknowledgements   11

Introduction   12
Structure of the book   12
The Walks   15
Maps and mapping   21
Mountain safety and the Country Code   22

The South-West Peninsula   25

The Quantocks   26
   Walk 1 Northern Quantock   27
   Walk 2 Crowcombe and Southern Quantock   34

The Exmoor National Park   42
   Walk 3 Dunster   44
   Walk 4 Dunkery Beacon   55
   Walk 5 The Doone Valley   63
   Walk 6 The Countisbury Cliffs   70
   Walk 7 Watersmeet   76
   Walk 8 Tarr Steps   82

Dartmoor   91
   Walk 9 Merrivale   93
   Walk 10 Haytor   101
   Walk 11 Postbridge and Cranmere Pool   106
   Walk 12 High Willhays   117
   Walk 13 Burrator and the Abbot's Way   124
   Walk 14 Dartmeet   134
   Walk 15 Lydford Gorge   140
   Walk 16 The Teign Valley   149
   Walk 17 Lustleigh Cleave   156

Devon   164
  Walk 18 Baggy Point   164
  Walk 19 Hartland Quay   171
  Walk 20 Torrington   177
  Walk 21 Dartmouth   185
  Walk 22 Slapton Ley   195

Bodmin Moor   205
  Walk 23 The Cheesewring and Kilmar Toor   206
  Walk 24 Brown Willy   215
  Walk 25 Rough Tor   221

Cornwall   229
  Walk 26 Truro   231
  Walk 27 Idless Wood   240
  Walk 28 The Bude Canal   242
  Walk 29 Tintagel   250
  Walk 30 Pentire Point and Port Isaac   261
  Walk 31 Polperro   269
  Walk 32 Lizard Point   276
  Walk 33 Zennor   286
  Walk 34 Men-an-Tol   295
  Walk 35 Chun Castle   307
  Walk 36 Lamorna Cove   310

Isles of Scilly   321
  Walk 37 Tresco   324
  Walk 38 St Mary's   330

Appendices   335
Appendix 1 The Dartmoor ranges   335
Appendix 2 Other walks on the South-West Peninsula   340
Appendix 3 Transport and weather   342
Appendix 4 Useful addresses   342

Index   346

Illustrations

	page
Weacombe	29
The Church House, Crowcombe	38
The Yarn Market, Dunster	51
Cottages near Gallox Bridge	54
Rowberrow from Dunkery Beacon	57
Oare Church	64
Watersmeet	83
Tarr Steps	88
A granite corbel, Swell Tor Siding	95
Haytor	104
Dartmoor ponies	111
The Beehive Hut	114
The Cranmere Pool letterbox	116
Meldon viaduct and the route of Walk 12	123
Nun's (or Siward's) Cross and Nun's Cross Farm ruins	128
The view east from Down Tor	131
The stepping stones at Dartmeet	139
Lydford Castle	146
Castle Drogo gardens	155
Hisley Bridge	158
Lustleigh	163
Woolacombe Bay	165
Slab Cove, Baggy Point	168
The Atlantic coast from Hartland Quay	174
The Torridge valley, Great Torrington	179
Dartmouth Castle	192
Slapton Sands	199
Slapton College	202
The Cheesewring	213
The Jamaica Inn, Bolventor	219
The logan rock on Louden Hill	225
Truro Cathedral	238
Bude Canal	247
The Old Post Office, Tintagel	260
The harbour, Port Isaac	265

The quay at Port Isaac   268
Nearing Polperro on Walk 31   271
Polperro   272
Kilcobben lifeboat station   283
The Wayside Museum, Zennor   290
Ding Dong Mine   304
Lanyon Quoit   306
Chun Castle   309
Guard-dog geese on Walk 36   314
The memorial cross near Lamorna Cove   317
Tresco Abbey gardens   326
Gig racing at St Mary's   331
A Dartmoor range notice board   337

(*Photographs taken by Richard Sale*)

Maps

The South-West Peninsula   16
Walk   1: Northern Quantock   30
Walk   2: Crowcombe and Southern Quantock   36
Walk   3: Dunster   46
Walk   4: Dunkery Beacon   60
Walk   5: The Doone Valley   66
Walk   6: The Countisbury Cliffs   72
Walk   7: Watersmeet   78
Walk   8: Tarr Steps   84
Walk   9: Merrivale   97
Walk 10: Haytor   103
Walk 11: Postbridge and Cranmere Pool   108
Walk 12: High Willhays   118
Walk 13: Burrator and the Abbot's Way   126
Walk 14: Dartmeet   136
Walk 15: Lydford Gorge   142
Walk 16: The Teign Valley   150
Walk 17: Lustleigh Cleave   160
Walk 18: Baggy Point   166
Walk 19: Hartland Quay   173
Walk 20: Torrington   181
Walk 21: Dartmouth   186
Walk 22: Slapton Ley   196
Walk 23: The Cheesewring and Kilmar Tor   208
Walk 24: Brown Willy   216
Walk 25: Rough Tor   222
Walk 26 and 27: Truro and Idless Wood   232
Walk 28: The Bude Canal   244
Walk 29: Tintagel   252
Walk 30: Pentire Point and Port Isaac   262
Walk 31: Polperro   274
Walk 32: Lizard Point   278
Walk 33: Zennor   288
Walks 34 and 35: Men-an-tol and Chun Castle   300
Walks 36: Lamorna Cove   312

Walk 37: Tresco   322
Walk 38: St Mary's   332
The Dartmoor Ranges   338

Acknowledgements

I would like to thank the staff of the libraries of Somerset, Devon and Cornwall for their assistance during the research for parts of this book.

I thank Julie and Tony Mills, Jan and Roger Francis, Mike Rogers and Susan Shorland for their assistance on the routes.

I thank Dave of The Printworks for all his help with the processing and printing of my films.

All photographs in this book were taken with Pentax camera equipment.

Introduction

This new volume of *Best Walks* uses the same selection criteria as were applied in previous volumes in the series. The three dozen routes have therefore been selected to explore the variation of scenery that the South-West Peninsula has to offer: a considerable variation, from sea cliff, through wooded valley to bleak upland moor.

The routes do not concentrate on the National Parks of Exmoor and Dartmoor, though, as might be expected, the Parks do provide a high proportion of the routes, nor do they specifically seek out 'unspoilt' countryside. Rather they seek to explore not only the varied geography of the West Country but the history of man in the area, from the Celtic saints to the smugglers.

Most of the routes are circular. Exceptions occur only where to have 'bent' a route would have affected its character or where a reasonable return route did not exist. In these (two) cases suggestions on transport are made.

Finally, while every effort has been made to produce comprehensive and intelligible descriptions, and to back these up with equally clear maps, it must be emphasized that these should not be seen as anything but a supplement to possession of the maps mentioned at the start of each walk. Should you go off route, for whatever reason, only possession of the correct map will assist you back on to the correct line, or back to your transport.

STRUCTURE OF THE BOOK

Because the area covered by the book is a large one, the walks have not been grouped together by category (see below for a definition of the walk categories) but by area or hill range. To help with a choice of route in the appropriate category, all the walks are given at the end of this section in increasing order of difficulty, i.e. the easiest first, the most difficult last.

Each of the areas or moor ranges is dealt with in a separate chapter, and the introduction to each chapter deals briefly with the particular historical, geographical or geological aspects of the area.

The walks have been divided into three categories, Easy, Intermediate and Difficult, the divisions making allowance not only for the time that a walk takes, but also for the terrain it crosses, and for the amount, and severity, of any climbing it involves. In broad terms, an Easy walk will take about two hours, an Intermediate walk up to twice as long, a good half-day's outing, while a Difficult walk will be, for most people, a long half-day's, or day's outing. As will be seen from the table of walks at the end of this section there are also a handful of walks that lie on the border between the categories. Those that lie between Easy and Intermediate are walks that cover easy ground, but take rather longer than other Easy walks, or ones that take the same time, but cover rather more difficult ground than those of the easier grade. In each case the walk does not really warrant the higher classification. The route that lies between Intermediate and Difficult covers rough ground with few landmarks but is, relatively, short and flat.

The time given to each walk has been calculated using Naismith's Formula, a well-known walking aid, which allows one hour for each 5 map-kilometres (3 map-miles) covered by an unladen walker and adds half an hour for each 300 m (1000 ft) of ascent. For most people this formula will under-estimate the time taken on a walk, and the under-estimation will increase as the time given for a walk increases. The reasons for this are several: firstly, no one will complete a walk in route-march style, but will pause occasionally to admire the view or watch the wildlife and no allowance for these stops has been made; secondly, the formula makes no allowance for the roughness or otherwise of the terrain or for the effects of the weather; thirdly, no allowance has been made for rest stops, and these may be both more frequent and longer on the longer walks; and finally, the formula assumes that the walker can maintain his level of performance indefinitely. While some people can maintain 'Naismith' walking for many hours at a stretch, many, especially those new to moorland walking, tire quickly and find not only that their rest stops increase and become longer but that they cover less ground while they are actually moving.

It is imperative, therefore, that the reader should use the walk-times as a guide only, and that newcomers to the area or to the sport should attempt lower-graded walks initially, and compare their actual performance with the given walk-time in order to gauge how long the more difficult walks will take them.

The Walks

Name/Area/Number	Length in miles	Ascent in feet	Time in hours	Terrain and special difficulties
EASY				
Truro Cornwall (26)	2	165	1	Town walk
St Mary's Isles of Scilly (38)	2	165	1	Paths
Idless Wood Cornwall (27)	2½	200	1	Paths
Torrington North Devon (20)	2	295	1	Paths
Polperro Cornwall (31)	3	305	1¼	Paths and lanes
Chun Castle Cornwall (35)	3½	300	1½	Paths and lanes, one section poorly defined
The Teign Valley Dartmoor (16)	4	500	1½	Paths, one section steep and loose
Hartland Quay North Devon (19)	2¾	600	1½	Paths, cliff section, exposed
Dartmeet Dartmoor (14)	3½	360	1½	Paths, one section undefined, Two sets of stepping-stones. Longer version offered
Men-an-Tol Cornwall (34)	4	230	1¾	Paths and lanes
Lydford Gorge Dartmoor (15)	3½	325	1½	Paths, one slippery section

THE SOUTH-WEST PENINSULA

Figures refer to Walk numbers

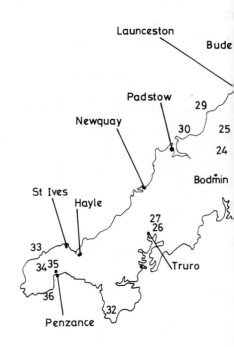

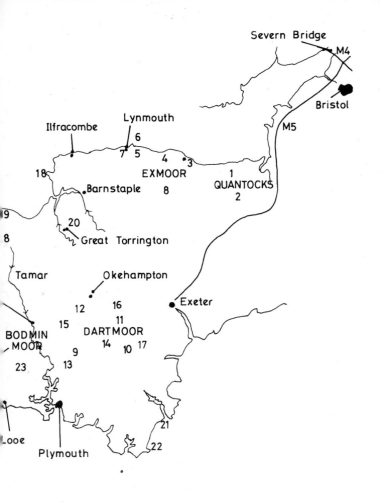

Severn Bridge

M4

Bristol

Ilfracombe

Lynmouth

6

7 5 4 •3

EXMOOR

18

•Barnstaple

8

1 QUANTOCKS

2

M5

19

20

•Great Torrington

8

Tamar

Okehampton

•

12 16

15 11

DARTMOOR

BODMIN

MOOR

14 10 17

23

9

13

Exeter

21

Looe

Plymouth

22

Name/Area/Number	Length in miles	Ascent in feet	Time in hours	Terrain and special difficulties
EASY				
Dunster Exmoor (3)	5	750	2¼	Paths
Watersmeet Exmoor (7)	5	920	2¼	Paths
Tresco Isles of Scilly (37)	6¼	325	2½	Paths
EASY/INTERMEDIATE				
Baggy Point North Devon (18)	4½	330	2	Paths, some indistinct. Longer version offered
Crowcombe and Southern Quantock Quantocks (2)	5½	1300	2½	Paths and lanes
Northern Quantock Quantocks (1)	6½	1300	3	Paths. Shorter version offered
Haytor Dartmoor (10)	3	600	1½	Paths, one section of rough moor
Merrivale Dartmoor (9)	4	300	1½	Paths, two sections of rough boggy moor. Unbridged stream to cross
Lamorna Cove Cornwall (36)	6	500	2¼	Paths and lanes. Cliff section exposed
INTERMEDIATE				
Ancient Penwith Cornwall (34/35)	7½	500	2¾	Paths and lanes, one section poorly defined

Name/Area/Number	Length in miles	Ascent in feet	Time in hours	Terrain and special difficulties
INTERMEDIATE				
The Bude Canal Cornwall (28)	8	330	3	Paths and towpath. One section poorly defined. Cliff section exposed
Slapton Ley South Devon (22)	8	525	3	Paths and shingle
Lustleigh Cleave Dartmoor (17)	7½	1000	3	Paths
Truro and Idless Wood Cornwall (26/27)	9	500	3½	Paths and lanes
Tarr Steps Exmoor (8)	8¾	325	3½	Paths and lanes. Riverside section can be wet
The Quantock Ridge Quantocks (1/2)	8	1000	3½	Paths
Dartmouth South Devon (21)	8	650	3¼	Paths and lanes. Shorter versions offered
The Doone Valley Exmoor (5)	8	650	3	Paths, one section of moor with undefined path
Tintagel Cornwall (29)	7½	500	2¾	Paths. Cliff section exposed
The Countisbury Cliffs Exmoor (6)	8	850	3¾	Paths. One steep ascent

Name/Area/Number	Length in miles	Ascent in feet	Time in hours	Terrain and special difficulties
INTERMEDIATE				
Zennor Cornwall (33)	6	650	2½	Paths, one section poorly defined. Cliff section exposed and rugged
INTERMEDIATE/DIFFICULT				
Brown Willy Bodmin Moor (24)	6¼	820	3½	Rough moor with good landmarks. Longer version offered
DIFFICULT				
Rough Tor Bodmin Moor (25)	7	500	3	Rough moor with good landmarks
The Cheesewring and Kilmar Tor Bodmin Moor (23)	8	820	3½	Paths, and rough moor with good landmarks
Lizard Point Cornwall (32)	8¾	1000	3½	Paths, one section boggy
Dunkery Beacon Exmoor (4)	10	2100	4¾	Paths
Pentire Point and Port Isaac Cornwall (30)	10½	1350	4½	Paths. Cliff sections very exposed
Burrator and the Abbot's Way Dartmoor (13)	10½	1500	4½	Paths and rough moor with indifferent landmarks. Longer version offered

Name/Area/Number	Length in miles	Ascent in feet	Time in hours	Terrain and special difficulties
DIFFICULT				
High Willhays Dartmoor (12)	12½	2000	5¼	Paths and rough moor with good landmarks
Postbridge and Cranmere Pool Dartmoor (11)	16	1150	6	Few paths. Rough moor with indifferent landmarks

MAPS AND MAPPING

The South-West Peninsula is covered by 10 Ordnance Survey 1:50,000 Landranger Sheets: Nos 180 and 181, 190–192 inclusive and 200–204 inclusive. The relevant map for each walk is listed at the start of each route. In addition, Darmoor, South Devon and the Scilly Isles are covered by 1:25,000 Outdoor Leisure Sheets. Again these, or the relevant Pathfinder 1:25,000 Sheet, are listed at the start of each route.

The maps given for each walk use conventional map signs, with the addition of the following:

∞∞∞	Intact wall	G	gate
○ ○ ○	broken wall	KG	kissing gate
+H+	fence or hedge	c	granite cattle grid
s	stile	_.._.._	indistinct path
– – –	distinct path	S	start point
…..	no path	③	feature of interest

Each map has a scale bar. They are drawn from personal observations, and so are not guaranteed to be absolutely to scale. Every effort has been made to ensure accuracy but from time to time fences are erected or, more unusually, taken down. The author would be grateful for any information on such changes so that the book can be kept up to date.

MOUNTAIN SAFETY AND THE COUNTY CODE

Though the moors of the South-West are low in comparison with the mountains of Wales, the Lake District and Scotland, they are real enough to a wet, cold and lost walker. That walker must be prepared for harsh conditions, particularly if he/she is on the moors in winter. All of the moors are close to the sea and are invariably windswept, giving a striking reduction in apparent temperature on the shelterless tops.

These comments are not made to make the hills seem a playground for supermen, or to dissuade anyone from walking on them. It is just that it would be irresponsible not to warn any newcomer to mountain areas of the tricks they can play. Be prepared: if you have not done so already, get a copy of *Safety on Mountains*, a very small booklet from the British Mountaineering Council that tackles the very large subject of individual responsibility and safety.

It is also important that anyone contemplating expeditions into mountainous areas should be able to use a map and compass. If you are not familiar with these critical items, you could do no better than obtain a copy of Kevin Walker's *Mountain Navigation Techniques*, published in the same Constable series as this guidebook.

The majority of the walks in the book follow distinct paths. Please keep to them. The Nationl Parks' only real pollution problem is people, and the cars that bring them. Under the sort of traffic some of the hills receive the laid pavements in towns would groan after a few months. So, if on any of the walks the path is diverted to allow the ground to recover, or if there is a section of constructed pathway, be sympthetic to the problems. Of course it would be better if there were no obvious, scarring paths but the only really successful method of reducing wear to zero would be to ban all walkers.

The Country Code
The Code was prepared by the Countryside Commission with the help and advice of the many organizations concerned with the welfare of the countryside.

Enjoy the country and respect its life and work
Guard against all risk of fire
Fasten all gates
Keep dogs under close control
Keep to public footpaths across all farmland
Use gates and stiles to cross field boundaries
Leave all livestock, machinery and crops alone
Take your litter home
Help to keep all water clean
Protect wildlife, plants and trees
Make no unnecessary noise

The South-West Peninsula

Virtually every area, or even county, of England claims to be the most beautiful, the most historic, the most *English* of them all. For each, in its own way, this is doubtless correct but for many of the visitors who flock to the South-West it is the counties of Cornwall, Devon and Somerset that represent idyllic England – a land of glorious scenery and quaint countryfolk. Cornwall has its sea cliffs, pixies and pasties, Devon its beaches and cream teas, and Somerset its cider orchards and a host of country pubs each filled with locals (yokels?) in smocks drinking scrumpy. For the tourist these generalizations can seem true – the tourist industry regularly goes out of its way to prove them true – but the visitor who gets behind the mask will find much more. Cornwall was the last stronghold of the Celts in England and has a collection of antiquities that is astonishing, set in a countryside that is surprisingly empty. And the Cornish seascapes are probably the finest in England. Devon has further exciting seascapes but also, by contrast, excellent wooded valleys and England's most famous stretch of upland moor – Dartmoor. Devon also has a share of Exmoor, a lower, more walker-friendly moor famous for its association with Lorna Doone. The county that shares Exmoor with Devon is Somerset, which has the Quantocks all to itself.

For the purposes of this book the whole of Somerset is not included; the dividing line between the Peninsula and the rest of England is taken as the M5 motorway. To the west of the M5 there is a 500-mile coastline that offers unrivalled opportunities for the walker. In addition to the two National Parks mentioned above, Dartmoor and Exmoor, there are Cornwall's Bodmin and Penwith Moors. And, to ensure a complete coverage, there are a couple of walks in the Isles of Scilly.

The Quantocks

Following the establishment of ten National Parks in the 1950s it was recognized that there were other areas of England and Wales which, for a variety of reasons – size, population density, etc. – were not suitable for designation as National Parks but were, scenically, outstanding. It was decided, therefore, to designate these as Areas of Outstanding Natural Beauty (AONB) and to provide a degree of protection for their natural habitats and scenic 'highspots' along the lines of those for the Parks. The first AONB to be designated, on 1 January 1957, was the Quantocks.

In the case of the Quantocks the reason that a National Park was not appropriate was size. The 'hills' – something of a misnomer for a raised, dissected plateau that forms a single north–south ridge – are just 20 km (12½ miles) long and barely 5 km (3 miles) wide. This forms a total land area of only 100 sq km (37½ sq miles) which by National Park standards is very small indeed. Within that area there is quite remarkable range of scenery; the result of the rapidly changing geology along the ridge's length. The Quantocks rose from a sea of New Red Sandstone as a geological island of Devonian rocks some 450 million years old. But that island appearance does not mean a homogeneity of rock. In fact there is a rapid variation. To the north are Hangman's Grits (named after their first discovery at Great and Little Hangman in north Devon) and quartzitic sandstones that are hard enough to have merited quarrying for road stone (the quarries are passed on Walk 1). The Grits have resisted erosion, giving a poor, acidic soil so that the northern end of the hills appears as a high, (relatively) barren moor, but drained by narrow stream valleys (combes) in which the vegetation is slightly lusher.

In the middle section the Grits give way to the Ilfracombe Beds, a mixture of sandstone and limestone – rocks which weather more easily and give a more sustaining soil. The vegetation here is both more varied and more plentiful. South again are the Morte shales, geologically the youngest, which are a softer rock weathered down to low, rounded hills with a deep, rich soil. But though these changes sound dramatic they are, in fact, very gradual and the walker who completes the Quantock ridge walk (a continuation of Walks 1 and 2, with a small additional section) could be forgiven for failing to realize that any change had taken place until he was asked to compare the view – both local and afar – at each end of his walk. Then he would recognize that at one end the local view was of short shrubs and windswept moor flowers, with South Wales and Exmoor visible, while at the other end it was of trees – trees thick enough to block out any far views.

As mentioned above, the Quantock ridge is a dissected plateau, with streams draining from the ridge watershed on both sides of the hills. Indeed, the name derives from this geography, stemming from *cantocks* (stream headlands), a name mentioned as early as the 7th century when it appeared (as *cantucudio*) in a charter of the West Saxon King, Centwine. These streams have formed combes that tend to be narrower at the northern end – though this generalization fails when account is taken of stream volume flow, i.e. bigger rivers cut bigger combes than do smaller ones. The combes are an impressive feature of the Quantocks, creating lush, wooded valleys that are a delight for both the plant-seeker and bird-watcher, and in which the patient visitor – particularly one who arrives at dawn or stays until twilight – can see deer. Completing Walk 2 very early one morning, with the dew just starting to rise as a light mist into the dawning sun, I stumbled into a small herd of red deer who were, for a long moment, more curious than afraid. It was a magical moment; I hope you will be as lucky.

Walk 1 Northern Quantock

On the northern end of the Quantocks the views include moor and sea, the combination that makes nearby Exmoor such a fine National Park. This walk visits the best of the viewpoints, together with a couple of beautiful, typically Quantock, combes. For a combination of Walks 1 and 2 see p. 41.

Walk category : Easy/Intermediate (3 hours or 2¼ hours if West
                 Quantoxhead is not visited)

Length : 10½ kms (6½ miles) – 8 kms (5 miles) if West
          Quantoxhead is not visited

Ascent : 400 m (1300 ft) – 300 m (1000 ft) if West Quantoxhead is
          not visited

Maps : Landranger Sheet 181, Pathfinder Sheet ST 04/14

Starting and finishing point : The car-park at 117 411. This car-
park is presently unmarked and is reached by taking the Bicknoller
road out of West Quantoxhead (first left after the Windmill Inn
when going west, i.e. towards Williton/Minehead) and then first
left again, up past the Staple plantation.

From the corner of the car-park take the path going south-west to
Weacombe. The path goes down through the Staple plantation to
join the seemingly over-named Weacombe Combe. Go left on the
path up the combe, a wider and less steep combe than is the
Quantock norm. Follow the path to Bicknoller Post, a parish
boundary marker. The village of Bicknoller is named for the beech
trees, which grow so beautifully locally. Ignore the crossing main
track that links the high points of the Quantock ridge and go
south-east on the path into Sheppard's Combe. Follow the path
that goes between the wooded escarpment of Lady's Edge and the
Black Ball wood for 2 kms (1¼ miles), entering Hodder's Combe,
one of Quantock's most famous combes, a tight valley filled with
superb oak trees. Hodder's Combe is formed around a stream
which is itself formed from the combined flows of streams down
Sheppard's, Slaughterhouse and Somerton Combes. Where this
stream performs a noticeable S-bend, use the ford to reach the left
bank and a path that climbs steeply up through the woods to open
ground (see (1) Viewpoint).

Weacombe

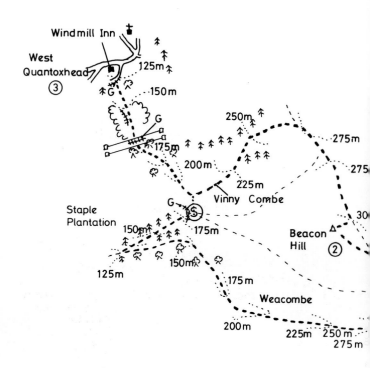

Windmill Inn

West
Quantoxhead
③

125m

150m

250m

275m

275

250m

225m

200m

175m

150m

G

Staple
Plantation

150m

G

125m

150m

175m

Vinny Combe

Beacon
Hill
②

30

175m

Weacombe

200m

225m 250m
275m

WALK 1   NORTHERN QUANTOCK

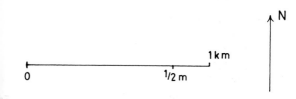

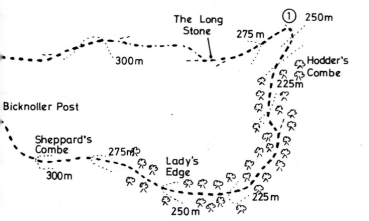

Longstone Hill

1 km

1/2 m

0

N

The Long
Stone

1 250m

275 m

300m

Hodder's
Combe

225m

Bicknoller Post

Sheppard's
Combe

275m

Lady's
Edge

300m

225m

250 m

When a clump of fir trees, planted in 1946 as a memorial to local men who had died in the 1939–45 War, comes into view, take a leftward (south-east) track that rises up the ridge of Longstone Hill. The Long Stone of the name, a standing stone of indeterminate age, is reached by taking the right fork at a Y-junction. Just beyond the Stone leave the track for a path to the right that leads directly to the Great Road, as the track from West Quantoxhead to Holford is somewhat exaggeratedly called.

At a track junction go north-west towards Beacon Hill (see (2) Beacon Hill). From the summit go back on to the main track and continue north, ignoring a path that goes south of the Vinny Combe plantation to reach one that goes north of it, edging it to reach Vinny Combe itself. As the stream in the combe swings right look for a steep break among the rhododendrons on the far bank and take it back to the car-park.

To extend the walk, do not take that path, but continue along the track by the stream, going under the power lines and through the (fenced off) disused quarry to emerge at the Windmill Inn in West Quantoxhead (see (3) West Quantoxhead). To return to the car-park retrace this route.

(1) *Viewpoint*

From here the view north-east extends to the Mendips, with Glastonbury Tor rising like a fantasy cone above the Somerset Levels, one of Britain's finest wetlands. But the view is dominated by Dowsborough, the high, tree-topped hill to the south-east, on the summit of which the lines of the superbly sited Iron Age hill fort can still be traced. An alternative local name for the hill fort, Danesborough, derives from a time when Viking raiders landed on the Somerset coast near Combwich. One story tells of these Danes coming inland to shelter in the fort. From here they were lured by local women to the cottages at the hill's foot and murdered one at a time. One young local fell in love with her Viking, a handsome young lad who played the harp, and hid him when the murderers arrived. A few days later he was discovered and killed; today his ghost haunts the hill fort where his harp can still be heard.

In the 19th century the area at the foot of Dowsborough became popular with the great poets of the age. Samuel Taylor Coleridge wrote the *Rime of the Ancient Mariner* in Nether Stowey – where the pub is called (but you've guessed!) the Ancient Mariner – and William and Dorothy Wordsworth stayed in Alfoxton, only to be moved on by the locals when their habit of taking walks at night convinced the neighbourhood they were French spies. (As an aside, the same thing happened to D. H. Lawrence – at a later time and in Cornwall – see note (3) of Walk 33.) Wordsworth knew of the story of the ghostly Dane who 'warbles songs of war/ That seem like songs of love'.

If ghosts interest you, you may also like to visit Walford's Gibbet, on the side of Dowsborough. Here hung the body of John Walford, executed for the murder of his simpleton wife whom he had been forced to marry despite his love for another village girl. His true love knelt beside the scaffold at his hanging. Dead Woman's Ditch, at 161 381, is said to derive its name from this murder.

Returning to the theme of Viking raiders, Hodder's Combe derives its name from Odda, a Saxon general of King Alfred who camped here while preparing to do battle with another raiding party. It is said that he lit a beacon fire on Longstone Hill, which is possible because it is actually a little higher than the neighbouring peak of Beacon Hill, which is more obviously named for such a fire.

(2) *Beacon Hill*
Though only just topping the 1000-ft contour at 302 m (1019 ft) high, Beacon Hill is a superb vantage point. Northward are the Welsh hills, while to the west are the moors of the Exmoor National Park. Dominating the coast below are the reactors of the Hinkley Point nuclear power stations. The two blue cubes are the older, Magnox, 'A' station; the grey building to the right is the newer Advance Gas-Cooled Reactor (AGR) station.

(3) *West Quantoxhead*
This straggling village is interesting mostly for its fine church and for having two names. The second name, St Audries, must be

from the church, you assume, so it comes as a surprise to discover that it is dedicated to St Etheldreda. The answer to this puzzle lies inside, after you have negotiated the delicate, delightful wrought iron gateway over which a fragile light seems likely to collapse and decapitate all who enter. St Etheldreda and St Audrey are the same person – the 7th-century Queen of Northumbria who became the first Abbess of Ely and died in 679. It seems odd that an eastern Saxon noblewoman should be associated with a Somerset church. Odder still is that the Queen's early liking for cheap jewellery – before she renounced materialism for a spiritual life (changing a bad habit for a nun's habit as it were) – gave us the word 'tawdry'.

   The church was built in 1856 of Somerset stone with an English oak roof, though some items from an older building were incorporated. The font is Norman, while two of the church's five bells are dated 1440. The organ is a working Kilton barrel organ, built in London in 1782 and originally installed in Kilve church. It is the only one in Somerset that is still playable. Beside the organ look for the plan of the village dated 1817. One of the cottages was owned, or at least occupied, by 'Evans near the Church (Waterman)'. Delightful.

Walk 2 Crowcombe and Southern Quantock

This walk visits the southern end of the long Quantock ridge, dropping down off the ridge to Crowcombe, one of the most interesting of the hill base villages. For a combination of Walks 1 and 2 see p. 41.

Walk category : Easy/Intermediate (2½ hours)

Length : 9 km (5½ miles)

Ascent : 400 m (1300 ft)

Maps : Landranger Sheet 181, Pathfinder Sheet 1236 (ST 03/13)

Starting and finishing point : At (140 366) the car-park behind
Church House, Crowcombe

From the car-park go through the gap beside Church House to the
village road. Opposite is the church; to the left and about 100 m
away is the cross (see (1) Crowcombe). Go right, and first left on
the only road that crosses the Quantock ridge. Follow this, bearing
left once, up Crowcombe Combe – as with Weacombe Combe on
Walk 1 this name seems a bit overdone – to reach the ridge track
at Crowcombe Combe Gate. Go right, along the ridge track which
goes over the high point of West Hill and then along the flank of
Great Hill. This ridge path is the old Drove Road and passes some
superb beech trees: it is, perhaps, the best section of walking on
the Quantocks.

Ignore tracks to the right that go down Triscombe Combe and
also a crossing road that is drivable to the east but not to the west
where it passes the huge scar of Triscombe Quarry. At the road's
end to the left is a car-park in which stands the easily missed
Triscombe Stone (see (2) Triscombe Stone). Beyond the stone the
old Drove Road is known as Alfred's Road (see (3) Alfred's
Road) but we leave it soon on a path going half right and directly
to the top of Will's Neck (see (4) Will's Neck).

From the summit go just north of west down the elegant ridge to
reach the narrow belt of trees at the base of the hill. Go through
them to the road near Triscombe. Go right, then left past the Blue
Ball Inn. Take the lane to the right and, after 100 m or so, go right
again up a track. Beyond a gate the obvious way is ahead but we
bear left on a path that goes through woodland. Pheasants are fed
here which makes the autumn walker feel like the Pied Piper.
Cross a fence, by way of a gate cunningly placed behind a tree, to
emerge on the lower slopes of Grant Hill. Follow the path to
where it joins a track going up Little Quantock Combe. Go left on
the combe track to reach a road. Go right and bear right after
200 m. Follow the road back to Crowcombe.

(1) *Crowcombe*
The first house in Crowcombe reached on the walk is also the most

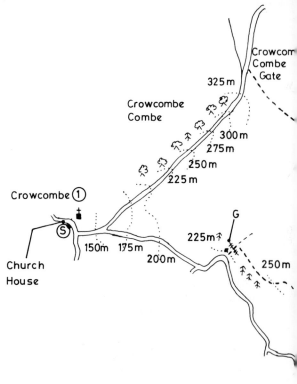

Crowcombe ①

Church
House

325 m

Crowcom
Combe
Gate

Crowcombe
Combe

300 m
275 m
250 m
225 m

150m   175m   200m

225m

G

250 m

WALK 2   CROWCOMBE AND
SOUTHERN QUANTOCK

Triscombe

Blue Ball
Inn

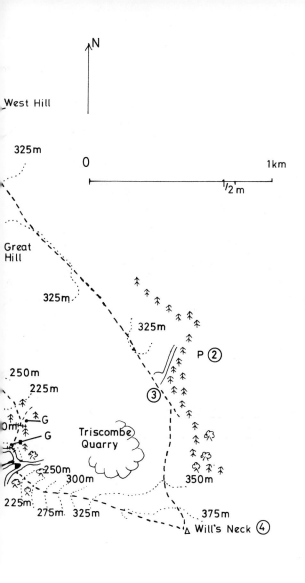

N

West Hill

325m

0   1km

½ m

Great
Hill

325m

325m

P ②

250m

225m

G

0m

G

Triscombe
Quarry

250m

300m

350m

225m

275m   325m

375m

△ Will's Neck ④

interesting: the Church House. This was certainly in existence by the early years of the 16th century and is probably late 15th-century. It is a simple construction on two floors. The upper floor is reached by an external stairway, the stone steps of which have centres hollowed out by the tramping of countless feet. Church houses, sometimes call church-ale houses, were built as village halls and the villagers used them for social gatherings at certain times of the year – saint's days, fair days, etc. – at which food and drink were available. All profits went to the upkeep of the church – hence church-ale. In the absence of shops the house was also used by travelling salesmen who showed off their goods under a dry roof. Though most villages had such houses very few now survive; indeed the only other one in Somerset is at Chew Magna, many miles to the north and now – by a decree best ignored – part of Avon. Crowcombe is lucky its own house survived for, having served for over a century as schoolroom above and poor house below, it was abandoned in the late 19th century and only rescued from near terminal decay during this century.

The Church of the Holy Ghost across from the house has a fine 14th-century tower that was once completed by a 24-m (80-ft) spire which was destroyed by lightning in 1725. The top section is preserved in the churchyard – near the east window. The tower is older than the rest of the church, the south aisle of which was described by Pevsner as the finest Late Perpendicular building in Somerset. Elsewhere, the font is late 14th-century and the pew ends are beautifully worked. The absence of stained glass is surprising but does offer an unusual, for a church, view of the wooded hills behind. In the churchyard, besides the spire top, there is an old preaching cross with sculpted figures. The cross's top is neither original nor as good. Beside the church is Crowcombe Court, originally built in the early 18th century and now a residential senior citizens' home. A few hundred metres or so to the west of the church is the 13th-century Crowcombe Market Cross. Its steps were once used as market stalls, and show signs of considerable wear.

The Church House, Crowcombe

(2) *Triscombe Stone*

It is easy to miss the stone as it is only about 0.6 m (just over 2 ft) high. There are several stories told about it, all revolving around its use by the Devil as a mustering-point for the Yeth Hounds, hounds of death who hunted the Quantocks. The hounds are accompanied by ghostly riders who ride at breakneck speed. To see, or even to hear, the hounds could mean death and, as they were thought to ride on moonless and stormy nights, the locals would walk miles in order to avoid the stone on such nights. Surprisingly, the locals also believed that it was a wishing-stone and would visit in daytime to sit on it and make a wish. The real purpose for erecting the stone here is unknown.

(3) *Alfred's Road*

In days before refrigeration and lorries, meat had to be delivered on the hoof and the animals were herded by drovers along drove roads. The Quantock ridge was such a road. The drovers herded not only cows and sheep, as would be expected, but pigs and even turkeys – the latter having their feet dipped in pitch to harden them for the journey. The name Alfred's Road is given to the drove road section south of Triscombe Stone, though the reason is far from clear. Before the time of Alfred, the Saxons controlled the area, though perhaps the ridge was followed by the king when he marched against an invading Viking army (see Note (1) of Walk 1). Alternatively, in keeping with the supernatural qualities of Triscombe Stone, the ridgeway could have been the *alferode*, the elf's road.

(4) *Will's Neck*

Will's Neck is the highest point on the Quantocks at 384 m (1260 ft) and is a fine viewpoint. On a good day the Mendips, Brecon Beacons, Exmoor and Dartmoor can all be seen, as can Pilsden Pen, Dorset's highest peak. The name is Saxon and has nothing to do with anyone called Will. To the Saxons all non-Saxons were the same: they called them *wallas*, which just means foreigners, a term they derived from their first meeting with a Celtic tribe, the Velcae. This word has given us Wales – the land of the foreigners according to the Saxons – and also the Vlachs in Romania, Valais in Switzerland and the Walloons in Belgium. It also gives us 'Will' here.

Walk 1/2 The Quantock Ridge

This is the real Quantock walk, a full traverse of the ridge. But unless a double traverse is planned – a long but worthwhile trip – two cars are needed. The first will be left as for the start of Walk 1; the second at the Lydeard Hill car-park.

Walk category : Intermediate (3½ hours)

Length : 13 km (8 miles)

Ascent : 300 m (1000 ft)

Maps : Landranger Sheet 181, Pathfinder Sheets as for Walks 1 and 2

Start and finishing points : Start as for Walk 1; finish at (181 838) the car-park on the southern flank of Lydeard Hill

Reverse Walk 1 to Beacon Hill and take the main ridge track to Bicknoller Post. Continue on the ridge path to join Walk 2 above Crowcombe. Follow Walk 2 to Will's Neck. From there take the track going south-east to the corner of a wood (Bagborough plantation). Walk along the northern edge of the wood to a gate and stile. Beyond, take the path that goes down the southern 'ridge' to reach the car-park through a gate.

The Exmoor National Park

Of all the National Parks of England and Wales, Exmoor has the greatest range of natural scenery. While it has none of the rugged grandeur of the mountains of Snowdonia or the Lake District, the bleak upland moors of Dartmoor or such an extent or range of sea cliff as the Pembrokeshire Coastal Park, Exmoor has a little of all of them and a bit more besides. Its 680 sq kms (265 sq miles) extend over both Somerset and Devon – though it includes more of the former county – stretching along the Bristol Channel coast from near Minehead to Combe Martin and as far south as Dulverton. The Park's upland is divided into two sections by the River Exe, which gives the moor its name, and by its tributary, the Quarm, with the Brendon Hills (not to be confused with Brendon Common, which lies in Doone country to the west) to the east and the main Exmoor plateau to the west. On its north-eastern edge Exmoor falls into gentle, wooded country studded with villages that are as beautiful as the scenery in which they are set, villages such as Selworthy and Dunster, to name but two. One of our walks starts in Dunster village.

Underlying Exmoor are rocks of the Devonian era, sandstones and grits. These hard, resistant rocks yield a poor, acidic soil that drains badly and supports a very limited vegetation. In the valleys that drain down from the moor the soil is a little better and overlies a sub-soil that is more clayey. This better drained, more nutrient-rich soil supports a greater range and growth of vegetation, making the river valleys, themselves more sheltered to give a better growing environment, greener and more lush, a real delight to the eye. In the valleys are the predominant tree but there are also stands of beech and ash as well as other, less numerous, species. Our walks take us to Watersmeet and Tarr Steps, each of which lie in good valleys. We also visit the Doone Valley on a walk that combines the lushness of the valleys with the bleakness of the moor. Another walk also combines the two features, taking in the superb valley of Horner Water and the moor's highest point, Dunkery Beacon.

On the high moor the vegetation is chiefly heather – ling and bell heather – with clumps of bilberry (known locally as whortleberry). The former offers tough walking – discouraged by the Park Authority and the National Trust, who own great tracts of the moor, in favour of walking on heather-free paths – but a glorious purple show when it blossoms. Here the animal life is limited: a few Exmoor ponies and, but rarely, deer. The latter, the native red deer together with introduced herds of roe, fallow and sika are mainly encountered in the wooded valleys. The red deer is still hunted by stag hounds on the moor, a pursuit that has given rise to a great deal of criticism of late, especially as much of the hunting takes place on National Trust land. It is generally agreed that a cull of the deer population is necessary in the absence of a natural predator (there has been no suggestion that the re-introduction of wolves would be a move calculated to meet with universal approval) but it is the nature of the cull that divides people. Is it acceptable in a caring, civilized society that an animal as magnificent as a red deer stag should be hunted to exhaustion and unpleasant death in order to provide an afternoon's recreation for a very few people? Arguments on the history of Exmoor as a Royal Forest (i.e. hunting ground) hold no water: in England today there is no need to employ such methods of killing to secure meat. The reader will have gathered on which side of the fence I stand and perhaps the matter should rest there.

Moorland birds are not abundant, despite the fact that over 200 species have been noted within the park's boundaries, but the buzzard is frequently seen, working the thermals of the up-slopes searching for a meal. The bird-watcher will choose the wooded valleys rather than the moor if he is after variety, and he will doubtless travel north to the coast to complete his survey, for there, with the moor still visible behind him, he can add razorbills to a list that may also include stonechat, dipper and kingfisher. And if he travels to the cliffs near Countisbury, as we do on Walk 6, he may also see, on the Glenthorne cliffs, the rare silver ragwort, rarest of over 900 species of flowers growing in the park.

Man is known to have lived on Exmoor since Mesolithic (Middle Stone Age) times, that is for about the last 8000 years, and may have been there even earlier. It was not until the Neolithic (New

Stone) Age that he left a tangible imprint on the landscape: on
Exmoor there are few Neolithic remains, though Bronze Age sites
are more abundant. Walk 5 passes several Bronze Age burial sites.
Walk 3 moves closer to our times by a millennium when it passes
through the Iron Age hill fort of Bat's Castle, while Dunster
Castle, on the same route, brings us forward by one more
millennium. The Doone Valley (Walk 5) was made famous by
events in the Middle Ages, while the Lynmouth flood (Lynmouth
is the start of Walk 7) brings us to a date within living memory.

Walk 3 Dunster

There are many villages in England that claim to be the prettiest in
the realm, or the archetypal version. Either description requires a
judgement, so they are both ultimately matters of opinion. I will
state mine, therefore, claiming that while some villages may be
prettier than Dunster few can measure up to its claim to be the
typical English village. All the ingredients are here: a fine castle,
well set above delightful cottages; an interesting church; and old
market house in the centre; an old mill on a stream that runs
under an elegant pack-horse bridge; superb surrounding country
with lots of trees; and a hill fort to further enhance the sense of
history. And, as if further recognition was needed, it also has
yards of yellow lines to keep the inevitable stream of cars at bay.

Walk category : Easy (2¼ hours)

Length : 8 km (5 miles)

Ascent : 230 m (750 ft)

Maps : Landranger Sheet 181, Pathfinder Sheet 1215 (SS84/94)

Starting and finishing point : The car-park at 992 439 to the left of
the road into Dunster from the north.
There is another car-park closer to
Gallox Bridge but use of that means
you may miss out on a walk through
the village.

Even before the walk starts the visitor will have noticed the Tower (see (1) Conygar Tower) on the hill above the north end of the village. The walk does not approach it, but goes left from the car-park and down High Street (see (2) Dunster). To the right is the Yarn Market (see (3) the Yarn Market), while about half-way down and also to the right is the Dunster Doll Museum. At the bottom of High Street the castle is straight ahead (see (4) Dunster Castle). Go right into Church Street passing, to the right, the beautiful old Nunnery (see (5) the Nunnery). Next to the right are the village gardens, originally part of Dunster's Benedictine Priory but bought by the villagers in 1980. Opposite the gardens is Harwood's clock and watch shop. It is now accepted that John Harwood patented the first automatic (self-winding) watch in 1924, in Switzerland. Next to the right is the church (see (6) St George's church), with, to the right beyond it, the Dovecote and Butter Cross (see also note (2)).

Bear left into West Street. A signed turning to the left (Mill Lane) leads to the mill (see (7) Dunster Mill) but our walk takes the next lane to the left (Park Street) down to Gallox Bridge (see (8) Gallox Bridge) beyond a fine row of thatched cottages. Go over the pedestrian-only bridge, pass more cottages and, at the path junction beyond, go over the stile to the left (signed for Carhampton) on a rising path through the deer park (see also note (2)). The path reaches a broad track. Go right (signed for Withycombe) passing a line of beech trees, to the right, known as King's Hedge (see (9) King's Hedge). After about 800 m (½ mile) there is a gate in a wall to the right. Go through and take a path that goes over Bat's Castle to reach Gallox Hill (see (10) Bat's Castle and Gallox Hill). A detour is needed to explore the second hill's summit, the path going across the right flank of the hill to reach woodland. At a fence with a gate go left, then almost immediately right through a gap to reach a path. Go left, then right on to a waymarked track. To the left soon is Black Ball, from where there is an excellent view over the River Avill – that flows under Gallox Bridge – and Grabbist Hill. Follow the track – it is part of an old coach road, one that due to lack of funds never got past Black Ball – to Gallox Bridge. To reach the start, reverse the outwards route through Dunster.

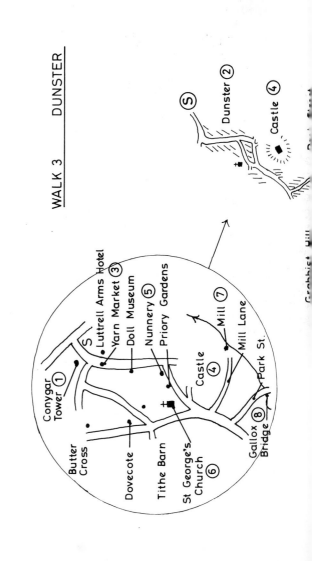

WALK 3   DUNSTER

Ⓢ

Dunster ②

Castle ④

Park Street

Conygar Tower ①
Luttrell Arms Hotel
Yarn Market ③
Doll Museum
Nunnery ⑤
Priory Gardens
Ⓢ
Butter Cross
Dovecote
Tithe Barn
St George's Church ⑥
Castle ④
Mill ⑦
Mill Lane
Gallox Bridge ⑧
Park St.

Grabbist Hill

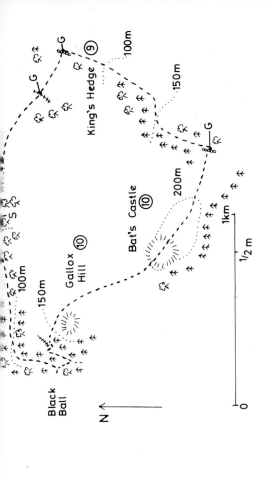

(1) *Conygar Tower*

The tower was built by a member of Dunster's Luttrell family in 1776 for the mighty sum of £192. It is named from the hill on which it stands and is a folly in the grand style, having been built for no better reason than to create a landmark. A local tale maintains that a subterranean passage links the tower and the castle. If that is so it is a very long tunnel.

(2) *Dunster*

Dunster is mentioned in the Domesday Book, though only as *Torre* – from the tor on top of the hill now topped by the castle. The addition to the name was probably derived from a corruption of the name de Mohun, the first Norman lords of the area. The de Mohun family built a keep on the hill, replacing an earlier, Saxon building, but in the 14th century they sold the estate to the Luttrells who have held it ever since. The Luttrells were responsible not only for the castle but also for the deer park through which the walk passes. The park – laid out in 1755 – was recreational (it was extensively and delightfully landscaped) but it also provided the castle with a ready supply of fresh venison. Deer can still be seen in the park though, as it is no longer bounded, they are much rarer. Interestingly, the first English book on hunting, *The Master of Game*, was written by Edward, Duke of York, a grandson of Edward III who was married to a de Mohun from Dunster Castle. Perhaps the duke had hunted locally before he sat down, around 1410, to write his work.

As befits a village that is such an epitome of Englishness, Dunster also had its monastic house, a Benedictine priory. Curiously the parish church of that time – from the late 12th century onwards – was actually shared between the village folk and the monks (who had the eastern half which was separated off from the western half). The priory was small, only a prior and three monks, and was dissolved in 1536. Of the priory itself there remains little that is substantial, though there are some interesting outbuildings. Part of the monks' quarters form a section of one Dunster house, and the tithe barn – a fine building behind the church – still stands, as does the dovecote. This charming round building with a conical slate roof, topped by what for all the world is an up-market bird-table, held 500 pairs of doves, a number which must have kept four monks very well fed. The dovecote stands close to the tithe barn and on the road to the Butter Cross, a medieval cross shaft. This may have been the original village market cross. One story suggests it was moved here when plague was rife, so as to act as a point of sale where farmers could leave goods in exchange for villagers' cash, without the two set of folk ever coming within reach of other.

Elsewhere, apart from visiting the sites mentioned in the other notes, the visitor is best left to wander, especially in the High Street which is delightful because of, rather than in spite of, its lack of plan.

(3) *The Yarn Market*

This wonderful building was built in the first years of the 17th century by a member of the Luttrell family as a market for cloth when the village was a centre for the local wool trade. The village was especially famous for the manufacture of cloth known as 'Dunster'. The market was damaged in the Civil War action of 1647 and some roofing timber still shows the impact of a cannonball..The restoration is noted on the weather vane, which is marked 'GL1647'. GL stands for George Luttrell.

Opposite the market is the Luttrell Arms Hotel, built for the Abbot of Cleeve Abbey but taken over by the Luttrell family in 1499.

(4) *Dunster Castle*

An inscription above the fireplace in the Great Hall of the castle expands on the Domesday Book entry for Dunster. It states that the first castle on the hill here was built by Aluric, a Saxon, in the time of Edward the Confessor. There is, however, a legend that an earlier Celtic fort stood here and was used by the Celtic saint Carantoc to exhibit a dragon that he had charmed from the sea on the orders of Arthur. Aluric's castle was supplanted by de Mohun's fortress in 1070. Of that first Norman building only a tower and part of a curtain wall remain, though there are other sections of the building that represent additions from the 13th century. One addition was the gatehouse, a formidable structure, one tower of which was known to have been used as a dungeon even before the discovery in 1869 of the skeleton of a seven-foot man who had been manacled to a wall with iron bands on his feet, hands and neck, and then walled up to die. The castle saw service during the war of Stephen and Matilda, when it was held for the Queen and successfully saw off a siege, and again during the Civil War when it was twice besieged. At first it was held for Parliament and withstood a Royalist siege in 1642 before the Luttrells changed sides in 1643. In 1645 it was besieged again, this time by Parliament. The siege lasted for six months, until long after all other West Country castles had surrendered and the King's cause was hopeless. Then near starvation caused the castle garrison to surrender, though they found the strength to march out with honour. Acknowledging the castle's great strength as a fortress, Cromwell had the castle slighted, a semi-demolition that included the razing of the original Normal keep. As an aside, the siege gave English military history one of its most bizarre moments. At one stage a Royalist ship sailed towards Dunster from Wales loaded with supplies meant to help break the siege. The ship put in locally but the crew were surprised by a really low tide and were left beached on the mud. At that stage a force of Parliamentarian cavalry arrived and attacked the ship, boarding and taking it. This incident is the only known record of cavalry defeating a man-of-war!

Between the war of Stephen and Matilda and the Civil War the castle had been extensively re-modelled, in Elizabethan times, with the domestic elements taking great precedence over the military elements. Then in Victorian times the whole building was re-structured by the architect Salvin to whom we owe the glorious views of the castle from a distance – most specifically from the deer park on the walk and from a lay-by on the A39 just to the east of the village, but also along the length of the High Street.

Inside, the castle is a fine mix of Elizabethan and later work,

The Yarn Market, Dunster

with wood panelling and plaster ceilings and, in the Leather Gallery, some remarkable leather 'tapestries'. One room was used by the Prince of Wales, later Charles II, during a stay in 1645 when the Civil War was going badly for his father.

Equally good are the castle gardens which include, among the more unusual plants, orange and lemon trees, camellias and magnolias. The site of the old Norman keep is now a bowling green.

(5) *The Nunnery*

This superb, triple-storeyed, double-overhung building is emphatically called the Nunnery despite its never having been so. Indeed there was never a house of nuns in Dunster. In fact the house was built in the mid 14th century as a guest house for Cleeve Abbey. It seems that only in the 17th century did the name 'the Old Nunnery' come to be applied to the building.

The overhangs are excellent: the slated frontages of the upper storeys are known as fish-scaling or pan-tiling, the latter a name that has come down to us as a type of roof tile.

(6) *St George's Church*

It is not known if Dunster had a Saxon church but it certainly had an early Norman one because records exist of the dispute that arose between the vicar and the prior over times of service and use of bells. The dispute over the bells was brought to a head when the villagers removed the bell ropes so that the monks could not toll them. The incensed prior wrote that 'to fulfill and satifie theire croked appetites, thei take up the bell roopis and said that the Priour and convent there should have no bellis there to ryng'. The dispute was taken to Glastonbury where an unsatisfactory decision was reached that the building should be divided into two. That decision has left us one of the longest rood screens in Britain, over 16 m (50 ft) long and massively constructed. The screen was built locally and erected in 1499. In its original form it supported a rood, or cross, that was three-figured.

By the time the screen was erected the original Norman church had been almost entirely rebuilt. The tower was rebuilt in 1443, with the nave and eastern section being remodelled in 1450 and the remainder in the decades that followed. Today, apart from a few small sections – chiefly the much-restored west door and some pillars – everything is 15th-century. The font is 16th-century, although the elegant cover is much later – probably 19th-century. The pews were carved in 1876 when there was a general, but tasteful, restoration. They are noteable for their wood carving, with no two being the same.

The church holds several monuments to members of the Luttrell family but the most interesting memorial is the cover slab from the grave of Adam of Cheddar, Dunster's Prior in the mid 14th century.

(7) *Dunster Mill*

The Domesday Book notes the existence of two mills in Dunster and it is thought likely that this is one of them – not the actual one but on the same site. Despite the history of the town's involvement in the wool trade this was a grist mill, for grinding wheat to flour.

The building the visitor sees is thought to be late 17th-century but had fallen into disrepair when it was acquired by the National Trust – as part of the castle estate – and needed extensive work by the present mill operator to make it serviceable. Today it is in full working order, with grinding taking place several times weekly. All the machinery and the process is fully explained to the visitor at this most fascinating site. Power to the mill is from two sequential overshot waterwheels fed from the River Avill. Overshot means the water is fed to the top of the wheel so the wheel rotates in the direction of water flow (in an undershot wheel it rotates against the flow). Dunster Mill is unusal in having two wheels, and the water feed allows one or other, or both, wheels to be used.

(8) *Gallox Bridge*

Gallox is a medieval pack-horse bridge whose name is believed to be a corruption of gallows and is called after the hill to the south – which is on the walk. Until Tudor times the bridge was known as Doddebridge, implying a mid 16th-century use of the hills for

execution, although one local legend suggests a later time, claiming that the gallows was first used during Judge Jeffery's Bloody Assize that followed the Monmouth rebellion. The Monmouth uprising, which reached such a final and bloody conclusion at Sedgemoor just the other side of the Quantocks, was a West Country affair, and it is highly likely that local men were involved.

(9) *King's Hedge*
The name here is something of a mystery; the most usual opinion that it represented the boundary between Royalist and Parliamentarian forces during the Civil War siege seems a little unlikely – though it has to be remembered that this was the age of the cannon (as well as of the archer) so attackers could not sit right under the walls. There are, however, numerous references to the king on Exmoor – King's way, King's wall and so on – almost in the way that Arthur is referred to in Wales (or Cornwall!), so the reference may not be explicit.

(10) *Bat's Castle and Gallox Hill*
The original fortification of both hillocks took place in the Iron Age but it is believed that Bat's Castle – the larger of the two at 3½ acres to the Gallox Hill site's 1 acre – was refortified during the Civil War. What gives rise to this conclusion is the parallel ditch arrangement on the east side of the earthworks. These ditches run up to a gateway and are virtually unique for an Iron Age hillfort. The name 'Bat's' is of unknown origin, while Gallox, as suggested in Note (8), probably derives from the hill's use as a gallows' site.

Walk 4 Dunkery Beacon

As a highest point Dunkery Beacon could expect splendid isolation or, at the very least, remoteness. In fact it suffers the double indignities of a road to within 70 m (225 ft) of its top, and barely rises above its surrounding moorland. Nevertheless, high

Cottages near Gallox Bridge

point of Exmoor it is and, as compensation, this splendid walk reaches it by way of the moor's highest and most remote church.

Walk category : Difficult (4¾ hours)

Length : 16 km (10 miles)

Ascent : 640 m (2100 ft)

Maps : Landranger Sheet 181, Pathfinder Sheet 1215 (SS84/94)

Starting and finishing point : The car-park in Horner, at 897 455

From the car-park go back to the road in Horner village (see (1) Horner). Go left and after 30 m go right down an unsigned, narrow lane to a bridge (see also Note (1)) over the beautiful Horner Water. It will be difficult to break away from this point but when you do, cross the bridge and go up the steep Cat's Scramble (see also Note (1)). Go left at the top on the obvious path which climbs steadily as it rounds two small combes. Ignore all turnings to left and right. The woodland here is superb, with oak and beech predominant but holly and other trees in evidence, and, as with all established broad-leaf woods, a good array of shorter shrubs. This section of woodland is well-stocked with red deer and the lucky walker may see one. As a rule, though, it is best to try patience rather than luck, so unless you have a great deal of time to spare keep moving and hoping.

A path (from Ley Hill) comes in on the right and shortly after a sign is reached pointing the way ahead (west) to Granny's Ride (see also Note (1)). The path is always clear and eventually narrows as it drops quite steeply to reach a footbridge over Horner Water. Go over the bridge and head for Stoke Pero, bearing left at a path-fork and then staying with the main path to reach a gate. Go through and turn right to reach Stoke Pero (see (2) Stoke Pero). Take the road out of the 'village' and, after reaching open ground to the right, choose any convenient point to cross that open ground so as to regain the road having cut off a considerable corner.

After rejoining the road, follow its right verge until open moor is reached on the left. (Here there is a distinct track to the left

Rowberrow from Dunkery Beacon

marked Dicky's Path to Webber's Post.) Continue along the road's verge for about 1200 m (¾ mile) to where an unsigned but obvious path leads off south-east (half-left) towards the Rowberrow summit on the horizon. *Note*: On this route, and indeed all walks on Exmoor, it is imperative to stay on the paths through the heather, as the heather itself is fragile as well as very difficult to walk over. Occasionally paths are closed; be sympathetic to these exercises in conservation.

Go over Rowberrow's shallow summit, passing the Bronze Age round barrows that give the hill its name, and continue along the broad path that leads to the cluttered summit of Dunkery Beacon (see (3) Dunkery Beacon). From here go north-east down the obvious wide track to reach a road. Go left and look for a path through the heather to the right that allows access to the unnamed summit topped by the How cairns (see also note (3)). Now descend northward along a mixture of indistinct and distinct, but not always useful, breaks to reach the car-park at Webber's Post, reached by crossing not one but two roads.

Go to the west end of the car-park, overlooking the Horner Water valley, and, after admiring the view, take the path to the right that leads obviously towards a distant signpost. Continue along the clear ridge path northward that goes past a seat commemorating the grant of a long lease on many acres of local land to the National Trust by Sir Thomas Acland. The path goes over Horner Hill – ignore all side turnings – to reach an obvious path junction about 500 m below the long, ridged top. Here go left and steeply down to reach a road, and go left into Horner. At the tea-shop to the right a short path leads back to the car-park.

(1) *Horner*

This beautiful, if somewhat overcrowded in summer, little village lies in the wooded valley of Horner Water that is equally picturesque. The pack-horse bridge taken by the walk could be medieval but is equally likely to be 17th- or 18th-century, and adds to the overall effect. The village is associated with the Acland family who rose from humble beginnings in the 15th century to owning so much land that it was said they could ride from Porlock

to Exeter without ever going over one of their own boundaries.
The family is credited (if credit is the appropriate word) with
having re-invented or popularized stag-hunting, but deserve
greater appreciation for the magnificent gesture of Sir Richard
Acland in 1944 when he gave the 5000 hectares (12,400 acres) of
the Holnicote Estate to the National Trust. This estate includes
virtually the whole of our walk as well as much more besides. The
Acland family were also responsible for the fancy names given to
many of the woodland and moorland paths. Cat's Scramble is said
to be named for 'Cat', a pony of the 1870s: Granny's Ride is
straightforward; while Dicky's Path that we passed was named for
Sir Richard Acland at the time of his 21st birthday in 1927 (though
it has to be said that the path is much older than its name).

(2) *Stoke Pero*
At 309 m (1913 ft) Stoke Pero is the highest church on Exmoor. It
is also the most remote – all the more so now that the little village
it once served has been reduced from its maximum of about 20
cottages to the solitary Church Farm. One tale, probably
apocryphal, recounts a visitor asking at Porlock for the best way to
Stoke Pero and being told that there was no best way.
Nevertheless, a congregation still assembles for the services held
here. In that sense the church is used more now than it was just
prior to its 19th-century restoration. Then, one story goes, few if
any people turned up. Indeed it is said that on one Sunday only
the vicar, the church warden and the parish clerk arrived and not
one of them had brought a key. The service, such as it was, was
held in the farm next door. The name Stoke is pre-Norman and
means displaced farm or village, Pero was added to the name
when the manor was given to a Norman family from Pirou in
Normandy itself. It is known that there was a pre-Norman church,
perhaps even a Celtic one, as the foundations of the 13th-century
(Norman) building were found to sit on an earlier churchyard. By
the late 19th century the church was ruinous but the Acland family
paid for its restoration which was carried out in 1896–97. Roofing
timber had to be brought from Porlock for the work and was
carried by a donkey called Zulu who made the trip twice daily for

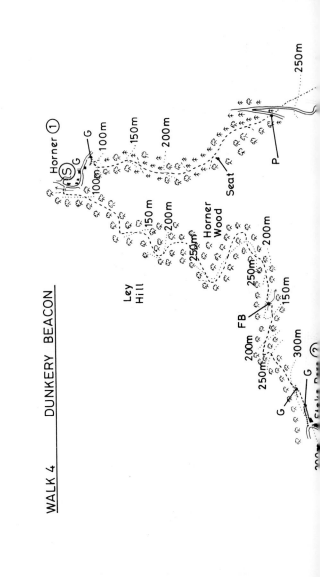

WALK 4   DUNKERY BEACON

Horner ①

S

G
G

100 m
100 m
150 m
200 m

Seat

P

250 m

Ley
Hill

Horner
Wood

150 m
200 m
250 m
250 m

250 m
250 m
200 m

FB
150 m

200 m
250 m
300 m

G
G

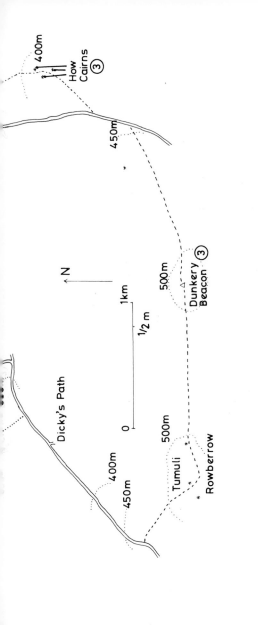

months. As a reward Zulu has his portrait hanging inside the church which, if not unique, is certainly unusual.

(3) *Dunkery Beacon*

The name Dunkery is said to derive from the Celtic *dun creagh*, a rocky hill, which is about as inappropriate a name as could be imagined. It is almost easier to believe the story of the Devil creating the hill with the shovelful of earth he removed from the Punchbowl to the south near Winsford. The 'Beacon' was added after successive signal fires, the earliest of which could perhaps go back to very ancient times. Of late, beacon fires have been built here to commemorate the Queen's Coronation and Jubilee, Royal weddings and to celebrate the centenary of the publication of *Lorna Doone*. The summit itself is crowned with a huge cairn, a trig point and a toposcope pointing out details of the view. On a good day this takes in the Mendips to the north-east, the Brecon Beacons to the north, and Dartmoor and Bodmin Moor to the south, as well as the Brendons and the Quantocks, the sea and, of course, the superb local scenery, most especially the valley of Horner Water and Horner Wood. The local high moor here is usually associated with the purple of ling, but in fact it is surprisingly prolific in terms of its wildflower population as the walker may see on his/her way from Rowberrow to the Beacon. The list includes not only bell heather, bilberry and gorse, as might be expected, but also tormentil, blue heather speedwell, heath spotted orchid, bog pimpernel and milkwort.

The ridge of moor of which Dunkery is the highest point was almost certainly a trackway in ancient times and the burial mounds along it indicate its importance in the Bronze Age. The last cairns we pass, Robin How and Joaney How, derive their second names from the Norse word for a barrow. The first names are harder to pin down, but it is speculated that they may be from Robin Hood and Little John who are often associated with such places. It may seem a long way from Sherwood Forest, but there is another, and distinct, use of the outlaw's name near Taunton.

Walk 5 The Doone Valley

For most visitors to the Exmoor National park the name 'Lorna
Doone' is synonymous with the area. Indeed visitors seem to be
evenly divided between those for whom the story is real and who
would be surprised if they could not find the place where John
Ridd and Carver Doone rode and fought, and those who are
surprised when they do, having been of the opinion that
Blackmore's work was just a story. In this walk we visit the real
Doone Valley, together with Oare Church, and examine the truth
behind the book. The second half of the walk, over Brendon
Common, is on the real Exmoor, a high plateau split often by
stream-filled combes but with wonderful views. The walking is
easy enough but the country is open and barren, the path
reasonable but not wonderful. Be cautious, especially if the
weather is closing in.

Walk category : Intermediate (3 hours)

Length : 13 km (8 miles)

Ascent : 200 m (650 ft)

Maps : Landranger Sheets 180 and 181 (though only Oare church
lies on 181). Pathfinder Sheets 1214 (SS64/74) and 1215
(SS84/94), though again only Oare church lies on the latter
map.

Starting and finishing point : The car-park in front of Lorna Doone
Farm, Malmsmead, at 792 478

Go over Malmsmead's delightful old pack-horse bridge or, if your
boots are up to it, through the ford, and head towards Oare. Pass
the Exmoor Natural History Centre, an excellent information
centre for local wildlife, to reach Parsonage Farm and Riding
Centre to the left. Go down past the farm and right over a
footbridge. Bear right to a gate and follow the path beyond along

the valley floor passing through several more gates to reach a road near Oare House (for all places associated with Lorna Doone see Note (2)). Go right to reach a T-junction. Go left to Oare Church (see (1) St Mary's church). Continue past the church for a few metres to reach a signed bridleway to the right. Follow the line of the right-hand hedge to a gate. Continue along the hedge in the next field to another gate, looking for the occasional yellow waymarkers. Beyond the next hedge the track goes round the head of a small wooded combe. Beyond a gate continue with the hedge to your right, bearing left with it to reach some old sheep pens. Beyond, the path falls to Cloud Farm, reaching it through a barn. Bear right before the farm house, cross a footbridge and go left along the track beyond. Soon you will pass the Blackmore Memorial Stone (see (2) R. D. Blackmore and *Lorna Doone*).

Beyond the stone, the path beside Badgworthy Water – a favourite haunt of dippers and kingfishers and the border between Somerset, to the east, and Devon – enters a good section of oak wood. Where a footbridge takes the path over a stream from Lank Combe, a stream heading for Badgworthy Water, the walker has reached the most probable site of the Doone Valley. A short detour here, no more than 30 m, reaches the water-slide that seems anything but the formidable barrier guarding the Doone family's secret combe. At the head of the combe, which is not followed by a Right of Way, is the Doone Gate rock.

Our route continues along Badgworthy Water to reach Hoccombe Combe and a sign, pointing to the right, to Brendon Common. The old ruins 100 m or so up the path here are the site of a medieval village which was once thought to have been the Doone family home. The path is straightforward, falling at first, then rising to a wall gate. Beyond this it becomes less distinct and care is needed to reach Lankcombe ford over the stream that flows through the Doone Valley. Beyond, there is a confusion of paths but an obvious signpost. Go right with this to Malmsmead. After about 800 m (½ mile) take the left fork where the track splits into three somewhat indistinct and unmarked paths. This path too soon

Oare Church

WALK 5   THE DOONE VALLEY

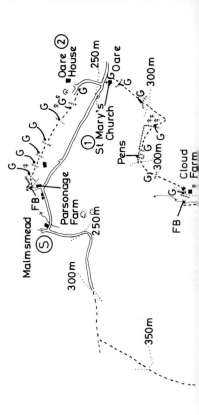

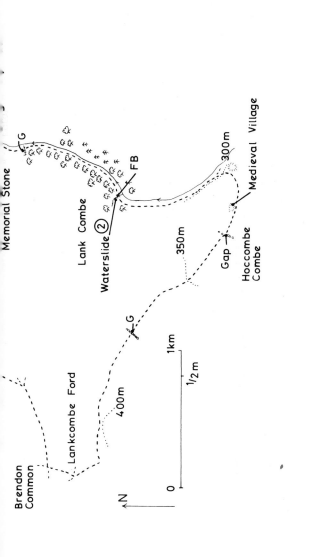

Memorial Stone

G

Lank Combe

FB

Waterslide ②

300m

Medieval Village

350m

Gap

Hoccombe Combe

G

Brendon Common

Lankcombe Ford

400m

N

1km

½ m

0

splits; bear left again. Another stream ford is reached. Cross and
follow the now more distinct track to a road. Go right on this back
to Malmsmead.

(1) *St Mary's Church*

The Domesday Book refers to Oare (as Are) but it is not known
whether there was a church here before the present building was
constructed in the 14th century. The tower is later, having been
built in the mid 19th century when the church was also extended –
a fact that helps the Lorna Doone story. Within the church, most
visitors are looking for the window through which Lorna was shot
(see Note (2) below) – it is dutifully marked with a card – and the
fine memorial tablet to Blackmore. But do take the time to find
the piscina – here the vicar washed the communion vessels. It is in
the shape of a head held by a pair of hands and represents the
Celtic saint Decumon. Legend had it that he sailed across the
Bristol Channel from South Wales accompanied only by a cow.
Landing at Watchet he set up a hermit's cell but was one day
beheaded by a thief. The saint picked up the severed head and
took it to a holy well to wash it. The piscina represents that final
carrying.

(2) *R.D. Blackmore and Lorna Doone*

Richard Doddridge Blackmore was born in 1825, the son of John
Blackmore, the curate of Longworth, Berkshire. Sadly, when
young Richard was only three months old his mother died and
much of the responsibility for his upbringing fell to his
grandparents, his grandfather – also John – being the rector of
Oare church. Richard was boarded at Blandells School, Tiverton
and spent holidays here on Exmoor, learning at first hand the old
stories of the Doones, a 17th-century family of local outlaws.
Richard qualified as a barrister after graduating from Oxford but
when ill-health forced him to give up his practice he turned to
writing full time. Though he lived in Middlesex he retained an
affection for Exmoor, visiting frequently before his death in 1900.
Lorna Doone remains Blackmore's most popular book.

Considerable research has now been carried out on the story of

Lorna Doone, as a consequence of which it is now established that the book is essentially factual, though elaborated to create a compelling drama. It is, therefore, 'faction' rather than fact or fiction. The facts are that a very small, perhaps only three or four, group of Scots under the leadership of a knight of Clan Stewart were outlawed in the early years of the 17th century as a result of a family feud. The head of the group, Sir James Stewart, took the Gaelic, poetic version of his name when he settled in a remote Exmoor valley, calling himself *Iain Ciar Duine* – Ian, the chosen man, a name which suited his bitterness at the loss of family lands – but retaining his knightly 'Sir'. The locals, not understanding the Gaelic, called him Sir Ensor Doone and the name stuck. The lands that Sir Ensor had lost were those of Lorne in North Argyll. This land – now called Lorn – was named for a Viking settler and had on occasion been called Lorna. In his Exmoor valley Sir Ensor's sons grew up to become real outlaws, holding the local county to ransom, while Sir Ensor dreamed of recapturing his former wealth and title. In an attempt to do so he kidnapped the daughter of the new lords, with the intention of marrying her to his eldest son Charles (Carver) when she came of age. To hide her identity she was called Lorna (from her lands) Doone (from Sir Ensor's newly acquired local name). It was this girl that John Ridd, a real man who truly was a local wrestling champion, met when he climbed the water-slide one day. In the story John marries Lorna, but only after Carver Doone has shot her at the altar, the Doones are defeated and their village burned, then John and Lorna live happily ever after. In reality most of this is also true: the Doones leaving Exmoor to return to Scotland and Lorna staying locally even when her true identity was known. As records from Oare church do not go back far enough no marriage record exists, so it is not definite that John and Lorna really did marry. Only in one respect did Blackmore positively alter the story, rather than just embellishing it. The real Lorna Doone was born in 1645 but in the book this is taken twenty years forward to 1665 so that the author could weave in some local intrigue about Monmouth's rebellion and Judge Jeffreys' Assize; these latter dates could not be altered. Of the places that occur in the book our walk passes quite a few.

Lorna Doone Farm is the residence of Nicholas Snowe, the (real) churchwarden; parts of the building are believed to be over 1000 years old. Oare church is as it was. The book does not actually specify that Lorna was shot through a window, so there is no real need to look too hard for this. If Carver Doone had shot her along the length of the church he would probably have walked away such was his reputation. Nevertheless, the fact that the church has been extended means that where the altar would have been in the 17th century would have left a bride visible from the moor's edge through the southern window. Opposite the church is Oare House, almost certainly the model for John Ridd's Plover's Barrows Farm. Further along the Oare Water valley Robber's Bridge, where John Ridd's father was murdered, not only exists but retains the name.

Badgworthy Water is the book's Bagworthy Water, where the young John went fishing. The locals pronounce the stream's name 'badgery' which explains the spelling change. The water-slide is at the entrance to Lank Combe as we have seen and the valley contains the ruins of medieval cottages, the old home of Sir Ensor and Carver Doone.

Walk 6 The Countisbury Cliffs

Devon reaches its most northerly point just north of Countisbury, a tiny hamlet at the top of the notorious hill rising from Lynmouth. East of Foreland Point, the actual northern tip, the cliff top is not followed, or even reached, by a road for about 10 kms (6¼ miles), a long way for England. The cliff edge is taken by the North Devon and Somerset Coastal Path, which in this section offers seclusion and magnificent seascapes.

Walk category : Intermediate (3¼ hours)

Length : 13 kms (8 miles)

Ascent : 260 m (850 ft)

Maps : Landranger Sheet 180, Pathfinder Sheet 1214 (SS64/74)

Starting and finishing point : At 747 497, the car-park opposite the
                                  Exmoor Sandpiper Inn at the top of
                                  Countisbury Hill

Before starting the walk spare a thought for those who have
negotiated Countisbury Hill under less than ideal circumstances
(see (1) Countisbury Hill). Now go out of the gate in the east wall
of the car-park and left to reach Countisbury church (see (2)
Countisbury church). The route goes through the churchyard – go
left of the church as you face it – to a stile in the yard wall. Beyond
is open clifftop moor. Bear right and climb Butter Hill – not on the
Coastal Path, but a superb vantage point (see (3) Viewpoint).
Descend the hill to the north to reach a huge landslip called Great
Red which forces the Coastal Path inland and eastward. A direct
route through to Foreland Point is possible – there is even an
unmaintained path – but the cliff here is grim and the attempt
should not be made if you are with children or are in any doubt
about the cliff or your abilities. A metalled road is reached at the
head of Caddow Combe. This is the lighthouse road and can be
followed to the lighthouse on Foreland Point. The lighthouse is
open to the public on afternoons and is a good place from which to
watch sea birds but is a disappointing viewpoint as it is set into,
rather than on, the headland.
    Follow the lighthouse road for about 300 m to where it doglegs
right. There go left on the Coastal Path to reach a stile near the
unseen Rodney's Cottage (a lime burner's cottage from the 19th
century, now a private house). Beyond, the country is superb,
mostly oak woodland, but with other broadleaf trees and some
rhododendron looking a little out of place. The shrub is being
systematically destroyed, to make the cliff area – the National
Trust's Glenthorne Estate – more native in appearance. In this
area the lucky visitor may catch a fleeting glimpse of a red deer.
The walk crosses several combes running down to the sea. First is
Chubhill Combe, then come Swannet Combe, Pudleep Gurt and
Wingate Combe. Near Pudleep Gurt (in fact about 150 m before
it) look for the distinctive oak tree that is slowly engulfing a
boulder. Look, too, for a landslip to the east of the Gurt which has

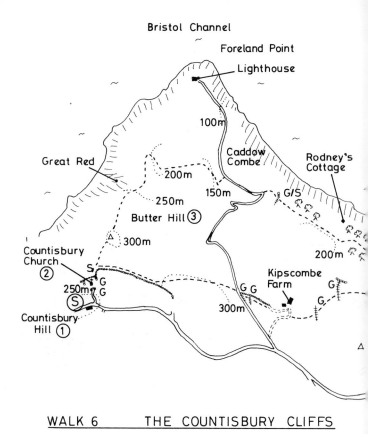

Bristol Channel

Foreland Point

Lighthouse

100m

Caddow Combe

Rodney's Cottage

Great Red

200m

150m

250m

G/S

Butter Hill ③

Countisbury Church ②

S

△ 300m

Kipscombe Farm

250m

G
G

Countisbury Hill ①

Ⓢ

G G

G

300m

G

△

WALK 6   THE COUNTISBURY CLIFFS

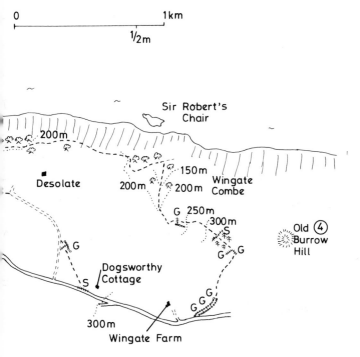

0   1km

½m

Sir Robert's
Chair

200m

150m

Desolate   Wingate
         200m   200m   Combe

G   250m

        300m
         S

G   Old ④
           Burrow
G   G   Hill

Dogsworthy
Cottage

S

G   G
300m   G G

Wingate Farm

necessitated a detour in the Coastal Path. The next big combe is Wingate and in the sea beneath it is Sir Robert's Chair, a tree-topped island. It is named for Sir Robert Chichester who was murdered near Lynton and is said to haunt this section of the cliff top, sometimes, it is said, driving a ghostly coach. Our walk follows the combe; look for the sign for White Gate (County Gate) and follow the path it points out uphill. The path rises steeply, very steeply, to a gate beyond which a sunken track continues to rise steeply to a stile into a small forest plantation. At the far end of this is a signpost. To the left is Old Burrow Hill (see (4) Old Burrow Hill). To the right is our route – now labelled as Black Gate/County Gate (why the change of colour?). The route is straightforward, the main road being reached beyond a muddy cattle pen.

Go right for about 800 m (½ mile) to reach a stile, right, just past Dogsworthy Cottage. There is a sign at the stile for Countisbury and the path beyond is waymarked in yellow. Follow the wall of the first field to a corner gate. Keep the wall to the right, pass a gate to Desolate (a somewhat pessimistically named farm) to reach another gate, and keep to the wall again in the next. When Kipscombe Farm is reached keep the buildings to the right, cross the farm road and follow a wall, right, to the lighthouse road. Cross and take the track ahead. Bear left after about 25 m and continue to a wall. Keep this to the left all the way to Countisbury church. Now follow the outward route the short distance to the start.

(1) *Countisbury Hill*

In the 19th century – and, indeed, until the 1914–18 War – a horse-drawn coach plied the coast between Lynmouth and Minehead, doing the journey in just three hours. The first team of horses was changed at the inn here. Just thinking about the effort involved, and it must have been little easier going down, brings on a sweat. Men could never, would never do it, you might say. You would be wrong.

On 12 January 1899 the *Forest Hall* got into difficulties in Porlock Bay and a call went out to launch the Lynmouth lifeboat.

Unfortunately the sea was swamping the slipway and launching
was impossible, but the coxwain, Jack Crocombe, decided to haul
the boat to Porlock for launching there. Helped by his crew, and
most of the population of Lynton and Lynmouth, Jack hauled the
3½-ton boat – a 10-m (33-ft), 10-oared boat called *Louisa* – up
Countisbury Hill on its wheeled launcher carriage. At the top they
found a section of moorland road to be too narrow for the
carriage, so the boat was taken off and hauled through on skids
while the carriage went through fields to the lane's end. The
journey of 15 miles to Porlock was completed in about 13 hours,
overnight, in appalling weather. The boat was launched
immediately, at 7 a.m., and successfully rescued the *Forest Hall*'s
crew. Each of the men on the *Louisa*'s crew, one of whom was
only sixteen years old, received a silver watch as a momento. A
replica of the *Louisa* can be seen in the Lynmouth Information
Centre.

(2) *Countisbury Church*
As someone once pointed out, the most remarkable thing about
this Early Foundation moorland church, dedicated to St John, is
its position. Inside I was especially touched by the pair of bell
clappers, all that could be salvaged when the bells were sold to pay
for the church's upkeep. What a *cri de cœur*.

   A notice points out that many of the *Louisa*'s crew (see Note (1)
above) are buried in the churchyard.

(3) *Viewpoint*
Butter Hill is topped by an ancient signal station, now in use
again, with a shelter which includes what looks like a 'What-the-
Butler-saw' device. Through it you can read the electricity meter!
The view from the hill is excellent in all directions but especially
westward past Wind Hill to Lynmouth and the coast beyond. It is
thought that the name Countisbury derives from the Iron Age fort
on top this hill near the headland. There is a story of a battle
fought locally in 878 when a Saxon force under Odda destroyed a
Viking army of 800 men under Hubba. The battle was fought near
the fort of *Arx Cynuit*, after the Saxons had been besieged by the

Danes and, desperate as their water had run out, charged out of
the fort, preferring death or victory to death by thirst. The victory
was the grandest over the Vikings in the reign of King Alfred and
academic opinion favours Wind Hill as its site.

(4) *Old Burrow Hill*

Firstly, do not be deceived by the Ordnance Survey. Despite their
insistence, the hill here is Old Burrow *not* Old Barrow. The hill is
topped by a small Roman fort probably built very early after the
Roman invasion (that is around 55 AD, Julius Caesar's foray of a
century before being little more than a recce despite his boast) as a
coastal look-out. The fort consisted of a roughly circular double
ditch and rampart defence about 100 m (328 ft) across surrounding
a rectangular ditch and rampart inner fort about 28 m by 26 m
(92 ft × 85 ft). The entrance to the inner fort was set on the
opposite side from that to the outer fort, and protected by a
wooden tower. No foundations from permanent buildings have
been found inside the fort, so it is thought likely that the defenders
lived in tents. However, a large field oven has been found. Coins
found at the site suggest only a three- or four-year Roman
presence and it is thought that the fort was used to support
operations by troop ships against the Silures of South Wales, a
Celtic tribe who held up the Roman conquest of Britain for several
years. It is not clear whether Old Burrow was abandoned when the
Silures were subdued or simply because the similar fort at
Martinhoe, about 13 km (8 miles) to the west, offered a better
view or better local weather for viewing.

Walk 7 Watersmeet

The paths along the East Lyn River from Lynmouth to
Watersmeet House offer one of the most famous walks on
Exmoor; the more so since both the valley's natural beauty and
Lynmouth's man-made attractions have had to be almost
completely re-constructed after the flood of 1952.

Walk category : Easy (2¼ hours)

Length : 8 km (5 miles)

Ascent : 280 m (920 ft)

Maps : Landranger Sheet 180, Pathfinder Sheet 1214 (SS 64/74)

Starting and finishing point : At 720 498, the car-park at the end of
                                   the Esplanade in Lynmouth. The
                                   walk can be shortened by about
                                   1½ km (1 mile) if the car-park beside
                                   Lyndale Bridge is used.

From the car-park go back along the Esplanade the way you
arrived, passing the bottom of the Cliff Railway (see (1)
Lynmouth) and the Park Information Centre and reaching
Lyndale Bridge (see (2) the Lyn Flood). Go down the steps into
the bridge car-park and through it to reach the East Lyn River
path. Follow this past a footbridge and on to the next bridge,
Woodside Bridge. Here the walker must cross to the river's right
(northern) bank as the left bank path leads to the A39. About
500 m further on is Overflow Pool from where water for the
Lynmouth power station (see also Note (1)) was drawn. The next
pool is Vellacott's, named for a local farmer who drowned in it
one night after losing his way.

   At the next bridge, Blackpool Bridge – named for a river
feature rather than the northern town – cross to the left (southern)
path again and follow this all the way to Watersmeet. About
200 m after Lynrock Bridge (the next bridge: do not cross) is
Shepherd's Bush Pool in which the corrosive nature of water borne
rocks can be clearly seen. Beyond the Pool the path follows the
river round two sharp bends before rushing Chiselcombe Bridge,
an ancient-looking structure opened in 1957 to replace the one lost
in the 1952 flood. At Bridge Pool just beyond the foundation of
the earlier bridge can be seen. Go over the next bridge – actually
over Hoar Oak Water – to reach a bridge over the East Lyn River,
beyond which is Watersmeet House (see (3) Watersmeet).

   Go back over the Hoar Oak Bridge, pausing to view the

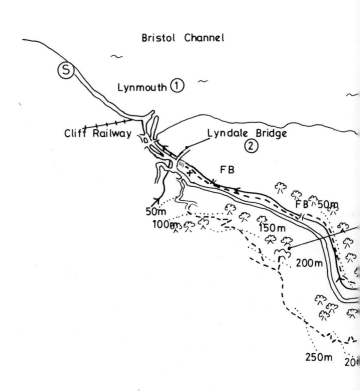

Bristol Channel

Lynmouth ①

Cliff Railway

Lyndale Bridge
②

FB

FB 50m

50m

100m

150m

200m

250m   20

WALK 7   WATERSMEET

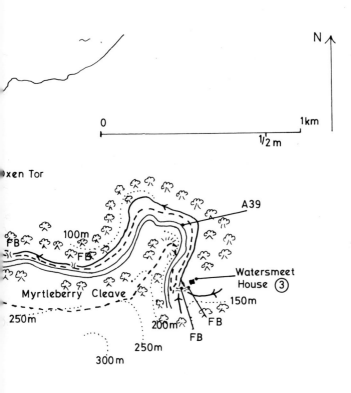

waterfalls, and ignore the path along the river's left bank in favour of one signed 'Lynton over the Cleaves'. Go up to and over the A39 (with care) and take the path signed 'Lynmouth, Lynton via Cleaves 3'. This path climbs to and through an old hill fort. Bear right beyond a seat on a zig-zag path upwards to reach easier ground through Myrtleberry Cleave. Beyond gates and a memorial further zig-zags take the path up again, the fine viewpoint of Oxen Tor soon being reached. Beyond this go right where the Lynton path bears left to descend rapidly to the alleys of east Lynmouth. Follow these down to reach Watersmeet Road opposite the village church, built only in the mid 19th century to avoid the villagers having to make the long journey up Countisbury Hill. Go left to reach the outward route and follow this back through the town.

(1) *Lynmouth*

Lynmouth is a prettily set old fishing village, though today it is largely given over to tourism. This might be considered a recent innovation but in fact it was the Napoleonic Wars, which prevented European tourism and forced the well-off to find more homegrown delights, that brought the first tourists. Lynmouth was one of the places they found. The Shelley Cottage Hotel, passed by the walk, stands on the site of a cottage rented by the poet and his young wife. In Shelley's case the trip was not wholly holiday, as he was being pursued by the government for having distributed pamphlets rife with revolutionary thoughts. In 1812 such behaviour was definitely suspect. In the village Shelley continued to write the pamphlets, distributing them, in part, by the apparently useless method of putting them in bottles and throwing them in the sea. After a stay of many weeks a kindly Lynmouth fisherman took the poet across to south Wales when arrest was imminent. A later literary connection is that R. D. Blackmore stayed in the Rising Sun Hotel at the bottom of Mars Hill, close to the walk.

The walk also passes the base of the cliff railway. In the mid 19th century the huge and steep hill from Lynmouth to Lynton was adversely affecting the tourist trade. A local engineer, Bob Janes, therefore decided to build a cliff railway to increase trade. It took him a very long time to persuade anyone to back the scheme but by 1887 money was available, and on Easter Monday 1890 the railway was ready. It rises 450 ft in 900 ft (metric measures do not seem right for something so delightfully Imperial), the motive power being the carriages themselves. Beneath each one is a 700-gallon water tank. The carriage at the top has its tank filled and it then hauls the lower carriage up. At the bottom the tank is emptied, while the top tank is filled again. The trip takes about 1½ minutes and on the first day cost 3 old pence up and 2 old pence down. Bob Janes' original design for hydraulic and emergency brakes was so good that despite the railway having transported millions of passengers, no one has ever been injured – though a dog once had its tail shortened when it wandered on to the track. In the same year as the railway opened, water from the East Lyn River was piped to a local generating station giving Lynmouth and Lynton electricity before many places in London had been connected. Near the railway's bottom station are two old lime kilns, Lynmouth having once been a centre for lime-burning. Lime was shipped in from south Wales, burned here and moved up on to Exmoor to 'sweeten' the soil.

Finally, look out for the Rhenish tower on the harbour. It is named for architecturally similar towers on the Rhine and was built early in the 19th century by one Colonel Rawdon as a lighthouse for the harbour and to store sea water that was used in the colonel's bath! The tower is actually a replica, the original having been destroyed in 1952.

(2) *The Lyn Flood*

In the first two weeks of August 1952 rain fell almost continually on Exmoor, raising the levels of the Hoar Oak, and the East and West Lyn Rivers. Then on 15 August the rain worsened. The day was the third wettest ever recorded in Britain, with almost 12 inches of rain falling on Exmoor. The drainage area of the rivers collected 3,000 million gallons (about 90 million tons) of water and it poured downstream as a huge wave. The Lyn rivers are very steep, averaging about 1 in 27 along their length, and the effect of water weight and gravity was devasting. Bridges, trees and buildings knocked over caused temporary dams and when these failed the water surge was even more powerful. With the water came an estimated 100,000 tons of rocks, some weighing 50 tons or more. When Lynmouth was struck it was washed away, daybreak revealing the loss of dozens of hotels and houses. Nineteen boats had been washed away, as had over 150 cars. Worst of all, 34 men, women and children had been killed.

The disaster brought assistance from all over the world: over £1.3 million (at 1952 prices) was collected for relief and in two years Lynmouth had been rebuilt. The story of the flood is told in the Flood Memorial Hall.

(3) *Watersmeet*

The whole of the riverside estate from Lynmouth to Watersmeet House was acquired over a period of years by the Reverend W.S. Halliday, a man of means who also subscribed to what might be termed the Romantic View of nature. In 1832 he built the House – which is now a National Trust shop and restaurant, the Trust having acquired the whole property over a period of years. Anciently, the area was home to charcoal burners and, as an old adit (horizontal shaft) opposite the House shows, one group of enthusiastic but unsuccessful iron ore miners. Today the whole area is a haven for plants and wildlife. The woods that border the river are mainly of sessile oak but with other broadleaves. There is also Irish spurge, Watersmeet being one of only two mainland British sites where this grows. The river itself is home to grey wagtails, dippers and kingishers.

Walk 8 Tarr Steps

Near the southern edge of the Exmoor National Park, the River Barle flows through some of the finest of the Park's scenery. It also flows through Withypool, a charming village, and under Tarr Steps, one of the Park's most picturesque and enigmatic bridges.

Walk category : Intermediate (3½ hours)

Watersmeet

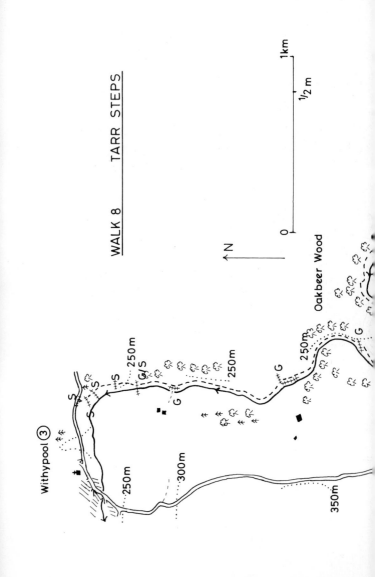

WALK 8   TARR STEPS

N

0   1/2 m   1km

Withypool ③

Oakbeer Wood

250m
G/S
S
S
S
250m
G
250m
250m
G
250m
G
250m
300m
350m

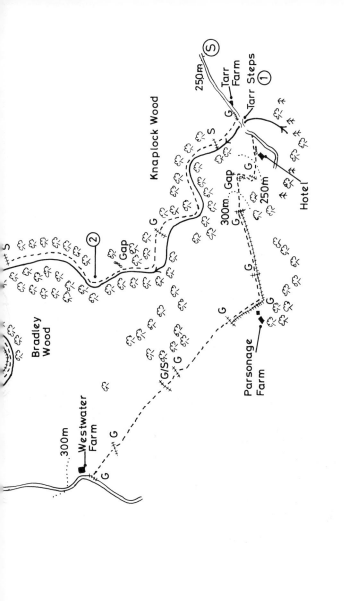

Length : 14 km (8¾ miles)

Ascent : 100 m (325 ft)

Maps : Landranger Sheet 181, Pathfinder Sheet 1235 (SS 83/93)

Starting and finishing point : The car-park at 872 324

From the car-park to back to the road and left down towards Tarr
Steps (see (1) Tarr Steps). Few will resist seeing the clapper bridge
immediately, but our route goes right before reaching it, taking
either the bridleway before Tarr Farm, or the footpath after it,
each marked with the yellow waymarkers of the Two Moors Way
(see (2) Two Moors Way). The route from here to Withypool –
about 7 km (4½ miles) – is straightforward, rarely leaving the
River Barle's eastern bank, well waymarked throughout and past
frequent signs pointing out that this is a Permissive Path not a
Right of Way. The going is occasionally difficult, especially after
heavy rain, but always delightful. As it nears Withypool the route
crosses four stiles in quick succession, the last one leading to a
road. Go left into the village (see (3) Withypool).

   Go through the village, crossing over the superb Barle bridge
and take the first turning left (for Hawkridge). This road – indeed
the whole return journey – is an alternative route for the Two
Moors Way. Follow the road to Westwater Farm. Cross the West
Water stream just beyond and take the yellow way-marked route,
left. The path heads in a straight line, south-east, and is well
waymarked as it follows a hedge/fence on the right across a series
of fields to a point just east of Parsonage Farm. There turn left,
and continue to follow field edges through two gates. At the end of
the third field a gap leds to a track to the right. Follow this around
the hotel to Tarr Steps. From there reverse the route to the car-
park.

(1) *Tarr Steps*
In 1968 the Post Office issued a set of commemorative stamps: the
4 old penny stamp (letter post) bore the image of Tarr Steps and

the bold title 'Prehistoric'. It is difficult to find a reference to the
causeway before, or immediately after, that date that does not
offer this view as though it were fact, but the truth is that no one
knows how old Tarr Steps are. In form the Steps are a very long
version of the clapper bridges more usually found on Dartmoor. In
fact this is the longest clapper bridge in Britain: over 36 m (120 ft)
long and comprising 17 slabs, the biggest of which weighs several
tons. The slabs average just over 2 m (about 7 ft) long and 1¼ m
(4 ft) wide and are held about a metre (3 ft) above the water by
piers placed on the stream bed. For all its size the bridge is oddly
sited: the River Barle can be successfully forded close to it for
most of the year, and less than a mile southward is another
crossing known to have been in use in the mid 12th century. This
latter fact lends weight to the argument that Tarr Steps are
contemporaries of their Dartmoor cousins which are believed to be
13th- or 14th-century. The name, too, seems to suggest a similarity
– Tarr from *tor*, the exposed slabs of rock found on moorland
summits: there is even some suggestion the causeway was once
called Torr Steps. Well, maybe. It is also suggested that Tarr is
from *tochar*, the Celtic word for a causeway. If the Iron Age Celts
had named the bridge then a Bronze Age construction becomes
more likely. One curious folk story also suggests a very early
construction date. The bridge, it says, was a ritual crossing rather
than a real one – the ford serving that purpose – and there was an
annual animal sacrifice (usually of a cat), the poor creature being
thrown across the river and killed on the far side before crossings
were allowed. It is such an unlikely story that there is a temptation
to believe it, but it does have an echo in a story told about Devil's
Bridge near Aberystwyth. The Devil was said to have built that for
an old woman, secretly claiming as his right the soul of the first
creature to cross it. The old woman was a canny lass, however,
and threw a bone across for her dog to chase. The dog hurried
over the bridge and was claimed, leaving the old woman to cross in
safety. Another Exmoor legend suggests that the Devil built Tarr
Steps so he could sunbathe near the river. Perhaps the old story is
not folk memory but a half-remembered Devil tale of which there
are many in the area. On nearby Winsford Hill is the Punchbowl

from which – as we noted on Walk 4 – the Devil shovelled earth to build Dunkery Beacon.

Overall, the weight of evidence suggests Tarr Steps are a medieval pack-horse bridge, but with just enough doubt to keep the interest high. In one sense the age of the bridge could be classified as 'recent' for severe flooding has required its rebuilding several times. The flood of 1952 that destroyed Lynmouth (see Note (2) to Walk 7) tore sixteen of the bridge's seventeen spans away. One stone, weighing over a ton, was moved nearly 50 m (164 ft) downstream. The restoration was as perfect as could be achieved and, using the best of modern equipment, difficult, merely adding to the wonder of the original construction.

Close to Tarr Steps, at 890 335, is the Caratacus stone, another enigmatic megalith. The stone, standing in a shelter erected to protect its inscription, is carved with the words *Carataci Nepus*, kinsman of Caratacus. Caratacus led the Welsh Celts against the Romans in the 1st century AD, yet the inscription is a 5th- or 6th-century work. The stone could be neolithic, 2000 years earlier than man or carving, and the inscription faces away from the old track it stands beside – was it once erected elsewhere? As with Tarr Steps we will never know for sure.

(2) *Two Moors Way*

The Two Moors Way is an unofficial – not adapted by the Countryside Commission, rather than private – long distance footpath that crosses Exmoor and Dartmoor. Its unofficial nature means it has never had the created footpath's advantage of avoiding road sections, but does not mean it is poorly maintained. In fact it is well waymarked throughout. The route starts, or finishes, at Lynmouth, crosses Exmoor by way of the East Lyn valley (following part of Walk 7), Hoar Oak Water and this walk. It links Exmoor to Dartmoor via West Anstey, Knowstone, Witheridge, Moreland Bishop and Drewsteignton, before crossing Dartmoor via the Teign Valley (following part of Walk 16), Hamel Down, the moorland just west of Widecombe, Ponsworthy, the

Tarr Steps

Dart Valley and Ugborough Moor to finish (or start) at Ivybridge.

The route avoids high Dartmoor, though it does cross the upland southern section, but has many plus points and is a fine walk worthy of consideration by anyone who loves the West Country.

(3) *Withypool*

The Domesday Book names three Saxon foresters of *Widepolla*, the willow pool, and it is thought that under the Normans the tiny village was the 'capital' of Exmoor. The Normans built a church but very little of this remains after substantial rebuilding in the 15th century. The fine carved font is probably original. The tower was rebuilt to celebrate the coronation of Edward VII in 1902 – or, at least, was built in the same year – and is short and squat. It comes as a relief to hear that this was not the architect's plan: the money ran out when the tower was this high! Since Withypool is about half-way around the walk, refreshments might be in order. If the walker uses the Royal Oak he will be following in famous footsteps. R.D. Blackmore wrote part of *Lorna Doone* here and in May 1946 General Dwight Eisenhower came, by horseback no less, for a pint after visiting American troops who were training on the moor.

Finally, on top of Withypool Hill to the west (right) of the road that takes the walk out of the village is one of Exmoor's very few stone circles. The circle, comprises about 40 very short stones, the tallest being barely 0.6 m (2 ft) high.

Dartmoor

Dartmoor became a National Park in October 1951, the Park covering some 940 sq km (365 sq miles) of granite moorland and the wooded valleys that drain it. The Park is an area rich in antiquities, studded with delightful villages and with any number of scenic highlights. Yet despite that it is a place of foreboding for many visitors who come no closer to it than the seat of a car, and gaze with a shudder at Princetown's drab, gaunt, clearly efficient prison. The reasons for this latter view are numerous. In 1586 William Campden described the moor as *squalida montana, Dertmore*, a phrase that needs no translation and did little to enamour the place to visitors. Down the years the message remained the same, culminating, if that is the right word, with the famous Plymouth tailor's quote in Sabine Baring-Gould's *Book of Dartmoor* (1900): 'I solemnly swear to you, Sir, nothing will ever induce me to set foot on Dartmoor again. If I chance to see it from the Hoe, Sir, I'll avert my eyes. How can people think to come here for pleasure – for pleasure, Sir! . . . only unwholesome-minded individuals can love Dartmoor.' It barely needed Conan Doyle to let loose the Hound of the Baskervilles for Dartmoor's popular fate to be sealed.

The reason for the bad press is geological. The basic rocks of Dartmoor were beneath the sea in the late Devonian and early Carboniferous eras. The delightfully named Variscan orogeny – an orogeny is a squeezing (and, therefore, folding) as a result of plate tectonics, the Variscan is just a distinguishing name – folded the area into the Cornubian Mountains around 300 million years ago and into the roots of these mountains poured the volcanic magma that would be, after overlying soft rock had weathered away, Dartmoor's granite. The Cornubian Mountains stretched from the Scilly Isles to Dartmoor and today six separate granitic 'bosses' are recognized, all of them connected below ground level (sometimes well below ground level) though the surface connection is more tenuous. Later in the book we shall visit Bodmin, a boss that is almost surface-connected to Dartmoor, and continue down the old mountain chain to the Scillies. Dartmoor granite comes in three

forms, the forms dependent upon the position of the rock as it
cooled relative to the cooler rocks into which the molten magma
intruded. The rock type, therefore, is dependent upon cooling
rate, which determines the crystal structure. Tor granite, that is
the rock that forms the most distinctive Dartmoor feature, is
coarse-grained, cooling having produced parallel jointing
invariably running horizontally and vertically relative to the moor's
surface. Granite is an impervious rock so the high plateau drains
poorly. The soil it produces is also thin and acidic, and supports a
small range of plants. In such a waterlogged environment the
decay of plant material is inhibited by lack of oxygen and by
leached acids which inhibit bacteria. The result is that dead plant
material does not decompose but forms a brown, mud-like layer –
peat. Much of Dartmoor is covered by peat bog, a frustrating
environment for the walker, a land of wet misery in which areas of
dry land seems to be randomly, and too intermittently, spread.
And to make matters worse, even when the walker moves into the
valleys things do not improve immediately, there the upland bog –
usually referred to as blanket bog – is replaced by mire bogs whose
whole surfaces move underfoot (giving them their other name,
featherbeds) and in which bright green oases of lush life turn out
to be a good deal less welcome when you arrive at them.

Does all this mean that the moor's reputation for being a dreary
place, a featureless morass of leg-clutching bogs is correct? Well,
yes, in part. It is certainly true that there are few who would
choose to be placed in the middle of a Dartmoor blanket bog as
darkness was falling on a winter's night. But in reality, if you are
cautious, stay on tracks or ridges and can 'read' the valley and
plateau floors a little, then Dartmoor is a fine place. It is especially
fine for the plant-lover. Though the high moor has a limited flora –
chiefly ling and bell heather, with a collection of hardy bog plants
– the moor margins have a superb collection of ferns and mosses.
For the animal- and bird-lover there is less delight. Apart from
Dartmoor ponies and a few moorland birds there will be little to
stop the heart.

Geographically, Dartmoor is split into two by the B3212/B3357
Moretonhampstead to Tavistock road, the northern area

containing the high land – including High Willhays, southern England's highest peak, and on the route of Walk 12; while the southern area has the best of the antiquities – some of which are visited by Walk 9, and lie close to Walk 13. Dartmoor's ancient sites could form the basis of a good-sized book and include fine stone circles and menhirs and, on Erme Plain, one of the longest stone rows in the world.

These sites indicate that despite its harshness the moor has been an inviting place for man for many centuries. He came here to worship, then to mine and finally to quarry stone. It is likely that over the years the climate has become colder and wetter, so that the Bronze Age folk would now be surprised by how few people live on the moor. In view of their circles and rows they might also be puzzled by the prison representing, as it does, an odd use for their sacred upland.

Note: The Dartmoor Military Ranges are dealt with separately in Appendix 1.

Walk 9 Merrivale

This short walk visits one of the best of Dartmoor's numerous prehistoric sites. The site is interesting for being at the one time extremely simple – it comprises 'only' standing stones – and at the same time extremely complex, with stone rows, circles, cairns and single stones. Merrivale is, therefore, a place that exemplifies the real mystery of such sites: the apparent sophistication of seemingly primitive men.

Walk category : Easy/Intermediate (1½ hours)

Length : 6½ km (4 miles)

Ascent : 90 m (300 ft)

Maps : Landranger Sheet 191, Outdoor Leisure Sheet 28

Starting and finishing point : At 561 749, a car-park on the southern side of the B3357 Princetown to Tavistock road.

Note: Though this walk is relatively short and involves little climbing, it covers a section of open moorland with poor or no paths. The section of old railway near the Swell Tor quarries is close to steep, unprotected quarry faces. The walk should not be taken lightly, especially if recent weather has been wet, or there are young children in your party.

From the car-park head south of west across open moor to the stone rows that soon become obvious, about 600 m ahead (see (1) The Merrivale Antiquities). Having traversed the rows, go south from their western end to the stone circle and menhir (see also Note (1)). Now go eastward for 300 m to another, but quite different, standing stone (see (2) The T/A Route), set among the clitter, as the litter of weathered granite chunks is known locally. As an aside, the walker who also knows North Wales will be interested to find that this local word for an untidy heap of stones is from the same root as 'glyder' in the peaks Glyder Fawr and Glyder Fach in the Snowdonia National Park. From the stone, head southward towards the obvious wall, crossing Long Ash Brook as you reach it and then following it to where it turns sharply right (westward). The ease of crossing of the brook is entirely weather dependent: if it has been dry, it is a mere step; if it has been wet it may well entail a long and frustrating detour; there is NO bridge. At the wall elbow go up the slope ahead to reach the obvious track-bed of an old railway (see (3) Plymouth and Dartmoor Railway) that contours around King's Tor. Follow the track-bed to where it forks and here go right on the less obvious track to enjoy fine views over the Walkham Valley. The main track is rejoined near a superb granite bridge. A little ahead now a broad grassy track goes left from the main track. This is the Swell Tor siding of the railway; take it. Along on the left side are a pile of beautifully finished granite corbels, originally cut for London Bridge, beyond which some of the old wooden sleepers, much rotted, are still in place. Be careful: some of the old, rusting studheads are also still here, and they can trip the unwary.

A granite corbel, Swell Tor Siding

Continue to a ruined building, right, where a track-bed goes off left through a narrow rock gorge to the Swell Tor quarries (see also Note (3)). The gorge itself is stagnant-pool-filled but a path runs up the gorge's left side for those wanting to visit the quarries.

Continue past ruin and gorge on the main (now somewhat fainter but still distinct) track. Go left and uphill where it forks – the track ahead finishes abruptly after a few yards – and bear right at the next fork. Left here goes back into the quarries, our route going down to reach a raised causeway between two halves of another quarry. To the right here is a steep drop with hanging moss which drips continuously into a dark pool. Round the next corner the track peters out into the moor but a more distinct track to the right is comfortably reached. To the right are the Foggin Tor quarries and the North Hessary Tor TV mast. Follow the new track back towards the point at which you reached it, exiting left to climb King's Tor if the temptation is too strong, and there go back down to the wall, recross the stream and head north-east across the final 600 m of open, very boggy moor to the car-park.

(1) *The Merivale Antiquities*

The northernmost of the Merrivale stone rows is a double row 182 m (600 ft) long, the stones being from 0.8 m (2¾ ft) to 1.4 m (4½ ft) apart. At its eastern end the rows is closed by a 'blocking' stone. The row is almost exactly straight and lies at an angle of 6½° to the E–W axis. The southernmost row is also double. It is 264 m (865 ft) long and is also closed at its eastern end. The southern row is at an angle of 8½°, i.e. it is not parallel to the northern row, the separation of the two varying from about 25 m (about 80 ft) at the east end to about 32 m (about 105 ft) at the west. Almost exactly half-way along the southern row – it is actually about 3 m (10 ft) closer to the east end – is a stone circle, within which is a small cairn. This feature is unique to Merrivale. From a small cairn near the western end of the southern row a less distinct single stone row 42 m (138 ft) long leads off south-west.

The rows were presumably ritualistic, since it is not conceivable that they represent a roadway, or the remains of housing. But what ritual? The non-parallel nature is strange but such a lack of

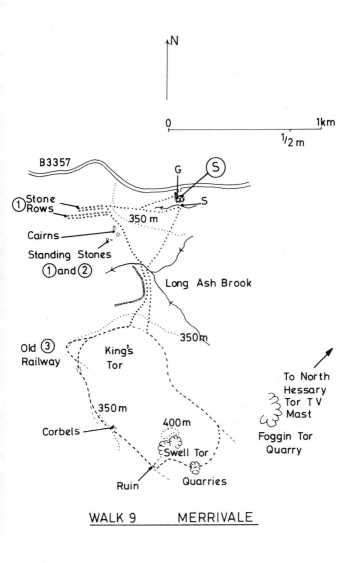

parallelism would be expected if the rows had been constructed to point to one spot on the horizon. Which spot? The best guess to date is that the rows indicate the rising point of the stellar group of the Pleiades (the Seven Sisters) at the time of the May sunrise. Supporting this theory is the known use of the stars to predict the May sun – the time of reaping – by ancient Greeks, who also used the November setting of the group to time their ploughing. Elsewhere in the ancient world the stars were also well known and deemed to be of great significance. It is even believed that in ancient times Australian Aborigines thought that the Pleiades were the reason for temperatures rising in summer, seeing them as more significant than the sun. One further piece of intriguing 'evidence' is that the Stonehenge cursus is also aligned to the rising of Pleiades. If the alignment is correct, then the reason for the two rows would be that there was a shift in observed position of the rise with time. If that is correct then the second row of the two (which would, if the theory is correct, have been the southern one) would have post-dated the first by about 200 years. However, it must be pointed out that this alignment is speculative rather than definite, and many scientists and laymen alike find it difficult to believe that Bronze Age folk could have been that interested in Pleiades.

In addition to the stone rows and the associated stone circle and cairn, there are a quite remarkable number of other features on this stretch of moorland. To the north and east are the remains of stone hut circles, the base stones of dwellings, as well as another stone circle to the south, the very prominent menhir (standing stone) on the route and a kistvaen about 20 m (65 ft) south of and 50 m (165 ft) east of the southern row's centre. A kistvaen is a burial chamber formed by creating a stone box using four stone slabs with another slab lid set into the ground. It is probable that in their original form these stone boxes – coffin is not the right word as the boxes are neither coffin size nor shape – would have been buried under a small earth mound.

(2) *The T/A Route*
The stone reached at this point of the walk looks like an ancient

menhir but is inscribed 'T' on one side and 'A' on the other. Prior to the creation of roads across Dartmoor the great wild expanse was crossed by tracks leading between the major towns situated on the moor's edge, tracks followed by travelling merchants and also by pack-horse teams. An Act of Parliament of 1696 allowed local magistrates to compel corporations (councils) to erect waymarking stones to assist travellers on the moor. In the Receiver Book of Plymouth Corporation for the year 1699–1700 there is an entry noting: 'Item paid towards defraying the charges of putting upp Moorestones on Dartmoor in the way leading from Plymouth towards Exon for guidance of Travellers passing that way the sume of £2-0-0.'

In this section of the moor these guide-stones were inscribed 'T' on the side facing Tavistock and 'A' on that facing Ashburton. The Turnpike built in 1792 superseded the track and the markers, no longer required, were occasionally commandeered as gateposts. Several still exist, however, on the section of old track going south-east from Merrivale Bridge.

It is interesting to note that when the early 18th-century track-makers were looking for a suitable waymark they chose a large standing stone, almost identical to the nearby menhir which pre-dates their own work by 3000–4000 years. The modern menhir, the TV mast on top of north Hessary Tor to the east, is, by contrast, completely different.

(3) *Plymouth and Dartmoor Railway*

Thomas Tyrwhitt was born at an Essex parsonage in 1762 and might have died unremarked had he not become a close friend of the Prince of Wales when the two were students at Oxford. The friendship led to Tyrwhitt's appointment as auditor for the Duchy of Cornwall in 1786. He arrived on Dartmoor shortly after, seeing in it not a bleak wilderness but an opportunity, and set about forming a small town in a wholly unsuitable position. In deference to his patron he called the settlement Prince's Town, though the locals soon shortened this to Princetown. It is likely that the unflourishing town would have died quietly but the early years of the 19th century were the times of the Napoleonic wars and at nearby Plymouth the floating prison hulks were overflowing with French prisoners of war whose number and condition were giving rise to concern. Tyrwhitt seized an opportunity, offering a solution to the problem in the building of a prison at Princetown. Work began in 1806 using stone from several local quarries, including those on Swell and Foggin Tors. The construction was long and difficult, hampered by bad moorland weather, difficulties with the site and transport problems, but none the less in 1809 the first prisoners – both French and American prisoners of war – were moved to the building. Sadly their conditions at Princetown were little better than they had been at Plymouth and epidemics were frequent. Eventually criticisms of the conditions grew so loud that wholesale policy changes were required – but by then Tyrwhitt was Sir Thomas and had been appointed as Black Rod.

His interest in Dartmoor and Princetown had not wholly ceased, however, and around 1820 he dreamed up an improbable scheme to blend several necessities and arrive at a virtue. A railway from Plymouth to Princetown could be used to export granite building stone and, at the same time, to import much needed coal to the town and to bring in lime. The lime was to be used to sweeten the moorland, so turning it into an arable paradise – most unlikely and, in the event, totally unworkable. Tyrwhitt's vision was translated into wonderful prose. The scheme would, he said, 'clothe with grain and grasses a spacious tract of land now lying barren, desolate and neglected'. The transformation would 'fill this unoccupied region with an industrious and hardy population' and 'create a profitable interchange of useful commodities between an improvable and extensive line of back-country, and a commercial seaport of the first capabilities, both natural and artificial'.

The list of useful commodities to be interchanged included not only lime and coal, but sea sand, timber and food inbound to the moor, and stone, peat, flax and hemp outbound. Tyrwhitt conceived a double road (twin track) but time and overwhelming expense narrowed this to a single, at first horse-drawn, railway. The time taken to build the track was so long that the Dartmoor quarries lost the contract to build London Bridge. Tyrwhitt was furious, calling the decision a gross injustice that implied that

Dartmoor granite was 'inferior in quality, more scanty in quantity, and more costly in working than the granite coming from Haytor or Aberdeen'. The reality was that with the railway not finished there was no way the Swell Tor quarries could compete with other sources. The railway was eventually completed in 1827. Fifty years later, after steam had reshaped the rail system, Princetown was linked with Yelverton and the Plymouth and Dartmoor Railway – the P & DR – became part of the GWR. This railway continued until 1956 when it finally closed. In its final years there was a halt at Ingra Tor, south of our walk, much favoured by walkers, who started on to the moor past a sign headed 'Great Western Railway Company NOTICE' which pointed out that in 'the interest of game preservation and for their own protection against snakes, dogs should be kept on a lead'. The snake warning was, I think, a slightly hopeful and definitely over-stated excuse.

On the track-bed we follow occasional sections where the old sleepers are intact and can cause the unwary walker a few problems but the superbly fashioned granite corbels that can be seen – most significantly a pile cut for London Bridge but left to the side of the track approaching Swell Tor – and the stone used on the Royal Oak siding, nearer to Swell Tor, are a real joy. Finally, as we are talking of Swell Tor, the quarries here were noted for the relative abundance of garnet in a form of granite, known as blue granite, which occurred as irregular lumps in the main rock mass.

Walk 10 Haytor

On its eastern edge Dartmoor falls into the Bovey valley, a delightful valley taken by Walk 17. But though the overall plateau height is decreasing quickly in this area the moor does not give in easily, throwing up tors almost within sight of its terminal edge. One of those, and indeed one of the best on the moor, is Haytor. This Tor, and the Down from which it rears up, is a delight, not spoiled even by the closeness of a road and of that most picturesque of honey-pots, Widecombe-in-the-Moor.

Walk category : Easy/Intermediate (1½ hours)

Length : 5 km (3 miles)

Ascent : 180 metres (600 feet)

Maps : Landranger Sheet 191, Outdoor Leisure Sheet 28

Starting and finishing point : At 759 766, the car-park by the side
of the road south of Haytor

From the car-park take the wide and obvious track up to the
skyline rocks of Haytor (see (1) Haytor). From the rocks Haytor
Quarry, down and right (north-east), is obvious, as is the track to
it. Take this to reach the quarries which can be visited by going
through a gate in the fence (see (2) Haytor Quarry and Railway).
From the gate go north-east and downhill to reach a Y-junction of
pathways. To the left is the track of the quarry's old granite
railway (see also Note (2)) which we follow northward. The track
to the right is also, but less obviously so, that of an old railway and
it meets the main Haytor line a little to the east of the point where
our walk will reach it.
    Follow the trackway to its junction with the main track and go
left. The track goes through an obvious cutting and then heads for
Holwell Tor ahead (about 800 m (½ mile) away). At this point
leave the track, going half-right (north-west) across pathless moor
to reach Smallacombe Rocks (see (3) Smallacombe Rocks). Now
head back towards Haytor to rejoin the trackway and turn right
along it to Holwell Quarry. Note that a direct route to Holwell is
not feasible because of the boggy nature of the intervening moor.
A path, of sort, heads off that way but do not be deceived: it soon
peters out and you will be forced south towards the track.
    From the Quarry climb up Holwell Tor and from it take a direct
line for Haytor crossing, on the way, another ancient quarry track
and the quarry it served, a quarry with the somewhat inelegant
name of Rubble Heap. Now continue across a moor covered, at

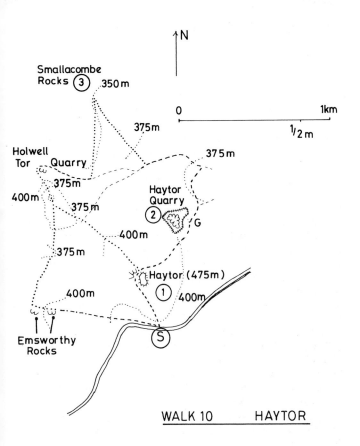

↑N

Smallacombe Rocks ③ .350m

375m

0   1km

½m

Holwell Tor   Quarry   375m

375m

400m

Haytor Quarry ②

375m

400m

G

375m

Haytor (475m) ①

400m

400m

Emsworthy Rocks

S

WALK 10   HAYTOR

the right time of year (August), with bilberries, back to Haytor and reverse the short outward track to the start.

   Note: As an alternative finish, go south to Emsworthy Rocks from where a green track leads directly back to the car-park.

(1) *Haytor*

Until fairly recently the spelling of the Tor was 'Hey' rather than 'Hay', and the former spelling is still occasionally used. In truth it matters little because both are only phonetic renderings of the local pronunciation of 'high', this being the High Tor. The Tor consists of two granite masses each with faces to tempt the rock-climber – 'Interrogation' (E2) on the lower (in altitude terms), more westerly block, is a fine test-piece – so caution is needed if you are with children. The higher mass is conveniently climbed – even having occasional iron spikes if you find the right route – for an excellent, if usually windy, view which takes in the whole of the route.

(2) *Haytor Quarry and Railway*

In 1792 one James Templar was granted an Act of Parliament to dig a canal from Bovey Tracey to the River Teign at Stover, a work completed in 1794 at his own expense. Later he also built, again at his own expense, the railway from the canal to Haytor, the excellence of its stone for building having been recognized. The railway was opened in 1820. It used granite rails, firstly because the cast iron rails then available were prone to breaking, and secondly because granite was readily available – there was a quarry full of it at track's end! Unusually, the track had the wheel flange on the rail, rather than the other way as is now the case, curves being produced by simply packing the rail with extra stone into which a correct rebate at the correct angle soon wore. The Haytor, and Holwell and Rubble Heap, stone was superb. It was used on London Bridge (to the great aggravation of the man who built Princetown, see Note (3) of Walk 9), where amongst other uses it forms the end blocks on which the City's coat-of-arms were mounted, and many places elsewhere. The problem was shipment. From the quarries the stone was shifted on horse-drawn, flat-bed carriages to Bovey Tracey, then placed on barges for canal and river shipment to Teignmouth, then off-loaded yet again to be put on ships for final export. Handling was expensive and ultimately the quarry became uneconomic. By 1858 it had closed. Today the quarry is a beautiful place, though caution is needed when exploring. The deep pools are home to dragonflies, trees and shrubs grow in the sheltered hollows, and even the bits of old machinery lying about seem to enhance the scene.

(3) *Smallacombe Rocks*
From the rocks the view is impressive, being especially good southward to Haytor and north-west to Hound Tor over the delightful Becka Brook valley. The summit plateau has the remains of some ancient huts, probably Bronze Age, from which the shards of pottery of a unique design have been excavated.

Walk 11 Postbridge and Cranmere Pool

On Walks 9 and 10 we sampled Dartmoor's wilder scenery. This route does rather more, penetrating the great tract of wild moorland that lies north of the B3212/3357 roads to reach one of the moor's most famous sites, Cranmere Pool.

This is a long and arduous walk, and should only be attempted by fit and experienced walkers.

Walk category : Difficult (6 hours)

Length : 25½ km (16 miles)

Ascent : 350 m (1150 ft)

Maps : Landranger Sheet 191, Outdoor Leisure Sheet 28

Starting and finishing point : The National Park car-park at
                                 Postbridge on the north side of the
                                 B3212 at 646 788

Note: Much of this walk lies within one of the Army's Dartmoor Firing Ranges. Please read Appendix 1 before setting out on the moor.

From the car-park go back on to the main road and left to Postbridge (see (1) Postbridge) and its clapper bridge. Go over the modern bridge beside it and immediately left through a gate. Follow the path through another gate and on towards Ringhill Farm. Blue-topped posts offer occasional help; go left along a wall near the farm, towards the East Dart River. Pass Hartyland Farm, right, and go right, through a gate at the field bottom. Go through two more gates by trees to reach open country. The path, indefinite at times, stays near the river, going around Hartland Tor to reach a stile beside a gap in a wall. As a 90° bend in the river is approached, Lade Hill Brook flows into the East Dart from the right (north). About 400 m up this valley of the Brook the Beehive Hut is reached (see (2) Beehive Hut). To the north of the hut – about 2 km (1¼ miles) across the moor – is the Grey Wethers stone circle (see also Note (2)).

Follow the main river around the 90° bend and continue to the East Dart waterfall, a tiny but potent fall, one of the best on the moor. Beyond, the path leads to Sandy Hole Pass. The pass is, in part, man-made; the stream has been dredged and banking has been built to confine the river and so increase its flowrate. This helped to drain Broada Marsh to the north, and the water was used to stream tin. Stream spoil heaps can still be seen at the base of the pass. The pass itself is an excellent stopping point and is also closely approached on the return journey. The leat that begins close to the waterfall took water to power waterwheels at mines to the south.

Take a path that goes across the top of the pass; then breaks away from the river, going north (half-right) to avoid boggy ground. Ahead now the path is barely discernible but can be followed with care to reach a peat pass on the right. Take this. Such peat passes were cut to allow a dry passage from one dry hill to another through an area of difficult moorland bog. North Dartmoor has many such passes and our walk will follow two

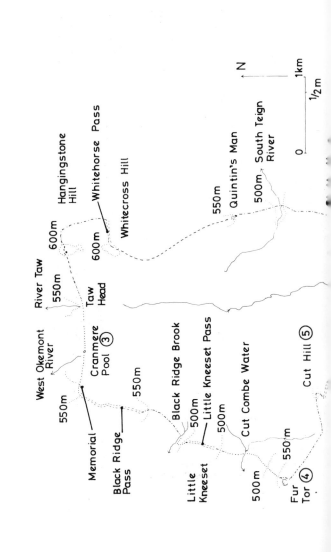

N

0   ½m   1km

River Taw

Hangingstone
Hill

Whitehorse Pass

600m

Whitecross Hill

600m

Whitecross Hill

550m
Quintin's Man

500m
South Teign
River

West Okemont
River

550m

Memorial

Cranmere
Pool ③

550m

Black Ridge
Pass

Black Ridge Brook

Little Kneeset Pass

Little
Kneeset

500m

500m

Cut Combe Water

500m

550m

Fur
Tor ④

Cut Hill ⑤

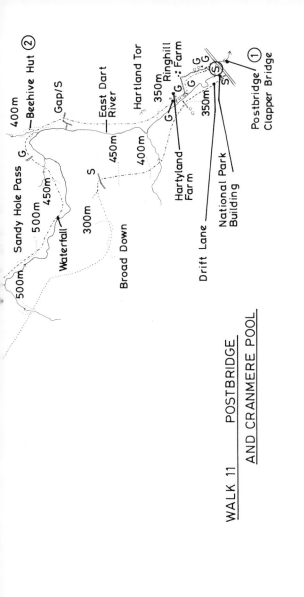

WALK 11   POSTBRIDGE

AND CRANMERE POOL

more. This one, Marsh Hill Pass – all the passes have names – is over 300 m (nearly 1000 ft) long. Close to the exit from the pass is Statts House, the ruins of an old peat-cutter's house. Go north along the shallow ridge of Winney's Down, then go gently downhill to the South Teign River. Keeping the Range Poles and Notice Board left, cross the river and follow the Range Poles to the top of Quintin's Man with its prominent hut and Range Flagpole (see Appendix 1). From the summit take the military track running west of north on to Whitehorse Hill where there is another Range Flagpole. Now go right with the track through the peat pass – called Whitehorse Hill and about 250 m long. Some of the passes are believed to have been hand cut in Saxon times; this one was bulldozer-cut in 1963 (though it did already exist in a shallower form). At the pass end, go left (north) to follow the hill flank before going up to the summit of Hangingstone Hill (see Note (3)). *Do not* attempt the direct summit ridge line to the Hill: it is miserably boggy.

From the observation post on the hill's summit take the indefinite path going west to Taw Head, staying as far north as possible to avoid the bog that is the birthplace of the East Dart River. Continue over trackless moor to the vaguely defined Cranmere Pool (see (3) Cranmere Pool). Now go west towards Great Kneeset, but before reaching it take the Black Ridge peat pass that heads southward for about 900 m (1000 yards). The start of the pass is marked by a memorial erected by Frank Philpotts (see Note (5)).

From the pass end head for the obvious rock mass of Fur Tor. The best route is to take a direct line down to Black Ridge Brook, but after crossing to bear right along the stream for 200 m to reach dry (drier?) ground to the left (south). Go ahead, then bear left around the bog to reach another peat pass that cuts across Little Kneeset just below its summit. At the pass end, head directly for Fur Tor, going down at first to cross Cut Combe Water, then steeply up to the Tor (see (4) Fur Tor).

From the top go south-east along the summit ridge, rounding

Dartmoor ponies

the head of the valley of Cut Combe Water to reach a path by
Range Poles on to Cut Hill (see (5) Cut Hill). Go right near the
Notice Board and head for the North Hessary Tor TV mast
(south) for 150 m to reach the North-West Passage peat pass,
marked by small cairns. Go along this and take the poorly defined
path at its end, aiming for two Range Poles. The path is soon lost;
continue with the West Dart valley to the left, staying high (and,
therefore, dryish). Go over a stream and pass a Range Pole. A
path is used soon but quickly ends. The East Dart Waterfall is a
landmark to the left as you go over Broad Down, the ground
falling gently south-east. Ahead now is a wall. Follow this to a stile
where it bends right; go over and follow a permissive path. Follow
the wall (left) and where it bends left keep ahead, crossing a leat
by clapper ridge and Braddon Lake (a stream) to reach a more
obvious track, Drift Lane, which leads directly back to the car-
park, which is reached over a stile to the left.

(1) *Postbridge*

Though there has been a human presence at Postbridge for many
centuries it was not until the late 18th century, when there was
commerical exploitation of local mines and the Moretonhampstead
to Tavistock turnpike was opened, that there was anything like a
hamlet or village. The turnpike – a private toll road – was never a
great commercial success (in the 1820s the Postbridge toll house
collected about £100 per year – a lot more than the Princetown
house but considerably less than on the roads off the moor to the
south) but did result in some local industry. The Hullet brothers
grew potatoes on the moor and extracted starch at a factory they
built here. They also built the Greyhound Inn, to the delight of
many a weary traveller. A couple of miles south of the village a
gunpowder factory was built, close to the site of Powder Mills
Farm. There, beside the farm road, the old mortar can still be
seen. This was used to check powder quality by firing a standard
iron ball and measuring the distance.

The village church, dedicated to St Gabriel, was built in 1867
and served not only as church, but as village hall and schoolroom.
The church stands north of the clapper bridge, the village's most

obvious and well-known feature. This is probably Dartmoor's most beautiful bridge, nine slabs of granite giving a span of 13 m (43 ft) at a height above the river that is much more than is often found. This was clearly to allow the bridge to be crossed even when the river was in spate. Note too the pillars, fashioned on the upstream side to create minimum resistance to flow. It seems that the bridge was very successful at withstanding winter's floods; the only recorded time it needed rebuilding was after some villagers dismantled it to use the slabs in a vain attempt to stop ducks swimming off downstream.

Close to the clapper bridge is a mould stone once used to form tin ingots at the Postbridge blowing house. The tin cast in the stone would have been pack-horsed across the moor to Chagford.

(2) *Beehive Hut*

Though well known, the Beehive Hut is poorly understood. It has been claimed to be very ancient but the quantity of surviving remains imply a much more recent construction date. Most experts now believe that the hut was built by medieval tinners working close to Sandy Hole Pass. It is thought that the hut was for tool storage rather than living, and that it would have been turf-covered for camouflage.

Nearby Grey Wethers consists of two circles, the northern one now having only nine stones (originally eighteen or more) and a diameter of 30 m (98 ft), the southern with seven stones (originally at least twenty-nine) and a diameter of 32 m (105 ft). The ridge top site is very evocative.

(3) *Cranmere Pool*

In the 17th century a Mayor of Okehampton, Benjamin Gayer, was found guilty of sheep stealing and sentenced to hang. He is said to have been hanged on Hangingstone Hill – hence the name – but his spirit was punished further, being required to empty Cranmere Pool with a sieve. That task was a good deal more thankless than it now seems, as at that time the pool was both deep and extensive. The peat that held it in place was breached – by storm or human hand – in the 19th century and much water ran

off leaving the pool today as a marshy area rather than a real pond. In very dry weather it can all but disappear; in very wet weather the pool seems to be everywhere, not least in both of your boots.

It is said that in ancient times the pool was visited by wives thought to have been unfaithful to their husbands. With an escort the women in question would come to the pool where they bathed in the dirty, cold water. The woman then visited the Scarhill and Grey Wethers Stone Circles. At the latter she knelt below a stone for judgement. If she was guilty the stone would fall and crush her.

Visits to the pool for more recreational reasons started, as far as written records are concerned, in 1789 when John Andrews, a Devonian lawyer, walked to it. Soon, with walking tours becoming all the rage, visits were more frequent. Most of these were guided visits and in 1854 one local guide, James Perrott, set up a cairn on which he placed a glass jar into which visitors could drop a card, and placed a visiting-book next to it. Various jars and bottles replaced the original until, in 1937, after an appeal by the *Western Morning News*, a stone box was erected. This, with a single change of door, still stands at the pool. The 'letterbox' caught the imagination – 'letterbox' because the intention was that you took a self-addressed postcard to the site and exchanged it for the one from the last visitor, taking his back to civilization for posting – with numerous other boxes being placed all over the moor. One estimate suggested that as many as 1500 permanent and temporary boxes existed by the 1980s, and letterbox visiting had become as popular as Munro bagging in Scotland. However, 1500 is obviously far too many to allow a reasonable chance to 'collect' the lot, and many people go only for a selected top ten or so. Of others, that at Fur Tor, also on our walk, is reckoned to be the most important. The Cranmere Pool and Fur Tor boxes are among the most inaccessible, the latter having the added value that the walker can spend hours searching for it. Some people also return from Cranmere having failed to find the box. You might expect, therefore, that I will give instructions on how to find them. You might expect that but . . .

The Beehive Hut

(4) *Fur Tor*

Fur Tor is one of the most impressive yet most inaccessible of tors and is said to be a site of natural energy by believers in Earth Magic. The local moor dwellers also believed the Tor was supernatural, being the home of the little people. As recently as the 1960s a walker claimed to have seen a pixie sitting at the top.

(5) *Cut Hill*

Fur Tor is so-called because it was the distant, the far ('Vur' in local dialect) tor. Cut Hill is named for its cut or peat pass. The plaque at the hill is to Frank Phillpotts who cut many such passages to help fox-hunters and moorsmen get about the moor.

Walk 12 High Willhays

As with Walk 11, this walk ventures on to the high wilderness of northern Dartmoor, visiting High Willhays – not only the highest peak on the moor but the highest in southern England.

   This is a long and arduous walk and should only be attempted by fit and experienced walkers.

Walk category : Difficult (5¼ hours)

Length : 20 km (12½ miles)

Ascent : 610 m (2000 ft)

Maps : Landranger Sheet 191, Outdoor Leisure Sheet 28

Starting and finishing point : At 563 918, the car-park near the
                                    Meldon Reservoir dam

Note: Much of this walk lies within one of the Army's Dartmoor Firing Ranges. Please read Appendix 1 before setting out on the moor.

The Cranmere Pool letterbox

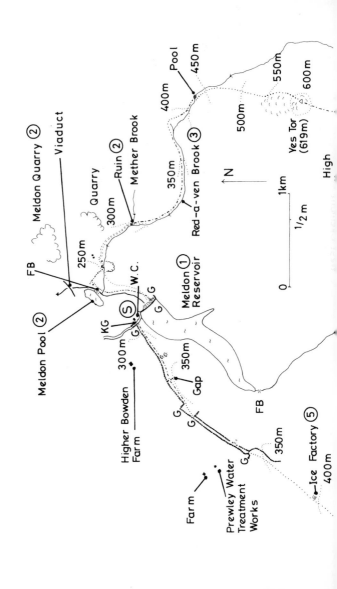

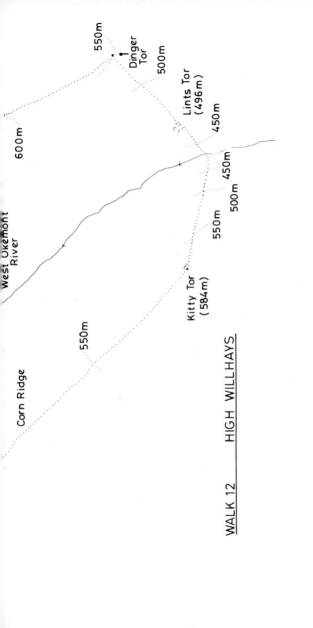

West Okement River

600m

550m

Dinger Tor

500m

Lints Tor
(496m)

450m

450m

500m

550m

Corn Ridge

550m

Kitty Tor
(584m)

WALK 12   HIGH WILLHAYS

Go past the toilets and through the gate to reach a lane. Go left to cross the reservoir dam (see (1) Meldon Reservoir). Go through the far gate, turn left and go through another gate to reach steps that lead down to the bottom of the dam. Follow the faint path along the outflow stream (the West Okemont River), go over an inflowing stream (Red-a-ven Brook) by stepping-stones and continue ahead, ignoring the track to the right. Over the bridge to the left about 50 m further on is the Meldon Pool, a filled limestone quarry (see (2) Meldon Quarry). Stay with the path until, at a telegraph pole just beyond a ruined building, a track is reached going sharply back to the right. Take this track, heading for a huge quarry across the brook (see also Note (2)).

Follow the brook (see (3) Red-a-ven Brook), a delightful stream with several small falls, past a Range Notice Board (close to which are the remains of an old mine (see also Note (2); be cautious if investigating) and over a small inflowing stream – Mether Brook. At one point the walker is forced left by a spring but the way is always close to the Brook. The ground steepens and a small artificial pool is reached. This is the Okehampton's old town reservoir; cross the brook just below it and continue along the other bank, staying close to the brook where the ground, paradoxically, is a little drier. At any suitable point – clear paths are some way behind us now – break right and up to the summit of Yes Tor with its trig-point, hut and Range Flagpole (see Appendix 1). The view from here is superb, extending over much of the moor, north to Exmoor and into Cornwall. Superb, that is, if you ignore the military bits and pieces and the churned-up ground.

Now go south to High Willhays (see (4) High Willhays) which reputedly has a letterbox (see Note (3) of Walk 11). Continue along the broad, but obvious, ridge going south-east to Dinger Tor: an obvious enough Tor, not least for its hut but as a high point representing little more then a blip at the end of a ridge. From the Tor head south-west to the more clearly defined Lints Tor that sits above the West Okemont River, the infeed for Meldon Reservoir. Crossing the river is the next hurdle, our next objective being Kitty Tor, due west from Lints across the valley. In all but the wettest weather the river is easily crossed and there is no need to go far south in order to find a convenient crossing. Go up to the hut and Range Flagpole on top of Kitty Tor.

Head north-west along the broad plateau towards the final rise of Corn Ridge. An alternative here is to go north and then to follow the edge of the West Okemont valley until the Corn Ridge end can be reached. Continue in the same line to Sourton Tors, crossing the line of King Way *en route*. From the Tors head north-east aiming for a long wall to the right of the clearly visible Prewley Water Treatment Plant. On the way look out for half-a-dozen shallow, now grass-filled troughs: the remains of an ice factory (see (5) Sourton Ice Factory). At the right corner of the wall line ahead a lane is entered. This is a more obvious section of King Way, an early route linking Tavistock to Okehampton across this corner of the moor. The lane's defining right wall ends after about 500 m, though the left wall remains. Follow this until another wall redefines the lane's right edge. Do not follow the lane here but go right with the wall, following it (it is on your left hand). Turn left with the wall and follow it back to the car-park.

(1) *Meldon Reservoir*

A little over ten years after Dartmoor had been made a National Park, the North Devon Water Board requested permission to construct a reservoir for Okehampton and District at Meldon, damming the West Okemont valley. This decision sparked a row over the right to develop such a scheme within the National Park boundary, especially since there were certain advantages in the use of an alternative site at Gorhuish, outside the Park. A select Committee of the House of Commons heard evidence and the Meldon site was chosen when it was found to be only about three-quarters of the cost of developing Gorhuish. The cost was £1.6 million, pricing destruction of a section of the National Park – and a fairly wholesale dumping of principles – at about £400,000 (at 1970 prices). The scheme was, it was said, a unique excursion into the Park, for a variety of unique reasons; since which, of course, there have been many other unique excursions in National Parks for equally unique sets of reasons.

The dam we cross is 200 m (660 ft) long, 44 m (144 ft) high and required 270,000 tons of concrete. The reservoir capacity is 300 million litres (nearly 700 million gallons) and its surface area about 25 hectares (around 60 acres).

(2) *Meldon Quarry*

There has been industrial activity in this area for centuries with some mining but chiefly the quarrying of limestone. Beyond the telegraph pole where the walk goes right up Red-a-ven-Brook is a fine, restored lime kiln. Meldon Pool is around 40 m (131 ft) deep and provided stone for several lime kilns, remains of which can be seen close to it. Today it is British Rail who operate the working quarry, extracting around 2000 tons of ballast stone daily. Ironically no trains now cross the ironwork Meldon viaduct, the line stopping at the quarry. The viaduct is 165 m (541 ft) long and 46 m (150 ft) at its highest. It was built in the years around 1874 and is a scheduled ancient monument.

The quarry to the left of our route was for the extraction of aplite, a mineral used in the ceramics and related industries. In the 1920s a glass bottle factory was set up next to the quarry to make use of the mineral. It was hoped that the factory would become the biggest in Britain but as with many of the local industries the actuality did not match up to the predictions and the factory failed.

The mine that the route passes was the Blackdown Copper mine first recorded in 1883. The mine had several names, Devon Copper, Wheal Maria, but none of them could change its fortunes and it soon failed.

(3) *Red-a-ven-Brook*

In an extreme but remarkably localized thunderstorm on 17 August 1917 the normal flow of the brook increased by an estimated 4,000-fold in volume, even though the West Okemont River was carrying no more than normal 'heavy rain' water. So much debris was carried down by the brook, boulders up to one ton being shifted huge distances, that it eventually dammed its old course and spread out to form a river over 80 m (262 ft) wide. One

Meldon viaduct and the route of Walk 12 seen from Meldon Dam

drainage ditch cut into the brook was expanded from 1.2 m wide by 1 metre (4 ft × 3 ft) deep to 63 m wide and 5 m deep (207 ft × 16½ ft) in the space of a few hours. Fortunately, unlike the similar flash flood at Lynmouth (see Note (2) of Walk 7) there was no village or town ahead of the water and the flood did little but change the local geography.

(4) *High Willhays*
The name of this somewhat undistinguished peak derives from the same Celtic root as Bodmin's Brown Willy (see Note (2) of Walk 24). But though undistinguished, the hill, at 621 m (2038 ft) is the highest English peak south of Kinder Scout, over 400 km (250 miles) away in the Peak District.

Those interested in the theory of ley lines (see Note (3) of Walk 34) will be interested to know that the Dragon Line, a supposed ley linking Stonehenge to Land's End, passes close to High Willhays, going across the southern end of its ridge close to Dinger Tor.

(5) *Sourton Ice Factory*
In the 19th century locals turned the high, exposed moor to their advantage by directing water from a nearby spring into shallow troughs which froze overnight for many months of the year and was ready for export to the fisherman of south Devon. Transportation was by horse downhill to Meldon and by the new railway to Plymouth. Mostly the ice melted *en route* and the factory (such as it was) was soon abandoned!

Walk 13 Burrator and the Abbot's Way

South of the cross-moorland road from Moretonhampstead to Tavistock by way of Princetown (the B3212 and B3357) the high Dartmoor plateau becomes a less high plateau. But it also loses some of the distinguishing high points and tors that makes the northern end a paradise for the well-equipped walker. The south is a less forgiving landscape, undulating but featureless – superb exploring rather than rambling country where use of map and compass rapidly become compulsory and inability to use them can be an embarrassment. The best walk here is, many would say, just to wander about for a day, visiting the ancient sites of which there are an abundance – the stone row on Erme Plains is 3.4 km (2.1 miles) long – or following rivers into their birthplace bogs.

Our route is less serious but no less committing, concentrating on the western edge of the plateau and following a section of the Abbot's Way.

Walk category : Difficult (4½ hours)

Length : 17 km (10½ miles) or 22 km (13¾ miles) if variants followed

Ascent : 460 m (1500 ft) or 500 m (1640 ft) if variants followed

Maps : Landranger Sheet 202, Outdoor Leisure Sheet 28

Starting and finishing point : At 568 695, the car-park by Norsworthy Bridge, at the stream inlet end of Burrator Reservoir

From the car-park go south along the strangely called Newleycombe Lake, and follow the road around a distinct right bend. The road approaches the tip of the reservoir (see (1) Burrator Reservoir) and as it does so a wall to the left leads off at right angles to the road. Take the track to the left here that leads through a wall gap to a gate, each waymarked in pink. Beyond the gate climb easily up Sheeps Tor (see (2) Sheeps Tor). From the summit a straightforward extension to the walk goes east to reach a wall and follows it around a rightward corner. Follow the line of the wall when the wall itself goes right again to reach, at 575 678 an extraordinary stone circle (see also Note (2)).

From the summit of Sheeps Tor take the indefinite path that heads for the south-east corner of the reservoir to reach a gate and lane (Joey's Lane) to the reservoir road. Go left into Sheepstor village (see also Note (2)).

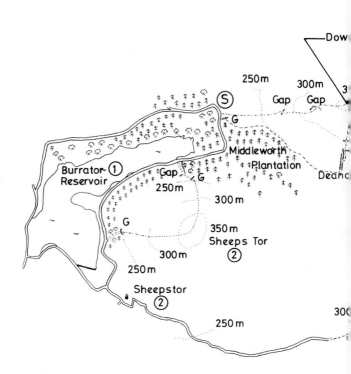

Dow

250 m
300 m
3
Gap   Gap

S
G

Middleworth
Plantation

Deanc

Burrator·
Reservoir ①

Gap
G
250 m

300 m

G
350 m
Sheeps Tor
300 m   ②

250 m

Sheepstor
②

250 m

300

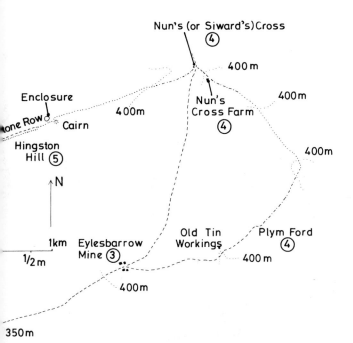

Nun's (or Siward's) Cross
④

400 m

400 m

Nun's
Cross Farm
④

400 m

Enclosure

Stone Row

Cairn

400m

Hingston
Hill ⑤

↑N

1km

½ m

Eylesbarrow
Mine ③

Old Tin
Workings

Plym Ford
④

400 m

400 m

350 m

Take the lane going east from the village and follow it, bearing left when a lane joins from the right, to its end just before a Scout Hut (marked on the OS map) among trees (not marked on the OS map). The walk continues along the track ahead to the ruins of Eylesbarrow tin mine at 599 681 (see (3) Eylesbarrow Mine). Before the mine is reached, after about 11½ km (1 mile), a track joins from the right. A fine extension of the walk – by about 2 km (1¼ miles) – follows this track to the ford over the Drizzle Stream and then contours to the left to reach one of Dartmoor's most concentrated prehistoric sites. There are two stone rows, each terminated by barrows at one end (north-east) and menhirs at the other (south-west). The most southerly menhir is, at 4 m (13 ft), the moor's tallest. Here too is the Giant's Basin, a huge burial cairn. From the Eylesbarrow Mine's ruin a second extension climbs Eylesbarrow itself for a fine view over the local moor.

From the mine ruin there is a choice. Take the path ahead for an easy trip to Siward's Cross. Better is to take the path going half-right (just south of east), passing the ruins of the miners' hostel (barracks?) and the mine officer's house, following it to Plym Ford where there are ancient ruins from a distant outpost of Eylesbarrow mine. The ford was taken by the Abbot's Way (see (4) Abbot's Way). From the ford take the path going north-east. This soon peters out. Now go north across the wild but beautiful moor. An ancient boundary ditch (see also Note (4)) is crossed close to another ancient cross before the ruin of Nun's Cross Farm and the cross itself (see also Note (4)) are reached. The farm reminds me of the old tale of the moorland cottage with the leaky roof in which a traveller sought (dubious) shelter from torrential rain. When he asked the owner why he did not mend the roof the reply was that only an idiot would work outside on a day like today. The exasperated traveller persisted: why did the farmer not mend the roof in dry weather? What, said the Dartmoor worthy, waste good time mending a roof that was not giving any trouble! From Nun's Cross our route crosses the moorland to the west.

Nun's (or Siward's) Cross and Nun's Cross Farm ruins

Head towards old mine hummocks, bearing left to find an obvious leat. Cross this where it emerges from the hillside – at a gate with Radon Gas warning notice. There it points directly at Down Tor, though the way soon becomes clear, the walker heading for the stone row on Hingston Hill (see (5) Hingston Hill).

From the end of the stone row continue to Down Tor, passing close to a wall to the left. From the summit it is claimed that 23 tors can be seen. From the tor there is a choice. Either go east of south from the summit to reach a steep, stony lane that drops down to the ruins of Deancombe. Bear right there along the path that follows the edge of the Middleworth plantation to reach the reservoir road at the car-park. Or take the obvious path that goes almost due west off the summit directly to the car-park. This is a more direct but less interesting route.

(1) *Burrator Reservoir*
In 1590 under the direction of Sir Francis Drake a water leat was cut from the River Meavy to supply drinking water to Plymouth. It is widely believed that the work (the leat was cut at the amazing rate of 1 mile per week) was the greatest of all Tudor feats of engineering. A section of the leat can still be seen below the dam of Burrator Reservoir. By an irony probably not lost on the Victorian engineers, who had a better grasp of historical perspective than many today, the reservoir produced by damming the Meavy valley also feeds Plymouth. Originally the reservoir, completed in 1898, had a capacity of about 650 million gallons but this was increased by 50% in 1928. The name Burrator means 'wooded tor', which could never have been truer than today, the area surrounding the reservoir being widely afforested and having an almost alpine beauty.

(2) *Sheeps Tor*
At the southern end of the ridge along Sheeps Tor (the name Sheeps is from *schittes*, a steep slope) is Pixies' Cave, a natural rock formation once, legend has it, used as a hiding-place by an

The view east from Down Tor

escaping Royalist during the Civil War. The tale that links the fairy folk with the cave suggests that if you leave a gift in the cave – a pin is the preferred offering – then the pixies will grant you a wish.

On Yellowmead Down, to the east of the summit, is a curious stone circle made up of four concentric rings of stones with diameters 6, 11½, 14½ and 20 m (20, 38, 48 and 65 ft). So close are the stones of the inner circle that they almost form a continuous ring. Surprisingly the arrangement is not unique; there is a similar one on Shoveldon to the west of Teigncombe Common.

The village at the foot of the tor, a village that shares its name, is an ancient tin-mining village. It is a delightful place: dark cottages grouped closed to a fine 16th-century church with a delicately pinnacled tower, a relatively common feature of moorland churches. The church, whose main pillars are of local granite, has an excellent rood screen – an exact copy in 1914 of a 15th-century screen – and a churchyard holding the tombs of three 19th- and 20th-century Rajahs of Sarawak. The first was James Brooke, born in 1803 in Bengal, the son of an East India Company judge. He was sent to Sarawak in 1839 to officially thank the Rajah for the help he had given some shipwrecked British sailors. Finding Sarawak in the grip of pirates and rebels he helped to bring calm and was asked to stay, being made Rajah in 1841. In 1848 on a trip to London he was made a KCB but continued to live in Sarawak until 1863 when he retired to this part of Dartmoor where he had bought an estate in 1859. He died in 1868. He was to have been succeeded by his nephew, John Brooke Johnson, but the younger man also died in 1868. The second Rajah was Charles Johnson, brother of John Brooke, who took the name Brooke upon succession. He in turn was succeeded by his son, Charles, who died in London in 1963. Strangely the tomb of the first Rajah is of Aberdeen not local granite.

On the outside church wall above the entrance porch is a strange mid-17th-century sundial/carving. It depicts a skull with bones in its mouth over an hourglass, corn-ears sprouting from the eye sockets, and represents 'Life from Death'. Outside the church the village cross was restored – look for the joins on the cross arms – and re-erected in 1911, after having served time as a rubbing-post for cows. It is very unusual in having a small relief cross on both sides.

(3) *Eylesbarrow Mine*
It is known that tin miners were at work in this area as early as the 12th century, and the mine was the last to operate on Dartmoor, closing in 1852. The ruins represent a comprehensive set of mine buildings, with not only an old blowing-house (see Note (3) of Walk 14) but a horizonal flue. The flue was built in this fashion because it was eventually recognized by mine owners that there was a significant loss of tin in the smoke that went up the chimney. They therefore built horizontal flues in which the heavy metal particles 'plated out' on the stone chimney walls. At regular intervals a worker would go in and scrape metal off the walls. Of all the jobs in the old mines this must have been one of the most unpleasant; the poor worker was exposed to an atmosphere in which the metal concentration was very high with inevitable effects on his lungs and internal organs.

(4) *Abbot's Way*
So entrenched is the name for the route across southern Dartmoor – it even appears on the OS maps – that it seems a heresy to challenge it, but it is a fact that the name dates from the 18th century while the abbot in question (of Buckfast Abbey) was history by the late 16th century. The name is based on the possibility that a route from Whitchurch Priory to Buckfast went this way, though there is evidence that the only 'sponsored' route stayed well north, going over Holne Moor (see Note (2) of Walk 14). It is probable that the name comes from a folk memory that 'jobbers', wool-carrying pack-horse leaders, came this way from Whitchurch carrying the prior's (and Abbott's) wool southwards, that tinners also used it, and that there are several crosses on the moorland near Nun's Cross (a minimum of 4, at least 3 of them not on Abbot's Way). Crosses were used as guide-posts by the monastic houses.

Nun's or Siward's Cross stands to the west of the ruined farm that bears its name. It is a superb medieval cross, dating at least from 1240 when it is mentioned in one of Dartmoor's first walking tours. The shaft has been repaired, following an act of blatant vandalism in the mid 19th century. The cross, over 2 m (6½ ft) high and almost 1 m (3¼ ft) across, has two names. Nun's is almost certainly not from a convent sister but from the Celtic *nant*, a small stream or shallow valley, which was probably applied to the area before the cross was erected. The second name, Siward, may also pre-date the cross as it refers to the Saxon Earl of Northumberland who owned estates locally. It may even be to the Earl's time that the *reave* – an ancient word allied to *rhine* (pronounced *rheen*) in Somerset and meaning a ditch – dates. The crosses may belong to the same period, the ditches having been used at that time on Dartmoor as estate boundaries.

(5) *Hingston Hill*

The sites here start, on the east side, with a cairn close to what the OS calls an enclosure. The former is a large – 16 m (52 ft) in diameter – burial chamber, the latter being a pear-shaped, walled pound about 43 m (141 ft) across. No evidence of hut cicles has been found inside the enclosure and its purpose is unknown. It is usually assumed to be an animal pound but such a use is questionable. To the west, and lined up with the cairn, is a superb stone row, about 350 m (383 yards) long, that ends, at its western end, with a tall menhir, 3 m (10 ft) high, that forms part of a stone circle. The circle is of the type known as a retaining circle because it encloses a burial. The circle is 11 m (36 ft) across.

Walk 14 Dartmeet

This excellent walk explores the high moors around the meeting place of the twin Dart rivers. But though excellent it is not without its problems as it uses two sets of stepping-stones to cross rivers. Check the stones at Dartmeet first: if these are barely passable, or even if the water is within an inch or two of the tops, come back on a drier day because you will not be able to cross Week Ford.

Walk category : Easy (1½ hours)

Length : 5½ km (3½ miles), but 8 km (5 miles) if Yar Tor is
          climbed

Ascent : 140 m (360 ft), but 240 m (1115 ft) if Yar Tor is climbed

Maps : Landranger Sheets 91 and 202, Outdoor Leisure Sheet 28

Starting and finishing point : The car-park at 672 733, beside the
                                bridge at Dartmeet

From the car-park walk back to the road and go right over the
bridge (see (1) Dartmeet) to reach an ancient petrol station to the
left. Take a signed path beyond the forecourt down to a gate.
Beyond there is another signpost. Its half-right facing arm
indicates posts up the field: this is the return journey. Bear left
with its other arm to stepping-stones over the West Dart River.
Note: *Do not* continue with the walk if the river here is only just
passable – the Week Ford stones sit 6–8 inches lower than these.
Over the stream the way is signed, going up through delightful
rocks and trees to a wall gap. Keep the field edge wall to the left
and continue to Combestone Farm, a beautifully sited building,
where another sign gives the line up hill to a gate by a shed.
Follow the track beyond to another gate out on to the moor. Go
obviously up to Combestone Tor ahead and left. When you arrive
you will find the view being shared by many who have driven to
the spot, the tor summit having a road and a car-park as part of its
furniture (see (2) Combestone Tor).
    Retrace the last section of the ascent to the final gate, go
through and left with the sign for the Week Ford stepping-stones.
The path here is at best very indistinct. To make the best progress,
go along a shallow gully to a gate at the bottom of the field. Now
go down to a bridge (of sorts) over what is more realistically
termed lying than flowing water. Beyond, a squat wall, right, gives
the way at first but soon bends away rightward and should not be
followed. Continue in the line of the wall, picking a way down to

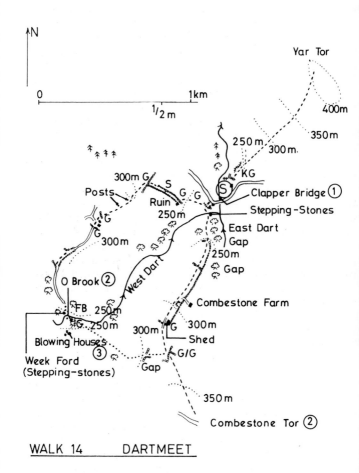

N

0   1km

½ m

Yar Tor

400m

350m

250m   300m.

KG

300m G   S

Posts

G   G

Ruin

250m

G

G

300m

O Brook ②

West Dart

FB   250m

G   250m

Blowing Houses

③

Week Ford
(Stepping-stones)

300m

Gap

G/G

Gap

S

Clapper Bridge ①

Stepping-Stones

East Dart

Gap

250m

Gap

Combestone Farm

300m

G   300m

Shed

350m

Combestone Tor ②

WALK 14   DARTMEET

the West Dart. It is not possible to go too far left as a fence is reached that must be followed to the river. Too far right and you are in a stream. At the river, go left, upstream, to reach a fence with a gate. Go through and over the O Brook (see also Note (2)) by a bridge close to where it joins the West Dart. Nearby on the far side – upstream and to the right by trees – are the ruins of an ancient blowing house (see (3) Blowing House). About 100 m further upstream are the Week Ford stepping-stones.

From the far side of the stepping-stones follow a path that soon becomes a lane. The left retaining wall goes off left but a sign points the way along the right wall to another lane. This ends at farm buildings. Go past the barn, shed and silage mound and bear right to a gate. In the field beyond, posts give the way to an enclosed lane that is followed to a stile. Go over and down the lane to a ruin on the right, opposite which enter a field. This has waymarking posts to lead you back to the signpost mentioned at the start. Reverse the outward few yards to reach the car-park.

To add another fine view to the walk, go north out of the car-park through the kissing-gate next to the driveway and take the path beyond that reaches open moor near a gate marked 'Private'. Climb easily to the summit of Yar Tor from where the views are superb in all directions.

(1) *Dartmeet*

The old clapper bridge which stands proud, if a little forlorn, beside the new bridge is a contemporary of all other Dartmoor clappers. Those who have already read Note (1) of Walk 8 will find this of little comfort, as the age of Tarr Steps described there is thought to lie between 700 and 3000 years. The Dartmeet clapper collapsed on 4 August 1826 when a flash flood after torrential rain brought down both water and trees to this point. The trees are said to have tangled with the bridge piers causing a local dam, the collapse of which caused a flood surge that wiped away the slabs. By then, however, the clapper was already redundant, having been replaced by the handsome bridge that takes cars, in single file, over the combined rivers. That bridge was built in 1792. Interestingly, as the stepping-stones crossed on the walk are almost certainly pre-clapper, the full succession of river crossings from pre-history through medieval to (almost) modern is displayed within a very few yards.

Many purists decry the car-park and the tourist throng who gaze at the clapper and move on having 'done Dartmeet'. To retain your small inner glow about being slightly superior to the non-walkers, you might notice how few of them actually ever see Dartmeet. The East and West Darts actually join about 100 m south of the bridges, a spot rarely visited by the tourist. To be fair, though, it is not actually on our walk either!

(2) *Combestone Tor*

The view northward to Dartmeet is impressive but that southward to the high moorland of Holne Moor and beyond is more so. This is rugged, uncompromising country, a land for the connoisseur, a walker who is experienced in finding his/her way about featureless, often treacherous country. Just south of the Tor there are the remains of Bronze Age hut circles and a stone row that is probably older. Nearer is Holne Cross which may mark a spot on a trackway used by travellers to Buckfast Abbey.

To the west the view is over the O Brook down the valley through which our walk continues. The brook has the distinction of having the shortest British name for a waterway.

(3) *Blowing House*

Early attempts at ore smelting usually managed little more than the production of a puddle of melted ore mixed with some remnant slag and charcoal, a mix that had to be resmelted. The next stage of metal refining was the blowing house where a forced draught increased the working temperature and pure metal was produced in a single process. The Week Ford ruins are of such blowing houses, the draught here being provided by a bellows worked from a water wheel. There were, in fact, two houses each powered by wheels about 3 m (10 ft) in diameter. Mould stones, used to cast the molten tin, can still be seen at the sites. The tin

The stepping stones at Dartmeet

ore was extracted locally but the smelter was never really profitable and had a short, somewhat indistinguished career.

Walk 15 Lydford Gorge

To offer as a 'best walk' one that crosses private lands, which the owner charges a fee for walking on, would appear to many to be sacreligious. I have sympathy with that view. I am reminded of the story of the American hotel which laid a path to a local beauty spot and created a balcony for visitors. A sign was erected proclaiming that the view had been brought to visitors by kind permission of Hotel X, to which someone had added the note: 'With a little help from God.' Here, however, the owner is the National Trust and the reason for the control of access is to maintain the scenic beauty and local ecology. The Trust argue that without protection the Gorge would long since have been destroyed. Maybe. What is certainly true is that the Gorge is a superb piece of country, one of the finest remaining river valleys draining down from High Dartmoor.

Walk category : Easy (1½ hours)

Length : 5½ kms (3½ miles)

Ascent : 100 m (325 ft)

Maps : Landranger Sheets 191 or 201, Outdoor Leisure Sheet 28 – almost! (The OL sheet covers about 90% of the route. To cover the whole at 1:25000 it is necessary to buy sheets SX48/58, which is hardly worthwhile.)

Starting and finishing point : Numerous! There are National Trust car-parks at 500 834 – the 'waterfall end' of the walk – and at 508 845 – the Lydford end. Better still is the car-park at 510 848 in Lydford village itself, and that is what the map and directions assume.

Note: The complete Gorge walk is only open from April to October. From November to March the 'waterfall end' only is open, with access to the short walk down to the White Lady Waterfall.

From the car-park go back to the village road (see (1) Lydford) and go left, passing the castle (see (2) Lydford Castle) and church (see (3) Lydford Church). Go down the hill (south-west) using the pavement on the left side of the road to reach Lydford Bridge and a first, and very good, view of the gorge. Beyond the bridge go right up the National Trust road to the shop where the entrance fee is payable. Now follow the Gorge Walk by going along the left bank of the River Lyd (see (4) Lydford Gorge) to reach a bridge of the old GWR railway line close to the second gorge entrance. There go right on another pathway that soon splits into two. To the right here is a quick but steep (stepped) way down to the waterfall; to the left is a longer, more gradual descent.

At the waterfall (see (5) White Lady Waterfall) cross the Lyd by bridge and follow the river's right bank. At one point the path goes through a short rock tunnel, near a section of the Gorge called Tunnel Falls. Further on, about 600 m, is Pixie Glen, a very beautiful section. A bridge is reached just after Pixie Glen; go over for a direct way back to the start. Ahead is a path to the Devil's Cauldron (see (6) Devil's Cauldron). The further you go on this path, the more artificial it becomes. Finally the Cauldron is reached by an out-and-back path that is, in part, a narrow metal bridge over an uncompromising drop, and a set of rock-cut steps that are slippery when wet (which is most times) and positioned above an equally unfriendly drop. Notices suggest that the Cauldron path is not for the faint-hearted but there is no real reason for this exaggeration; the approach needs care but no experienced walker or sensible, careful visitor is likely to have much difficulty.

After viewing the Cauldron a straightforward path leads back to start of the Gorge Walk. To return to Lydford reverse the outward walk.

WALK 15   LYDFORD GORGE

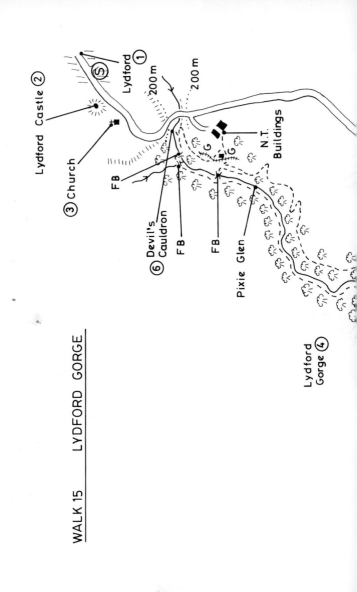

Lydford ①

Ⓢ Lydford

Lydford Castle ②

Church ③

Devil's Cauldron ⑥

Pixie Glen

N.T. Buildings

Lydford Gorge ④

FB

200 m
200 m

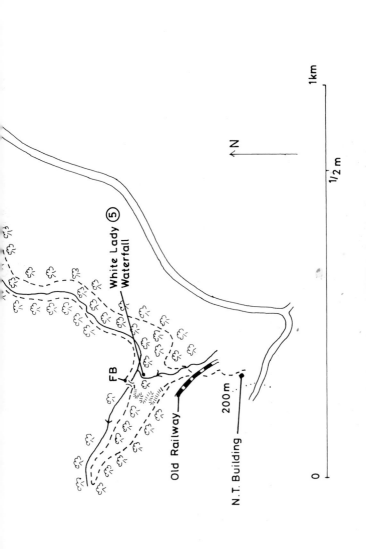

White Lady Waterfall ⑤

FB

Old Railway

200 m

N.T. Building

N

0   ½ m   1km

(1) *Lydford*

The naturally defensive position of Lydford, where a ridge of the
land was well protected by the Lyd and its tributary stream, was
noted by the Saxons when they needed a site from which to defend
the extreme boundary of Wessex from the Celtic lands of
Cornwall. As a consequence of its important position Lydford
became one of the four burghs of Devon, along with Barnstaple,
Totnes and Exeter. The remains of the Saxon defensive
earthworks, probably dating from the 9th century, can still be
seen; they follow the River Lyd to the south-east and its tributary
to the south-west and west, but lie close to the junction of Silver
Street and the main village street on the north-east side. Silver
Street itself is a reminder of Lydford Mint, a royal mint set up in
the late 10th century to produce silver coins known as Lydford
pennies. The village pub, the Castle Inn, has four of these and
there are many more in the British Museum. By far the largest
number is in the Royal Stockholm Museum, the Vikings having
obtained them either during the course of local raids, or as
Donegeld, the payment made by Saxons kings to persuade the
Norse raiders to raid elsewhere.

When the Normans came, they reinforced the Saxon ramparts,
placing their own earliest castle at the western corner of the old
fort. The remains of the stone keep – Lydford Castle, see note (3)
below – is not a part of that castle but dates from a time when
Lydford was the site of the Stannary Courts, which dealt with
abuses of local mining laws, and the Forest Courts, which
administered the laws of the Dartmoor Forest. At Lydford the
mines yielded not only the tin from which the name 'Stannary'
derives – from the Latin name for tin, *stannum* – but silver, copper
and some lead. By the mid 17th-century the mines had failed and
the village went into a serious decline. Shortly after it was
described as a 'mean miserable village of about 20 houses'. It isn't
much bigger now but is hardly mean and by no means miserable.

(2) *Lydford Castle*

The castle was, in fact, never a castle in the accepted sense and
was never so-called by its builders. To them it was a 'strong

building', a prison. The strong building was erected in 1195, prisoners being kept on two floors. A century later a ditch was added for extra security. Today's visitor sees just a shell, and a light and airy shell at that. It is safe to assume, however, that it was seen differently by the earliest occupants. Then, without much light, without any heat and, for many, without much hope, it must have been a bleak place. The lack of hope derived from 'Lydford Law' which was meted out to the prisoners. A local poem spoke of Lydford Law:

> I oft have heard of Lydford Law,
> How in the morn they hang and draw
> And sit in judgement after

The poem goes on to suggest that the law was so harsh that it was better to be stoned or pressed, or even to be hanged, than to be sent to Lydford Castle for judgement. One man who felt the power of the Stannary Court was Richard Strode, MP for Plympton. He spoke out against the pollution of streams with mine waste – proving that even 'green' issues are not new – and was imprisoned in the castle on a unspecified charge for his trouble. As a direct result of this incident a law was passed that allows free speech on any topic in Parliament.

(3) *Lydford Church*

The church is dedicated to St Petrock, a Celtic saint said to have been born in south Wales, who landed near the mouth of the Camel in the early 6th century and preached in Devon and Cornwall. There are nearly thirty churches in the counties dedicated to him, as well as one in Somerset and a couple in Wales itself.

Of Petrock's church in Lydford nothing remains. Nor does anything of the late Saxon church; the earliest work now surviving is 13th-century. This early work can be seen in the chancel and the west wall of the nave, the main fabric dating from a complete rebuild in the 15th century when the tower was also added. To minimize inconvenience during the building of the tower it was

actually placed 2 ft from the church, the gap being bridged only after completion. This short bridging section can best be seen from the outside. Inside, the most noteable features are the beautifully carved pew ends which date from earlier this century. The most unusual feature is the Lydford stocks preserved in the tower. The stocks could accomodate up to four n'er-do-wells at a time, and could also handle differing-sized legs.

Outside, most visitors will want to see the Watchmaker's Tomb, though the inscription for which it is famous is difficult to read as it is on top of the table tomb. The tomb is of George Routleigh, a Launceston clock and watchmaker, and the inscription runs:

Here lies in horizontal position
The outside case of
George Routleigh, watchmaker
Whose abilities in that line were an honour
To his profession
Integrity was the mainspring
And prudence the regulator
Of all the actions of his life
Humane, generous and liberal
His hand never stopped
Till he had relieved distress
So nicely regulated were all his motions
That he never went wrong
Except when set agoing
By people
Who did not know
His key
Even then he was easily
Set right again
He had the art of disposing his time
So well
That his hours glided away
In one continual round

Lydford Castle

Of pleasure and delight
Till an unlucky minute put a period to
His existence
He departed this life
Nov. 14. 1802
Aged 57
Wound up
In hopes of being taken in hand
By his maker
And of being thoroughly cleaned, repaired
And set agoing
In the world to come

Many visitors believe the inscription is unique or original. In fact it
is neither, having been first written down in America many years
before Routleigh's death. It is, of course, none the worse for that.

Routleigh appears to have plenty of neighbours in the
churchyard but all may not be what it seems. Lydford was one of
few local churchs and several corpse roads ran across the moors to
it. Rumours abounded that on occasions the bearers, fed-up with
hauling their heavy and troublesome load, would tip the corpse
into a moorland bog, carry the easiet, empty coffin to the village
outskirts and then refill it with stones to the correct weight.

(4) *Lydford Gorge*

The gorge was formed by the erosion of the underlying rock by the
River Lyd, a process that started about half a million years ago
when the Lyd was 'captured' by another stream. The narrow,
steep gorge offers some of the finest natural scenery in Devon and
is a complete contrast to not only the coast and high moors of the
county, but also to the more pastoral 'cream tea' country for which
it is famous. Pixie Glen, where the river is wide and shallow, is
one of the most beautiful spots, though Tunnel Falls, where the
river is fast, deep and enclosed in superb mossy banks, is more
dramatic. The outward part of our walk is further from the river
and offers the better long views.

Within the Gorge the dragonflies and butterflies are very good –

the latter include the silver-washed frittary and purple hairstreak –
as is the bird life with numerous arboreal species: tree creepers,
nuthatches and woodpeckers as well as warblers, wagtails, finches
and wrens. In summer tree pipits are often seen, and the river is
home to the dipper. The visitor will usually see grey squirrels and,
rarely, red deer and mink. The latter will be a local fur farm
escapee that has taken up residence and split the conservationists
into two groups. Overall, it is now believed it would have been
better if mink had not escaped, though direct evidence for its
affecting the otter population, which is now very small, is lacking.

(5) *White Lady Waterfall*

The fall is a delicate skein of water dropping 30 m (nearly 100 ft)
down a steeply impending rock wall. The name derives from a
local legend that anyone falling over the falls and seeing a ghostly
lady in white will not drown in the river. That must be wrong, as
anyone going over the falls would be unlikely to survive long
enough to drown. The National Trust version of the story
maintains that seeing the lady saves you from drowning if you fall
in the river at this point. That seems more plausible but the river
here is so shallow it is difficult to conceive of anyone drowning in
it. Perhaps the White Lady is a particularly active ghost.

(6) *Devil's Cauldron*

Ignoring the fanciful name, the like of which never much improved
one of Nature's better endeavours, the Cauldron really is very
good. The river at this point tumbles into a narrow, dimly lit rocky
ravine where the swirling of centuries has smoothed out walls and
hollows and produced 'pot-holes' as carried rocks have smashed
into the river bed and sides. The moss and lichen that thrive in the
wet, dark ravine add to the interest.

Walk 16 The Teign Valley

The essential Devonian river is, for many people, the Dart – rising
on Dartmoor and reaching the sea at the beautiful small, old port
of Dartmouth. Two walks in this book reinforce that view! Yet

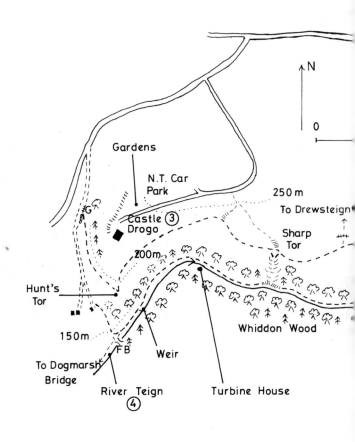

Gardens

N.T. Car Park

250 m

To Drewsteign*

Castle ③ Drogo

Sharp Tor

200m

Hunt's Tor

Whiddon Wood

150m

FB

Weir

To Dogmarsh Bridge

River Teign ④

Turbine House

WALK 16   THE TEIGN VALLEY

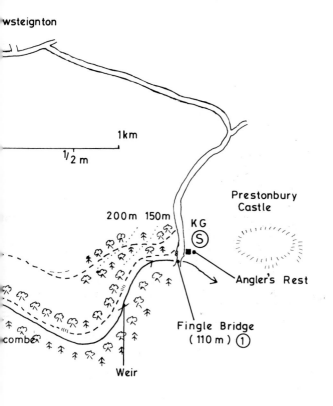

wsteignton

1km

1/2 m

Prestonbury
Castle

200m 150m

KG
(S)

Angler's Rest

Fingle Bridge
(110 m) (1)

combe

Weir

Cranbrook
Castle (2)

there is another river whose valley, certainly in its earliest stages, is as lovely as, though different from, the Dart. That river is the Teign.

Walk category : Easy (1½ hours)

Length : 6½ km (4 miles)

Ascent : 150 m (500 ft)

Maps : Landranger Sheet 191, Outdoor Leisure Sheet 28

Starting and finishing point : At 742 899, Fingle Bridge. There is roadside parking close to the bridge and the Anglers' Rest Inn beside it. The bridge is reached by a narrow road from Drewsteignton.

From the bridge (see (1) Fingle Bridge) go north along the road towards Drewsteignton for about 150 m to reach, to the left, a bridleway signposted as the Hunter's Path. Follow this up through trees to open hillside above the Teign Valley which is seen in all its beauty for almost the whole of its gorge-like section from Coombe to Fingle Bridge. Continue to Sharp Tor, an even better viewpoint to the left, and a tor of shale rather than granite. From the tor the eye is drawn across the valley to Cranbrook Castle set on a hill that rises far above the trees of Hannicombe Wood (see (2) Cranbrook Castle).

   Beyond Sharp Tor signed steps to the right allow access to Drogo Castle (see (3) Drogo Castle) which has been in view for a little while. Unfortunately the only reasonable way to return to the route after visiting the castle is to reverse to this point. Continue along the well-worn path to Hunt's Tor, a pile of granite rocks that sits below the ridge on which sits Drogo Castle. The name is correct by the way: it is the Ordnance Survey's name 'Hunter's Tor' that is wrong. At the tor the path swings sharply right and descends steeply to a tributary stream of the Teign. A signpost is reached pointing out the Fisherman's Path. Go south along this new path. Bear left for Gibhouse at a track junction. Gibhouse is a pleasant thatched cottage: go left on a path just before it to reach the Teign near an iron bridge and weir. Do not cross but take the Fisherman's Path along the river's left bank (see (4) Teign Valley), a walk that is, for the most part, straightforward, but does have a stepped section across the steeply falling and erosion-shattered flank of Sharp Tor.

(1) *Fingle Bridge*

This is so obviously a convenient crossing-point of the Teign that it comes as a surprise to discover that Fingle Bridge is the first bridge on the site, and that it only dates from Elizabethan times. It is a granite-built pack-horse bridge, sturdy against winter's rushing water and yet from the banks on either side, as elegant as could be conceived by artist rather than by engineer.

Surprisingly, in view of its apparent remoteness, the Upper Teign Valley saw considerable, if limited, action during the Civil War. An engraved cross on a granite rock just south of the bridge – on the old road to Moretonhampstead – marks the spot where one local Royalist died, while the Roundhead poet, Sidney Godolphin, of the family who later provided Charles II with a minister, died after being shot in a skirmish at the Coombe end of the walk.

(2) *Cranbrook Castle*

Cranbrook is one of two Iron Age hillforts which defend the tight Teign Valley. The other, Prestonbury, stands to the east of Fingle Bridge and dominates the view in that direction on the early part of the Hunter's Path.

(3) *Castle Drogo*

After the Normans had conquered England the new king, William, gave the Saxon estates to his relatives and those knights who had supported him. The town at the upper end of the Teign Valley eventually passed to a grandson of Richard, Duke of Normandy, named Drogo, a man who also spelt his name Dru and Drew, and gave his name to the town, Drew's Teign town – Drewsteignton.

Eight centuries later one Richard Peek was rector of Drewsteignton and his cousin Juluis Drewe used to visit him. Drewe became a very rich man after starting a successful grocery store chain in the last years of the 19th century. He became convinced that he was a descendant of Drogo and decided to build a castle named for the Norman lord. To realize his dream Drewe called in the man who was to become the foremost architect of his day, Edwin Lutyens. The idea was that Lutyens would build what Drewe wanted, but World War I took its toll on the sheer size of Drewe's plan, and Lutyens' better judgement reduced it still further. What we see, therefore, is more subdued then it might have been. Forty years after its completion the Drewe family gave the castle and its estate to the National Trust who still own and administer it.

The approach to the castle is superb, a *rond-point* being reached on the narrow road – all local roads are narrow, interesting tests of skill and patience – from Sandy Park on the A382 and Drewsteignton. From the *rond-point* a long curving drive, at one point going through an ilex grove, leads to the castle, an effect now somewhat spoilt by the funnelling of all visitors through the NT car-park and shop. That funnelling does mean though that the visitor sees the castle gardens before seeing the castle itself. The gardens are excellent, starting with a croquet lawn – equipment available at the shop – and continuing to a formal, terraced rose garden.

The castle is beyond the rose garden, set right on the long tip of the ridge above the Teign Valley. It is of granite, which gives its squat appearance a sombre look. Inside, the bare granite walls seem at odds with some of the richer furnishings, a curious blend of medieval castle reality and 20th-century luxury. Yet there is much to admire and interest: long corridors that draw the eye, the elegant drawing-room, the fascinating kitchen and scullery, and, best of all, the bath/shower unit in the bathroom.

Castle Drogo gardens

(4) *Teign Valley*

The upper reaches of the Hunter's Path is the haunt of stonechat, whinchat and meadow pipit. Until recently there were several pairs of nightjar here too, but sadly these are, as elsewhere, very rare now. In the woodland of the valley, which is still mainly of oak and birch, all three woodpeckers can be seen, as can tree creepers and the occasional crossbill. On the river itself the kingfisher can still be seen, though infrequently, as can dippers and several wagtails. Thankfully, the otter is still a local animal though there is also a thriving and increasing population of mink. Fallow deer are often seen in the valley's woodland.

In the woods the wood white and silver-washed fritillary butterflies have pride of place, though several hairstreaks and other fritalleries can also be seen. The plant life is almost too numerous to list – it must have been a delight to the Reverend Keble Martin, creator of one of Britain's finest wild flower books, who once served at Drewsteignton church – but do look out for the royal fern.

Walk 17 Lustleigh Cleave

On the eastern edge of Dartmoor, close to the National Park Office – which lies outside the park (!) near Bovey Tracey – the River Bovey flows through a wooded gorge overlooked by a ridge of high moor. The valley is an important plant area and has been designated as an SSI (Site of Special Scientific Interest). Our walk follows the best part of that valley from Lustleigh village, returning to the village along the moorland ridge.

Walk category : Intermediate (3 hours)

Length : 12 km (7½ miles)

Ascent : 300 m (1000 ft)

Maps : Landranger Sheet 191, Outdoor Leisure Sheet 28

Starting and finishing point : The church, Lustleigh village. In
summer months the village can be
very crowded and, as there is no
official car-park, choked with cars.
Arrive early or late or (and better) go
in spring or autumn.

From the church go south over a barely noticed stone bridge and
then uphill towards Rudge. At a crossroads – actually a T-junction
of roads, but the bridleway ahead is concreted – go ahead to reach
Hisley Farm. Gates lead into and out of the farm on to a path that
is followed downhill to the tiny Hisley packbridge. Go over,
through the gate ahead and turn right on the path signed for
Manaton. This path leads to Becka Falls, a pleasant enough
waterfall, but a spot made just a little too twee by its popularity.
The walk does not go that far, however, taking a wooden bridge to
the right – over Becka Brook rather than the River Bovey that
Hisley packbridge crossed – about 500 m futher on. Go over the
bridge and bear right on a path that follows the brook before
swinging through 180° to join the River Bovey. Continue through
delightful woodland to Clambridge.

  Clambridge looks as though it were designed and constructed by
Boy Scouts as part of a badge course. Cross it with enthusiasm to
reach a path junction. Ahead is a short-cut to Sharpitor but our
walk goes left along the Bovey on a path that is not always very
well defined but, because it keeps close to the river, can be
followed comfortably, apart from the odd fallen tree and mossy
boulder. To the left the Bovey is excellent, clambering noisily over
its own large boulders. About 1200 m (¾ mile) from Clambridge a
poorly defined and unsigned path, left, leads to Horsham Steps, a
series of boulders that form a natural (?) stepping-stone bridge
across the Bovey on the main walk. Foxworthy Mill is passed, a
gate giving access to a continuation of the path to Foxworthy with
its thatched cottages. Take the bridlepath past cottages, signed for
Peck Farm, and follow it, with improving views to the left, to a
junction of tracks. Go right to Peck Farm where a gate, signed for
a bridlepath, gives access to a field. Cross this to a gate and

continue to another gate. Do not go through this, but bear right with the wall on your left, to Hunter's Tor, an excellent viewpoint and topped by the remains of an Iron Age hill fort.

From the tor there is a choice: bear left along the field edge, a route of little merit, or go ahead to take the ridge edge with superb views into the Bovey Valley below, but with a profusion of aggressive gorse. Follow the ridge path past Raven's Tor and Harton Chest, and on to Sharpitor (see (1) Sharpitor). From the tor follow the path through a section of fine oakwood to a signed gate and take the narrow path beyond to a lane. Go right to a Y-junction and there take the left fork, marked as Unsuitable for Motor Vehicles, which leads back to Lustleigh (see (2) Lustleigh). Just beyond the Baptist church is a T-junction. Go left to return to the church of St John the Baptist.

(1) *Sharpitor*
On its map the Ordnance Survey adds 'Nut Crackers (Logan Stone)' beneath the tor's name but sadly this information is out of date. Until 1951 there was indeed a logan stone here – for an explanation of logans see Note (2) of Walk 25 – one that moved far enough and smoothly enough to crack nuts. This almost explains the name, the stone having been known locally as the Nutcracker, without the OS's plural. The logan, it is said, was beautifully poised above the Cleave but sadly in 1951 drunken vandals toppled it into the valley. The rock was broken but the outraged locals organized a rescue bid. Even more sadly the bid failed, the rock being further broken and the pieces going even further down into the valley. Now only the confusing name remains.

From Sharpitor the view of the Bovey valley is exquisite and it is a surprise to learn that the name Cleave derives not from the way the river cleaves through the country, but from an ancient name for a cliff.

Hisley Bridge

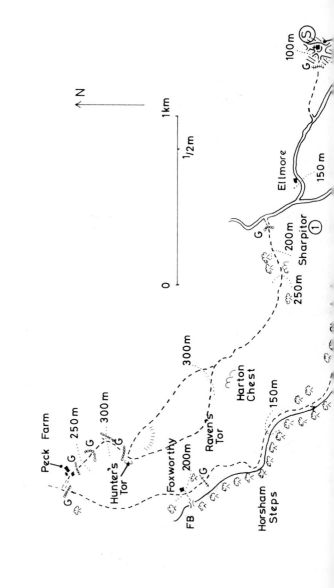

N

Peck Farm

250m

300m

G

G

G

Hunter's Tor

300m

Foxworthy

200m

G

FB

Raven's Tor

Harton Chest

150m

Horsham Steps

Sharpitor

200m

250m

300m

G

①

Ellmore

150m

100m

G

S

G

0   ½m   1km

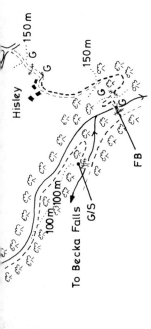

Hisley

150 m

150 m

G

G

G

G

G

FB

100 m 100 m

To Becka Falls

G/S

WALK 17   LUSTLEIGH CLEAVE

(2) *Lustleigh*

It comes as no surprise to discover that Lustleigh has been a popular spot with tourists since Victorian times as its thatched cottages, tight roads and central church are the epitome of the pretty English village. The church, to St John the Baptist, is set in an elliptical churchyard and entered through a 13th-century porch. Inside, there is an elegant Norman font and several interesting effigies. In the north aisle are a knight and lady definitely from the late 13th century, while in the south transept is a slightly later one of Sir William le Prout who died in 1316. The chuch's fine rood screen is 16th-century and required considerable restoration in 1895, a restoration that did full justice to the original work. The church's tower, such a feature of the village, is probably 14th-century, perhaps 15th.

   North of, and close to, the church is the 14th-century church house (see Note (1) of Walk 2), the upper floor of which was removed later last century. Elsewhere, the Manor House – on Mapstone Hill north-west of the village – is a fine 15th-century house with a minstrel gallery, while in the opposite direction Wreyland Old Hall is a century earlier.

   Finally, within the village itself, Primrose Cottage serves irresistible cream teas, with a range of naughty cakes.

Devon

Our next five walks visit that part of Devon which lies off the high moors of Dartmoor and Exmoor. Though there is much low-lying country, the walker is inevitably drawn towards the coasts. In the north the cliffs are high, the seascapes magnificent, the walking airy, while in the south the coast is more subdued. This southern coast is the land of the holidaying tourist, but also of the sea-faring Devonian, the land of Drake. Walk 21 visits Dartmouth which, while not having associations with Drake, is a fine old sea port. As a contrast, Walk 20 moves inland, tracing a short route along the River Torridge, one of the waters that defines the Land of the Two Rivers, home of *Tarka the Otter*.

Walk 18 Baggy Point

West of the Exmoor National Park the North Devon and Somerset Coastal Path goes through Ilfracombe and then rounds Morte Point to head south along Woolacombe Beach. At the southern end is Baggy Point where there is a quick taste of the high cliff scenery that will become familiar further south in Cornwall. The walk takes in the best of the rocky seascapes and offers the opportunity to visit Croyde, a holiday resort close to one of Britain's best surfing beaches.

Walk category : Easy/Intermediate (2 hours)

Length : 7 km (4½ miles) or 8½ km (5½ miles) if Croyde is visited

Ascent : 100 m (330 ft)

Maps : Landranger Sheet 180, Pathfinder Sheets 1233 (SS43/53) and 1213 (SS44/54)

Starting and finishing point : The National Trust's Baggy Point carpark at 435 396

Woolacombe Bay

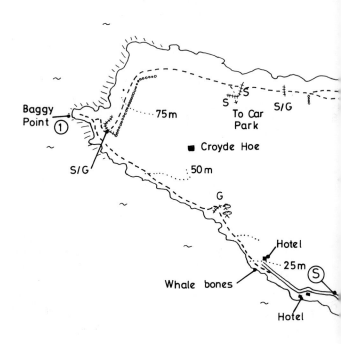

Willer's Stone

Baggy
Point
①

S/G

75m

To Car
Park

S

S

S/G

■ Croyde Hoe

50 m

G

Hotel

25m

Ⓢ

Whale bones

Hotel

Croyde Bay

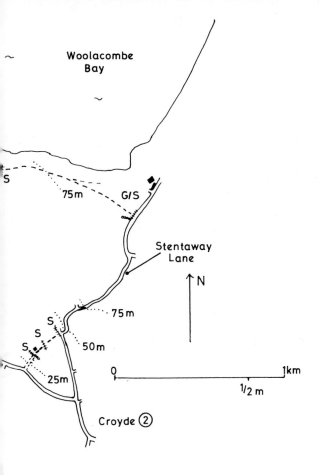

Woolacombe
Bay

S

75 m

G/S

Stentaway
Lane

↑ N

75 m

S
S

S

50 m

25 m

0   1 km

¹/₂ m

Croyde ②

WALK 18   BAGGY POINT

Go out of the car-park and right along the lane. Look out for the
wild cabbage growing here. Surprisingly, the cabbage thrives in the
salty air – and I thought the only time cabbage and salt enjoyed
each other's company was in the saucepan. Beside the road near
the turn-off to the second hotel passed are the bleached bones of a
whale beached or washed up on Croyde Bay in 1915. The route
now follows a gravel path prepared for wheelchairs, and soon,
below the cliffs at the path edge, is a 50-ton boulder that is famous
in geological circles. It is a huge glacial erratic: that is a rock
brought to the area by ice movements during the last Ice Age and
which is therefore quite different in type from the local rock.

Just beyond a gate in a small area of shrubs a rising path leaves
the gravel path; a shortened route returns to this point. The
prepared path soon reaches the cliffs of Baggy Point (see (1)
Baggy Point). The climbing fraternity divides the cliffs up into
areas with names that the OS omits from its maps. The first,
broken, area of slabs is Long Rock Slabs, the clear viewpoint
overlooking Slab Cove, on the slab of which – a superb 300-ft
sweep of rock – is 'Heart of the Sun', the area's best climb. Next
come Baggy Hole and Promontory Slab, then Concrete Wall and
Scattling Zawn. These final areas are not seen by the walker who
is forced inland by a fence, crossed by stile or gate, and must
content himself with a view of the coastguard practise pole (see
also Note (1)) unless he seeks out the cliff edge. The prepared
path also ends at the viewpoint.

The view from the grass above the cliffs is tremendous. To the
north, but to sea, is Willer's (Wheeler's) Stone (see also Note (1)).
The walk follows the Coastal Path in the No Man's Land between
the cliff edge to the left and a wall to the right, with an expanding
view of Woolacombe Bay. At a signpost pointing right for 'Car-
Park' a shortened version of the walk goes over a stile and follows
a path across farmland to arrive back at the prepared path. When
what is in fact a holiday apartment complex comes into view –
down and left, and with its own car-park close to the sands of the
bay – there is slight confusion. A path heads downhill towards the

Slab Cove, Baggy Point

buildings but the Coastal Path actually stays close to the wall, following it to a minor road.

Go right, and right again at a junction after about 200 m or so. This is Stentaway Lane, the least satisfactory part of the walk as it is narrow and high-sided. Luckily it lasts for little more than 600 m. The roads goes sharply right, then equally sharply left – walkers wishing to visit Croyde (see (2) Croyde) should go with the road here. Ahead is a footpath sign (labelled FP21); go over the stile and follow the path to a road. Go down the road and turn right at the bottom on to a road that leads back to the car-park.

(1) *Baggy Point*

Baggy Point is sandstone, part of the Devonian/Old Red Sandstone belt that sweeps across north Devon below highest Exmoor. The area is a favourite haunt of rock climbers; the steep faces and sweeping slabs draws them magnetically. The white posts on the cliffs represent the ends of a restricted area for the climbers during the sea bird nesting period from mid-March to mid-June. Birds that breed regularly here include several species of gull, fulmars, shags and cormorants. Gannets are often seen, while the 'inland' cliff area is a favourite with skylarks.

The rock ridge going north-west from the Point is Baggy Leap on which, in 1799, HMS *Weazle* was wrecked, her crew of 106 dying in one of Devon's most appalling disasters. The white pole on the cliff top near the point is a coastguard training mast where exercises with rescue rockets and breeches buoys take place. Only when you gaze down at the rocks and think about the *Weazle* do you realize that such exercises are not games.

To the north of the headland that finishes at Baggy Point is a pair of rocks that are another hazard to shipping, rocks only uncovered at low tides. On the OS maps these rocks are called Wheeler's Stone but the real name is Willer's Stone. Willer was William Luscombe, a sailor on the *Bessie Gould*. One day, as his ship neared the rocks, Willer jumped overboard, landed on them and claimed them for Queen Victoria. History does not appear to record Her Majesty's response, and Willer himself slides gently from history.

(2) *Croyde*
The headlands of Saunton Down and Baggy Point enclose, pincer-like, little Croyde Bay which is almost as long as it is wide. This trick of local geography stacks water up into the bay's mouth, the length of the beach-line then allowing wave patterns to develop. As a result, any reasonable day will see surfers and canoeists in droves riding the high, long waves into the Bay. At the Bay's back is the village of Croyde Bay, a pure holiday resort. Further back is Croyde, also a holiday resort, but one that has maintained its own charm and character despite having had to sacrifice some of its more seaward areas to the visiting trade. Dotted around are several typically Devonian thatched cottages, and the local craft industries are well represented. In the main street, the Gem Rock and Shell Museum is worth a visit for its collection of stones, both local and from much further afield, and its displays of jewellery.

Walk 19 Hartland Quay

Except where a couple of minor bureaucratic decisions have decreed otherwise, the River Tamar is the border between Devon and Cornwall for all of its length. The Tamar rises on the flank of Hendon Moor and from there the boundary-maker had to decide whether to continue the river's line north, to reach the west 6 miles away near Clovelly, or to go the shortest route, 4 miles west, following Marsland Water to the sea. He did the latter and so Hartland Point is not the last cliff bastion of Cornwall, but Devon's most impressive, most uncompromising section of high cliff. Our walk does not visit the point – though it can be easily reached from it, by following the Coastal Path – but goes a mile or so south, where the cliffs are almost as tall, but the inland area is just a little more interesting.

Walk category : Easy (1½ hours)

Length : 4½ km (2¾ miles)

Ascent : 180 m (600 ft)

Maps : Landranger Sheet 190, Pathfinder Sheet SS22/32

Starting and finishing point :   The car-park at 222 248, at Hartland
                                   Quay, reached by a toll road from the
                                   end of the road west of Stoke village.
                                   The toll road is single-track, steep,
                                   has blind hairpins and can be
                                   miserable in summer, but the journey
                                   is worth the effort.

From Hartland Quay (see (1) Hartland Quay) the walk follows the
Coastal Path which, exasperatingly, goes back up the slope down
which the toll road dropped. At the top is the Rocket Apparatus
House once used, as the name suggests, to house life-saving
equipment. A line was attached to the rocket which was fired out
to the ship in distress. A breeches buoy was then used to rescue
the crew. From the house go north on the Coastal Path which goes
over a shallow mound to reach Warren Cliff, a very pleasant
section of cliff-walking. On Warren Down is Warren Tower, a
structure about which almost nothing is known. It appears to be
too early to have been a folly, though it was used as a summer-
house by the owners of Hartland Abbey, and may have been first
constructed as a look-out – when the local area was plagued by
pirate attacks, the cove that was later the site of Hartland Quay
was an obvious landing site. But that seems to me to leave too
many questions unanswered. Why build a tower at all? The cliff
offers a perfectly respectable look-out, the extra few feet of tower
making precious little difference to the view, and more to the
point, did the local population really have the resource not only to
build but permanently staff a look-out on the off-chance that
pirates might attack?
   As the Path starts to descend be careful not to take a path off to
the right that appears to be heading for the prominent tower of
Stoke church: it does not. You must drop down to the sea at
Dyer's Lookout. The Coastal Path goes inland along a stream to a
stile. Here we leave it, continuing along the stream, which is
delightful, through an equally delightful small beech wood. The

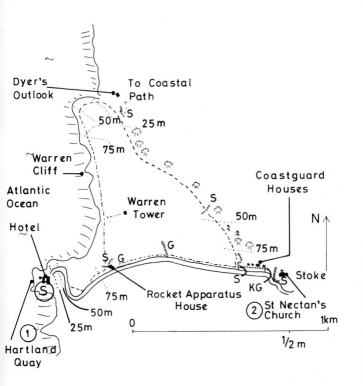

Dyer's Outlook

To Coastal Path

50m S   25m

75m

Warren Cliff

Atlantic Ocean

Warren Tower

Coastguard Houses

S

50m

N↑

Hotel

S G

G

75m

S G

S

KG

S

Stoke

Rocket Apparatus House

75m

50m

25m

1

Hartland Quay

0

St Nectan's Church
2

1km

1/2 m

WALK 19   HARTLAND QUAY

stream itself, Abbey River, is named for Hartland Abbey, the monks from which widened it in several places to form fish ponds, and used it to power cloth mills.

The path reaches a row of old coastguard houses. Pass in front of these on a curious section of path between the houses and a grass bank, to reach Stoke church (see (2) St Nectan's Church). To return to the car-park, go back along the coastguard house path and continue along the field edge all the way back to the Rocket House. From there reverse the short section of Coastal Path to Hartland Quay.

(1) *Hartland Quay*

The tightly confined old quay area is surrounded by some of the most impressive rock scenery in Devon. The sandstone of Baggy Point has been replaced here by tougher millstone rocks which give the cliffs a harder-edged and more angular set. Earth movements which have resulted in the folding of the strata have merely enhanced the dramatic effect, bands of rock going from horizontal to vertical in just a few metres of cliff face. Overall, the effect is to have created one of the most geologically interesting and, at the same time, visually attractive seascapes on the whole of the south-west peninsula.

But Hartland Quay is more than just a visual delight. The advantages of this small, (relatively) calm bay were seen by earliest sea travellers, but it was not until the mid 16th century that it was decided to exploit the potential commercially. Then a small group of eminent sailors, which included Walter Raleigh, Francis Drake and John Hawkins, petitioned Parliament for the right to construct a port. The port was a resounding success and soon a community had built up – fishermen using the quay as a good dock; coast guards; dockers servicing the ships that brought in coal, lime (there were lime kilns at the Quay), timber and other building materials – in 1616 the lead to repair St Nectan's Church roof was brought into Hartland Quay. The exports were chiefly agricultural: corn and malt, and processed fish. Eventually

The Atlantic coast from Hartland Quay

Hartland Quay was so important that a bank was formed, authorized to issue its own banknotes.

Ultimately, bigger ships meant that other ports usurped Hartland's trade and the quay fell into disrepair. Lack of repair sounds the death-knell for sea-resisting structures: storms caused damage which, being unrepaired, allow greater damage at the next occasion. Finally two violent storms in 1887 and 1896 completely demolished the Elizabethan port. What exists today is a new, very recent, smaller quay for crab and lobster fishing.

The hotel that now stands at the Quay was constructed around the old port offices and cottages. It offers an unrivalled view of the cliffs and must be an exciting place to wake up. Close by is the Quay museum with good exhibits on the local geology and natural history, and on the history of the coast and the Quay.

(2) *St Nectan's Church*

Nectan was a 6th-century Celtic saint who, legend has it, had 23 brothers and sisters, all of whom became hermits and most of whom were sanctified. Nectan set up his hermitage near where Stoke now stands – though more likely in the wooded river valley below – and there he was murdered by robbers. In the best tradition of Celtic sainthood, the murder was by beheading, and Nectan's body picked up the head to wash it off in a spring. Blood from the head caused stains on nearby stones that are still said to be visible, and the spring flows with miraculous water. Not surpisingly, the robbers were impressed and promptly gave up their evil ways. The actual burial spot of the saint is disputed: was it near Stoke or at St Nectan's Glen on Walk 29?

When the Saxons had taken the area, King Cnut – of wave-commanding fame – gave the local lands to Gytha, a high-born Saxon lady, on her marriage to the Earl Godwin. Gytha was the mother of Harold Godwinson who become King Harold, the last Saxon king before the Norman Conquest and loser at Hastings. Earl Godwin survived a life-threatening shipwreck in 1050 and in grateful thanks Countess Gytha had a collegiate church built near what is now the Abbey River. The church was dedicated to St Nectan, and was home to twelve monks. After the Normans had taken the area this monastic house was refounded as an Augustinan abbey in the mid 12th century. Of this abbey, dissolved in 1539, nothing but a small fragment of cloister remains, that being incorporated in the 18th/19th century mansion called Hartland Abbey that lies about 800 m east of Stoke. Though private, this house is open in the summer months, usually on Wednesdays and Sundays, but please check locally if you plan to visit.

St Nectan's church on our walk, in the parish church of Stoke and Hartland, stands on the 11th-century site, but was built in the late 14th century. In keeping with the spirit of Gytha's original church, the tower was built high and prominent, to act as a landmark to local sailors. At 39 m (128 ft) the church is the highest for many miles and would grace a cathedral with its slender, elegant, perpendicular lines. The tower walls are 1.7 m (5½ ft) thick, which is remarkable considering its base size, 7.9 m (26 ft) square. Inside the superb font is 12th-century Norman, while the fine rood screen is 15th-century. The altar tomb in the chancel was brought here from the abbey. Those interested in the development of publishing in Britain will be interested to see the memorial to Allen Lane, who started Penguin Books. Finally, the 'Pope's Chamber' over the north porch contains some interesting old relics: sections of a Jacobean pulpit, the old parish stocks, some old tiles and remnants of leaded glass, a 17th-century Turkish ransom note for Christian prisoners and parts of the original church barrel organ.

Walk 20 Torrington

As they swing southward the cliffs of the north Devon Coast are split by the estuaries of the rivers Torridge and Taw which create broad, shallow inlets where expanses of sand replace cliffs for several miles. Inland, and between the rivers, is the Land of the Two Rivers, an area of Devon farmland that is bleaker than the cream teas land further south. Here Henry Williamson set *Tarka the Otter*, his most famous book, choosing to prefix the name of his otter-hero with *Ta*, the ancient local name for a river (as in Taw,

Torridge, Tamar and Teign). The two rivers were famous for their fishing and for their otter-hunting – though, perhaps, the latter should be infamous rather than famous – with the Taw as the 'Gentleman's River', with inns strategically sited for hunt lunches. Our walk visits the 'less gentlemanly' (?!) Torridge, choosing a section near the town of Great Torrington.

Walk category : Easy (1 hour)

Length : 3¼ km (2 miles)

Ascent : 90 m (295 ft)

Maps : Landranger Sheet 180, Pathfinder Sheet SS41/51

Starting and finishing point : The Castle Hill car-park in Torrington, at 497 189. There is a second car-park at 494 189, a little to the west, that can also be used.

From the car-park go south to a tarmac path high above the River Torridge. Go left. At the fork just a few metres along take the right branch downhill and follow it around a 180° bend to the Waterloo Memorial (see (1) Waterloo Memorial). Go left – as seen from the approach path to the Memorial – on a metalled path that leads down to the A386 road, but before reaching this go right and down steps to reach a stony track beside a stream. At the Torridge (see (2) *Tarka the Otter*) go right on the broad track. At one point steps lead down to a launch-point by the river. The much vandalized plaque notes that the concrete structure was paid for by the women of Torrington during the Mayoralty of Austin R.O. Flaherty, 1927–28. There ought to be a good story here but I have yet to find it.

   Continue on the broad track until a clear tarmac path leads off left to the fine Taddiport Bridge. Cross this to visit the chapel of St

The Torridge valley, Great Torrington

Mary Magdalen (see (3) Torrington Leper Hospital). Return to
the tarmac path and go along it to the broad track and then go up
the path opposite that rises back to the castle walls (see (4) Great
Torrington) and the car-park.

(1) *Waterloo Memorial*

An inscribed tablet on the western face of the memorial records
that it was erected in June 1818 to commemorate the battle of
Waterloo in June 1815. The tablet is finished with 'Peace to the
Souls of the HEROES!!!' The memorial is a black stone square
pyramid with inset false archways. It is dour and squat, hardly
great architecture. I don't like the inscription either.

(2) *Tarka the Otter*

Henry Williamson settled in Georgeham, a village inland from
Croyde, after his return from the 1914–18 War. There he wrote a
book dealing with the life and death of an otter among the otter
hunts in the Land of the Two Rivers. When the book was
published it won the Hawthorden Prize in 1928. The book was
Tarka the Otter. Though Williamson lived to the north of the
Torridge it was that river that he loved and he had his animal-hero
born in a holt near the canal bridge on the river between Weare
Gifford and Landcross, two hamlets about 3 km (2 miles) apart,
Weare Gifford being about 5 km (3 miles) downriver from Great
Torrington. At the end of the book the waters of Torridge close
over the heads of Tarka and Deadlock the otter-hound as they
fight their last battle close to Landcross. Williamson wrote further
books, several of which also document animal lives – *Salar the
Salmon, Chakchek the Peregrine* – all of which, and most
especially *The Lone Swallows*, evoke the atmosphere of North
Devon in the first half of this century. In later life Williamson
moved to Norfolk, but when he died in 1977 he was buried at
Georgeham.
  This is not the forum to discuss *Tarka the Otter*. Suffice to say
that it is a book about which opinions vary widely, some seeing in
it an indictment of the hunting of beautiful creatures written by a
man appalled by the casual, senseless slaughter of the trenches,

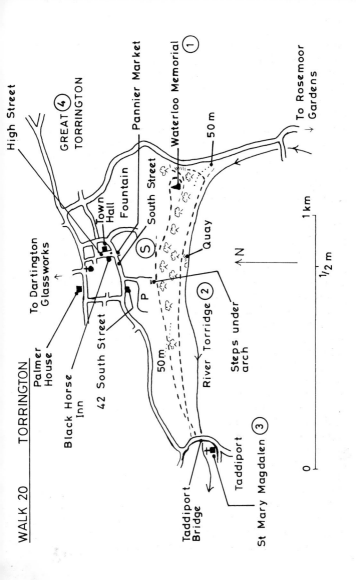

WALK 20   TORRINGTON

High Street

GREAT ④ TORRINGTON

Pannier Market

Waterloo Memorial ①

To Rosemoor Gardens

50 m

Palmer House

Town Hall

Fountain

South Street

To Dartington Glassworks

Black Horse Inn

42 South Street

S

Quay

P

N

1 km

½ m

0

River Torridge ②

50 m

Steps under arch

Taddiport Bridge

Taddiport

St Mary Magdalen ③

while others see a glorification of country virtues, including otter-hunting. It is best to form your own opinion.

An interesting project that takes its name from the otter has recently set up headquarters in Great Torrington – in the Eric Palmer Community Centre (see Note (4) below) – with the aim of promoting conservation as well as recreation and tourism in north Devon. One aspect of the Tarka Project is of great interest to walkers, as it involves the waymarking of the Tarka Trail, a 290-km (180-mile) walk. The walk will be a figure-of-eight centred on Barnstaple, going east and then north to Lynton and returning via Ilfracombe, and south through Bideford and Great Torrington to Okehampton, returning on a route to the east.

(3) *Torrington Leper Hospital*

In the 13th century the first bridge over the Torridge was built, and it is speculated that this was to reach a leper hospital set up on the southern bank. It is not until 1418, however, that the hospital is first referred to in print, though a chaplain at a chantry chapel in Taddiport is mentioned a century earlier. At the time of building of the hospital, the early Middle Ages, the disease was unusual but by no means unheard of in England and hospitals were frequently set up in remote places, as here where the river formed a good natural barrier to infection. In addition to the hospital and chapel the 'colony' would have had a farm, two green strips close to the chapel site being the remnants of that farm.

The hospital is referred to occasionally through to the mid 17th century, by which time the disease had been eradicated in England. The buildings then fell in disuse and were eventually demolished. All that now remains is the chapel, a tiny building measuring barely 9 × 3½ m (29½ × 11½ ft). The chapel has some 14th-century work, though the squat, embattled tower is 15th-century. The original doorway is to the right of present door (viewing from inside) and, as can be seen, was barely 1½ m (5 ft) high. The Ten Commandments that adorn the wall of the northern (organ) alcove are 16th-century; the spellings are delightfully eccentric. The present Taddiport Bridge is 16th- or 17th-century; beside it is the Dairy Crest Torrington Creamery on the site of north Devon's first-ever butter factory, built in 1874 to supply London and the Midlands

Finally, the name. Many believe that Taddiport derives from 'Toad Pit', the unkind name given by the people of Torrington to their unfortunate – and, doubtless, unwelcome – neighbours.

(4) *Great Torrington*

Though there are some strategic advantages to the town's position they are not vast, and there is no evidence of any major fortress or town before the coming of the Normans. Early in the 12th century the Norman lord of the area built the first recorded castle – on the aptly named Castle Hill – though this was dismantled in 1228 by order of the king as no permission for its construction had been given. Not until another century had passed was an official castle raised, by Roger de Merton. Roger's castle may have been acceptable but it did not trouble the pages of history. When Civil War raged around Torrington neither side saw fit to mention it, so by the mid 17th century even the real town castle had presumably ceased to exist. Most visitors to the town who park in the Castle Hill car-park assume the impressive castellated walls above the Torridge are the remains of the castle. They are not, having been built in the 18th century. The only tangible reminder of the Norman fortress is the Eric Palmer Community Centre, in the corner of Castle Street and the road to the car-park, which incorporates the castle chapel.

But this lack of clear strategic advantages did not prevent Torrington from becoming an important town. Its position in the Torridge valley, on a major route through Devon, made it an important commercial centre. It was granted a market in the 12th century and was the most important market town in north Devon by the 14th, and the largest in the whole county, after Exeter, by the 16th. Today it still has an important cattle market, and a well-known May Fair is held on the first Thursday in May. This commercial success led to the construction of merchant's houses, always the ones at the peak of the popular fashion of the day, though a great fire in 1724 means that most buildings post-date that event. Palmer House in New Street was built in 1752 for town lawyer John Palmer, a brother-in-law of Sir Joshua Reynolds and saw visits not only by the greater painter but by Dr Johnson. It is a superb brick house. Almost as good is the Town Hall, a stone and brick building that protrudes into High Street. The Hall, extensively revamped in the mid 19th century, houses the town museum. Opposite the Hall is the excellent Black Horse Inn, parts of which date from the late 17th century, the first building having escaped the full ravages of the fire. Between the inn and Hall is a fountain erected in 1870. In South Street, at the bottom of High Street and *en route* to both car-parks, poetry lovers will make a pilgrimage to No. 42, once the home of William Cory Johnson, the 19th-century poet, while few will fail to notice the Pannier Market with its original iron gates.

Torrington church dates from the late 17th century, but in this case the reason is not fire but explosion. In the Civil War Torrington had been staunchly royalist but in 1646 fell to a Parliamentarian army under Sir Thomas Fairfax, the fall of the town signalling the virtual end of West Country support for the Royalist cause. Fairfax captured many Royalists, about 200 of whom he imprisoned in the church, unaware that it had been used by the Royalist leader, Lord Hopton, as a powder-store. The store was accidentally ignited, many of the prisoners and their guards being killed and the church demolished. The long mound in the churchyard is believed to lay above the mass burial of the victims.

Torrington has much to offer the visitor: in addition to the town museum there is the world-famous Dartington Crystal. The factory can be visited, there are glass-blowing exhibitions, a museum of glass and early Dartington work, a restaurant and shop. The Plough is an Arts Centre and theatre, while younger visitors may like to try the live steam miniature railway at Mill Lodge, to the south of the town, just off the Exeter road. Also that way is the Royal Horticultural Society's Rosemoor Garden, a 40-acre benefaction of Lady Anne Palmer. Lady Palmer's original 8-acre garden is now being supplemented by development of a 32-acre meadow holding included in the gift. No gardener (and few, if any, others) should miss this National Garden.

Walk 21 Dartmouth

Walk 19 visits Dartmeet. Here we go down river, starting our walk at Dartmouth, arguably the most beautiful old port in Devon, and continuing along the South Devon Coastal Path that follows the Dart until it becomes lost in the sea. The Coastal Path in this area follows a section of Heritage Coast. Heritage Coasts are designated by the Countryside Commission for their beauty, wildlife and historical interest. This walk, and the one that follows it, show that all three aspects apply equally well.

Walk category : Intermediate (3¼ hours)

Length : 13 km (8 miles)

Ascent : 200 m (650 ft)

Maps : Landranger Sheet 202, Outdoor Leisure Sheet 20

Starting and finishing point : Coronation Park, at the northern end
                                 of Dartmouth

A shortened version of the walk (shortened to 8 km (5 miles)) uses the minibus shuttle service from Stoke Fleming (The Green Dragon) to Dartmouth (Townstal Road Garage). The bus is regular: approximately hourly but variable, daily (except Saturdays) in summer from 8 a.m. to 5 p.m.

From the Park follow the North Embankment down river towards the town (see (1) Darmouth – this note includes suggestions on what to see within the town, excluding those items covered in other notes). Take Mayor's Avenue into the town, turning left as it ends to reach the Butterwalk (see (2) Dartmouth Museum) in Duke Street. Now head for the Boatfloat, going round to its river side to reach South Embankment and following this to its end. Go right, then left to reach Bayards Cove (see (3) Bayards Cove).
    Steps from the fort at Bayards Cove lead up to Newcomen

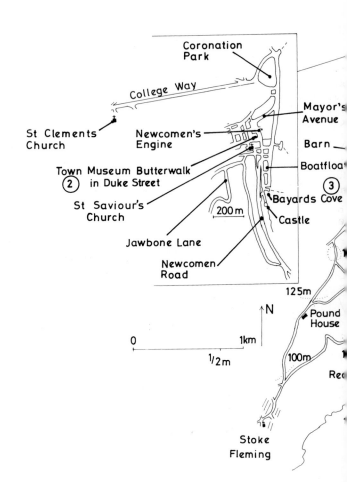

Britannia Royal
Naval College

Coronation
Park

College Way

St Clements
Church

Newcomen's
Engine

Mayor's
Avenue

Barn

Boatfloa

Town Museum Butterwalk
in Duke Street

②

St Saviour's
Church

③

Bayards Cove

Castle

Jawbone Lane

200 m

Newcomen
Road

125m

↑N

Pound
House

0   1km

100m

½m

Rec

Stoke
Fleming

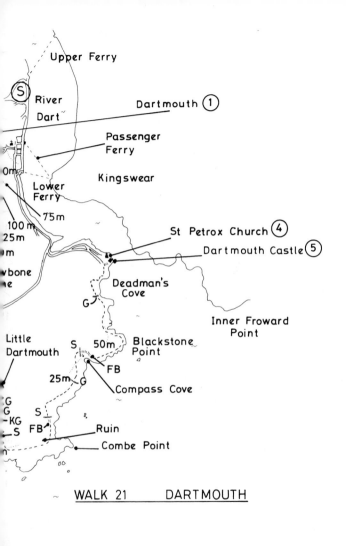

Upper Ferry

(S) River Dart

Dartmouth (1)

Passenger Ferry

Kingswear

Lower Ferry

0m

75m

100m
25m
m

bone
e

St Petrox Church (4)

Dartmouth Castle (5)

Deadman's Cove

G

Inner Froward Point

Little Dartmouth

S   50m   Blackstone Point

FB

25m G

Compass Cove

G
G
KG
S

S

FB

Ruin

Combe Point

WALK 21   DARTMOUTH

Road. Go left, following the road, which becomes South Town
and then Warfleet Road, to reach Castle Road on the left. Follow
this to St Petrox church (see (4) St Petrox Church) and the castle
(see (5) Dartmouth Castle).

Opposite the castle's ticket office the Coastal Path is reached.
Follow this well-marked and trodden path to Deadman's Cove –
from where there is a superb view across the Dart estuary to
Kingswear Castle on the eastern side – and on to Blackstone Point
– where, in the 17th century, there was a gun battery – and
Compass Cove, above which are some old cottages once occupied
by the Revenue men. At Compass Cove the Coastal Path goes
right, over a stile, where the path descends to the cove itself,
reaching a point from where the tower, a 19th-century navagation
beacon inland of Inner Froward Point across the Dart, can be
seen.

The path continues straightforwardly to Combe Point where
maps promise a coastguard lookout: only a few bricks remain.
Beyond the old lookout the path turns inland going over a stile
and through gates to reach a car-park (at 873 492). Go out on to
the road and left along it to reach Stoke Fleming (see (6) Stoke
Fleming).

If you are continuing the walk (which offers superb views of
Dartmouth in its latter stages), follow the verge – on the right side –
of the main road, A379, towards Dartmouth, transferring with the
verge to the left side when the Pound House is reached. Go past
the B3205 to the right, and then turnings to the right, the left and
again to the right, to reach Jawbone Hill on the right. The lane is
not named at this point but is marked as 'Unsuitable for Vehicles'.
The hill falls sharply (1 in 4) into Dartmouth at its lower end but, as
compensation, it offers excellent views, especially of the Britannia
Royal Naval College. When Crowther's Hill is reached, go right.
Bear left to Smith Street, taking the first left to visit St Saviour's
church before crossing Dartmouth to reach the starting point.

(1) *Dartmouth*
Though the Dart is a beautiful river and its estuary is wide,
Dartmouth is a most unlikely place for a significant port, built as it

is on a steep hill. The earliest, Saxon, settlement was Townstal, above the river which in those days had muddy, awkward banks. On land reclaimed from those tidal banks the earliest fishing port grew up, Dartmouth proper only coming into existence as more land was reclaimed giving a flat ledge for development, and a more usable river channel. By the 12th century the port had became important enough to be the natural focus for ships departing for both the Second and Third Crusades. In 1341 Edward III granted it borough status, chiefly, it would seem, because of the town's decision to offer him two manned warships for 40 days each year. This offer, at the very least, was taken up in 1346 when Dartmouth supplied 31 ships to the siege of Calais, a number bettered by only two other English ports. Indeed, its enthusiasm for the English king's cause in France led to several reprisal raids and the need to fortify the river mouth. At this time, the late 14th century, the town mayor was John Hawley whom most literary experts now see as the model for Chaucer's *Shipman*.

When peace came, Dartmouth expanded its trade, first to France and the Mediterranean and then to the New World. In 1620 the *Mayflower* and *Speedwell* berthed in the port, loaded with the Pilgrim Fathers *en route* to America and freedom from religious persecutions. The docking was due to the need for urgent repairs to the *Speedwell*. On the basis of the visit, Dartmouth has often claimed to be the port of embarkation of the Fathers but the claim does not stand up to scrutiny: the *Speedwell* made it only as far as Plymouth where its unseaworthiness became overwhelmingly apparent. All the passengers transferred to the *Mayflower* and the journey began in earnest.

Increases in ship sizes and the sophistication of inland transport brought about the decline of the port, the fine docking being unable, eventually, to overcome the difficulties of moving goods out of the town up the steep valley sides. Only as a naval port, where such things are of less importance, did Dartmouth remain important. In 1863 a Royal Naval College was set up in an old wooden warship, the *Britannia*, the ship being joined by another, the *Hindustan* the following year. In 1899 it was decided to move to more permanent quarters and the huge college that dominates the town from many angles was built, by Sir Aston Webb, designer of the V & A Museum and Admiralty Arch. The college – taking the name *Britannia* from the earliest ship – has often been criticized for its unfortunate choice of materials (different from anything else in the town) and its form (or, rather, lack of it). Perhaps the safest description is 'imposing'.

Our walk starts under the college, near the Higher, or Upper, Ferry. Dartmouth has three ferries, each of some interest. The Lower Ferry starts from Bayards Cove (see note (3) below); the Passenger Ferry links Dartmouth to Kingswear station. When railways came to Devon it was soon seen that a rail link would be an advantage to Dartmouth. Sadly, the valley was too steep to get the trains in, so Dartmouth had to be ferry-linked to Kingswear. However, it was possible to buy a ticket for Dartmouth, and the building beside the Boatfloat was a real station, even though there were no trains! The Higher Ferry is chain drawn. With the coming of the age of steam an engine was installed to haul the chain and, hence, the ferry, but it proved so unreliable that a return was made to the earlier source of power: a horse in a treadmill.

The oldest of Dartmouth's churches is St Clement's at Townstal, an early 14th-century building once held by the monks of Torre Abbey, but the best is St Saviour's, near where the walk re-enters the town. This late 14th-century building is an absolute delight, both inside and out.

Elsewhere, almost any walk among Dartmouth's narrow, steep streets will reveal a worthwhile little corner. It is difficult to chose a favourite spot, but the 16th/17th-century frontage of the Quay beside the Boatfloat, and Fairfax Street are personal choices. Lovers of industrial archaeology should visit Newcomen's steam engine. Thomas Newcomen was a Dartmouth man, born in 1663 and plying trade as an ironmonger in the town. He was also a spare time inventor and in 1712 built a very early steam engine for use in mines as a water pump. Newcomen was, therefore, one of the pioneers of the industrial revolution, and to celebrate the tricentenary of his birth Dartmouth erected an engine house in the Royal Avenue Gardens, inside which is a working engine of Newcomen design.

(2) *Dartmouth Museum*

In Duke Street the Butterwalk is one of Dartmouth's most photographed features. This superb block of shops/houses has its first floor supported by the columns of the walk itself, while a second, overhung, storey is topped by gabled or fanlighted roofs. The wood carving of the frontage, while not being in the league of Michelangelo, has a wonderful vibrancy. Not surprisingly, the Butterwalk has been described as the pick of Devon's 17th-century domestic architecture. At No. 6 is Dartmouth Museum. Three rooms contain the collection of Percy Russell, a local historian. The King's Room – worth visiting for the panelling and plasterwork alone – has models illustrating the history of the sailing ship and several good canvases. The Holdsworth Room has momentoes of the Holdsworth family, an important local family in the 18th and 19th centuries, and of Thomas Newcomen, as well as several more ship models. There are yet more models in the Lewis Stock Room, mostly made by Stock himself. Finally, if you are wondering about the stairway access, the steps were deliberately made uneven so that any unwanted night-time visitors would trip and wake the household dogs!

(3) *Bayards Cove*

This small cove has a nautical history that could well be the envy of many large ports. From here Crusaders sailed, as did Walter Raleigh on trips to the Americas. The Pilgrim Fathers came this way and the early trips of the East India Company were from here. And if all that were not enough the cove formed the backdrop for the BBC series *The Onedin Line*.

Close to where the Lower Ferry's very narrow slip road enters the Cove is Agincourt House, a fine, though much restored, 15th-century house. The Custom House dates from the early 18th century.

At the far end of the cobbled quay is Bearcove Castle; the name Bearcove is the local dialect rendering of the longer name. The castle was built in Henry VIII's time, after the main castle, as a second line of defence. It consisted of massive walls, through holes in which eleven flat-bed – rather than wheeled-trolley – mounted

cannons protected the river. In 1940 the castle was used as a machine-gun post, but quickly abandoned when it was realized that the field of fire through the walls was very limited; the earliest defenders had noticed the same problem.

(4) St Petrox Church

Petrox, as with Clement and Clarus to whom the other Dartmouth churches are dedicated, was a Celtic saint and it is possible that he had a cell near this spot in the late 6th century. Of early churches there is no sign, but it is known that one existed in 1192, and it is conjectured that it was built to celebrate the successful return of St Petrox's remains from Brittany. The remains had been stolen from Bodmin by Breton monks (!) and were returned by order of the king. It seems likely that they were landed at Dartmouth. That earliest chapel – which showed a light at night for the guidance of fishermen – fell into disrepair and it was not until the mid 17th century that it was rebuilt. It was used as a castle grain store during the Civil War and required considerable work following the peace that followed, though what we see retains the 17th-century design. Inside there are several fine brasses.

(5) Dartmouth Castle

The first thing that the visitor to the castle sees is a ruined tower and old wall set next to what is now the car-park. These formed part of a fortress built in the 14th century, one of the spasmodic attempts to defend the mouth of the river during the Hundred Years War. It was not until 1462 that the king granted £30 for the building of a proper defence. The stone and sand for the construction were brought by barge and in twelve years the castle was complete. The castle is interesting because it was the first in Britain to be designed to have cannon as a primary armament. In design the castle was functional: a tower section, half-round, half square, with cramped living-quarters and gun platforms to both sides. Some of the guns are original, though most would have been flat-bed mounted when the castle was new.

Dartmouth Castle

The 'companion' castle of Kingswear was started some 10 years after Dartmouth and the combination of the two would certainly have deterred an attack up-river. In addition there was a chain across the river-mouth that could be hauled up to the water-line to impede shipping, both for defensive reasons and to keep them in the line of the guns. Though it is often stated that the chain was slung between the castles, this was not the case. The eastern end was attached to the rocks below the old fort of Gommerock almost directly across the river from Dartmouth Castle, the hauling equipment being in the latter.

Modifications were made to the castle over many years, a huge earthwork being added during the Civil War. It can still be seen on Gallant's Bower, above and to the west of the castle. Dartmouth was Royalist, the Gallant's Bower fort being destroyed when the town fell to the Parliamentarians. In 1672, when a Dutch invasion was feared, an extra battery was added to the castle, this battery being enlarged and strengthened in 1861 to form the fortress that takes up half of the visit for those buying a ticket to the castle. Finally, in 1940 the castle was used again as part of the coastal defences.

(6) *Stoke Fleming*

The village is thought to have been named for an early defended house (stockade) of the le Fleming family. That the family existed is borne out by the historical archives – they are mentioned in 1218 – but the name implies a Low Country rather than Norman origin. The village church, to St Peter, is delightful, with a fine 13th-century tower. As at St Petrox, the tower was said to have held a light in past centuries – but not as a navigation light here; Stoke Fleming's light was to give the all clear to the village's smugglers. Inside the church is a brass, to John Corp, dated 1361, the oldest dated brass in Devon and Cornwall. The churchyard holds the grave of George Parker Bidder, born 1806 in Moretonhampstead, who was famous in the early 19th century as the 'Calculating Boy' for his ability to perform complex mental arithmetic. Bidder put his mathematical skill to use as a civil engineer, his works including London's Victoria Docks, and the London to

Birmingham Railway which he built with Robert Stephenson. Opposite the church is the Green Dragon, a fine village pub which was a firm favourite with the father of the author during trips when the youngster was having the delights of Devon explained at first-hand.

Close to the village are the Blackpool Sands, a superb crescent of fine sand, one of the best of local bathing beaches. The sheltered nature of this bay – for the pleasure of visiting which the tripper has to pay – led to its use as an invasion spot in 1404 when a small Breton army landed. The locals rapidly armed themselves and fought off the invaders. To celebrate the victory the king, Henry IV, had a *Te Deum* sung at Westminster Abbey.

Walk 22 Slapton Ley

This fine walk, unfortunately a straight line walk with little chance of a circular route, takes a high shingle ridge between the sea of Start Bay, a windsurfer's paradise, and the freshwater Ley, one of Devon's foremost natural history sites. The walk continues to the ruggedly beautiful Start Point, the southern headland defining the bay of the same name, passing, *en route*, a Sherman tank, a memorial to the area's use as a pre-D-Day practice ground. The walk therefore combines the three requirements – beauty, history and wildlife – that define a Heritage Coast.

Walk category : Intermediate (3 hours)

Length : 13 km (8 miles) – one way only

Ascent : 160 m (525 ft)

Maps : Landranger Sheet 202, Outdoor Leisure Sheet 20

Starting and finishing point : The Strete Gate car-park at 634 457.
There are also car-parks on Slapton
Sands (829 442), at Torcross
(824 424) and at Start Point
(820 377).

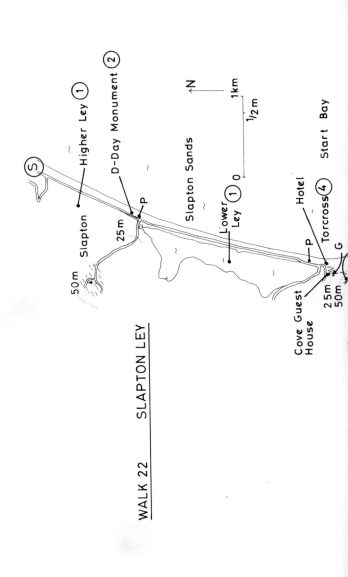

WALK 22 SLAPTON LEY

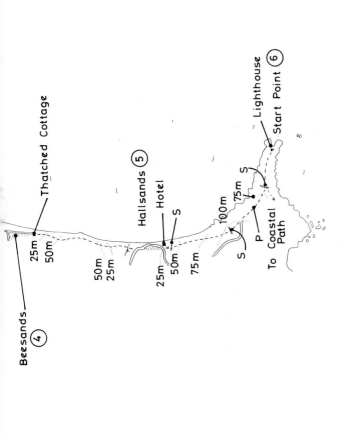

Beesands ④

Thatched Cottage

25m
50m

50m
25m

Hallsands ⑤

Hotel
S

25m
50m
75m

100m
75m S

S

P

To Coastal
Path

Lighthouse

Start Point ⑥

Those not wishing to reverse the full length of the route can consider the use of two cars – one at Strete Gate, one at Start Point – to reduce the walk to the quoted mileage. Western National buses that run between Torcross and Slapton can also be used to reduce the full double mileage. If that option is used the total mileage is reduced from 16 to 12 miles. From the car-park head south, either along the west, the Ley side, or the east, the sea side, of the main road. This first section of the walk traverses Higher Ley (see (1) Slapton Ley). Just beyond the memorial (see (2) D-Day) a minor road off right visits Slapton village (see (3) Slapton) where there is a pub for elevenses. Continue southward, again using either the Ley or sea side, of the road, to reach Torcross with its Sherman tank memorial (see (4) Torcross). Go up steps to the right of the hotel to reach the Coastal Path that goes round past Cove Guest House. The Path continues by skirting an old quarry and going to and through the Beesands Caravan Park. To the right here is Widdicombe Ley, a final expanse of freshwater. The reeds around its fringe were once used by crab-fisherman for building pots.

Beyond the village of Beesands – badly damaged by the storms that hit the area in 1979 (see also note (4)) – the Path is straightforward, going along the cliff edge before dropping down across the shingle to reach Hallsands (see (5) Hallsands). Beyond, it is straightforward walking all the way to Start Point (see (6) Start Point) where the lighthouse is reached by leaving the Coastal Path.

(1) *Slapton Ley*
Changing sea levels have caused a shingle ridge to be formed at the back of Slapton beach – a beach that is usually, and somewhat inappropriately, termed Slapton Sands. The ridging effect is readily experienced by the swimmer here: the beach shelves in a dramatic style that, together with the shingly undertow, can give the unwary a real fright. The shallow valley formed behind the high ridge has been filled by streams to form a freshwater lagoon

Slapton Sands

known by the local name of Ley. Slapton Ley is divided into two sections, Higher and Lower, by the embankment that takes the road into Slapton village. At the edge of the water the shingle bank is home to the birdlife that forms the major natural attraction. During the winter months the Ley is home to migratory warblers, firecrests, ducks, grebes and, occasionally, divers, while in summer the nesting populations in the reed form an impressive list that now includes Cetti's and Savi's warblers. Notable rarities that have taken shelter here include purple herons and little bitterns. A Nature Trail along part of the inland edge of Lower Ley can be reached from the road to Slapton village. Information on this trail and on other aspects of the Ley's natural history are available from the Field Studies Centre, to the right as you enter Slapton village. The Centre administers a Nature Reserve that covers the Ley and nearby France Wood, the reserve having been designated as an SSSI (Site of Special Scientific Interest).

There is also a public bird-hide on the Ley near the Torcross car-park.

(2) *D-Day*

In late 1943 the similarity between Slapton Sands and Omaha Beach, Normandy, was noted by the Allied High Command, and the order was given to evacuate the whole area so that American forces could practice assault manœuvres – with live ammunition – on the beach and surrounding fields. At Slapton the villagers were told on 13 November 1943 to be out of the area by 20 December – just in time for Christmas. Despite the lack of able-bodied young men and heavy winter rain, the evacuation was completed and for six months American landing-craft brought troops ashore while off-shore vessels shelled the local area. The devastation was surprisingly slight – at least as far as habitation was concerned – though the cost in human terms was more severe. Only in recent years have the details of the disaster that overtook one unit discovered by a roving German surface boat come to light. The Sherman tank at Totnes is still the only real memorial to the 800 or so men who died. The memorial on the beach here is from the USA to the local people as a 'lasting tribute' to their self-sacrifice.

The monument was erected in 1954. For the locals a more tangible, and at the time more welcome, thank-you had been the boxes of blankets and household goods that the Americans sent when the villagers returned.

War is no laughing matter, but one story from the period must be told. It concerned a proverbial little old lady in a car who ignored the prohibition order and drove into the Slapton area. She met a huge column of military vehicles in a very narrow lane but before she had a chance to either reverse or explain, she and her car had been picked up by a mobile crane and dumped in the adjacent field!

(3) *Slapton*

At one time the village of Slapton reached down to the end of the access road, a group of 16th-century buildings known as the Slapton Cellars – and used chiefly as fisherman's storage rooms – sitting virtually on the shingle. In time a pub was added, fishermen recently come ashore being convivial folk. The pub, the Sands Hotel, become the Royal Sands when the young Prince of Wales (later Edward VII) stayed briefly. Sadly, none of the buildings survived the D-Day landing practice. The local story of the destruction tells of 'Pincher', a local dog, who, seeking old haunts, strayed into the restricted area and set off a series of land-mine explosions. The blast all but wrecked the hotel and probably did Pincher no good at all, though history does not record his fate.

Slapton is a delightful village, the cottages in Brook Street and near the church being especially attractive. The church itself is early 14th-century – though tiles were found during one period of restoration that imply an earlier, perhaps 10th-century, church – and dedicated to St James the Great. In the porch is a sanctuary ring dating from the time when felons could seek sanctuary in a church by grasping such a ring.

The prominent tower in the village is all that now remains of a College of Chantry. Such small monastic houses were occasionally set up by noblemen to house priests who would say masses on behalf of the founder's soul, and that of anyone else he wished to name, in perpetuity. Slapton's College was endowed by Sir Guy de

Brien who was born in the first decade of the 14th century and died in the last decade, a quite astonishing life span for the time. Sir Guy was a steward of Edward III and a much trusted and respected man. He acquired land in Gloucestershire by marriage and is buried in Tewkesbury Abbey.

In 1373 Sir Guy granted ten shillings yearly rent to four chaplains 'to celebrate divine service daily in the chapel of St Mary within the manor of Slapton', with a celebratory mass to be said for the founder and his wife on 31 May annually. The practice lasted until the time of Henry VIII when the College suffered the fate of all other monastic houses and was dissolved. Today all that remains of the building is the ruined tower which lies on private land and cannot, therefore, be visited. Visitors will have to make do with a visit to the inn, said to incorporate the remains of cottages in which the masons and workmen building the College were houses.

(4) *Torcross*

The Sherman tank memorial at Torcross was retrieved from the sea in 1984. The village itself was once a small fishing port and later had a coaching inn. Today it is largely a tourist stop-over. Torcross, as with nearby Beesends, was very badly damaged by storms in 1951 and again in 1979. After the latter storms a defensive sea wall was built, a wall that was inaugurated (that cannot be the right word, but it seems better than opened) by the Queen in 1980.

(5) *Hallsands*

The history of Hallsands at the end of the 19th and beginning of the 20th centuries is almost an object lesson in green politics, as a notice board beside the Coastal Path records. The story began in 1892 when a company was granted a licence to dredge shingle in the bay for the building of Plymouth's Devonport Docks. Within a remarkably short time over half a million tons of material had been dredged out. During the same time the shingle ridge in front

Slapton College

of the 37 houses of Hallsands dropped by about 4 m (13 ft),
opening the village to the sea. The villagers complained, but a
panel of inquiry in 1901 found that the dredging was not to blame.
That winter the sea started to cause damage and a second inquiry
in 1902 stopped the dredging. It was too late, and despite an
emergency sea wall a storm in 1917 destroyed the village. No
proper compensation was ever paid and fewer than half the
villagers were re-housed locally. There are no new problems, it
would seem, just recycled old ones.

(6) *Start Point*

The name of the headland is from the Saxon *steart*, a tail – as in
redstart – probably from its position at the base of Start Bay. The
lighthouse here is Devon's most southerly light. It was built in
1836 and its beam is visible for more than 20 miles. But despite its
presence a storm in 1891 wrecked five ships off the Point, though
the storm was such that there was little that the ships could have
done to avoid the rocks. Three centuries earlier a priate met his
end at the Point, though the circumstances were quite different.
The pirate, Henry Meige, was hanged here for piracy, his body
being gibbetted in chains to rot.

Bodmin Moor

Bodmin is the second of the granite moors of the South-West that we visit, and its geology and geography is similar to that already described for Dartmoor. Indeed, so similar is it that the very best quote about a Bodmin bog is from the same Sabine Baring-Gould who supplied us with one on Dartmoor. In the *Book of Cornwall*, though, the Reverend Gentleman gives us an experience of his own rather than one gleaned from another. He sank into a Bodmin bog, going in up to his waist quickly and then more gradually to his armpits. He saved himself by placing his six-foot bamboo walking stick across the surface and using it to negotiate a way to dry land. He hauled himself out, but the 'suction had been so great as to tear the leather gaiters off my legs'. It is easy to smile but the description has little in it to suggest exaggeration and does appear to have been life-threatening.

Despite that experience Bodmin is more benign than Dartmoor. It has bogs but they are fewer and more separated, the moor being a lower, more congenial place for walking. It is also smaller, about 250 sq km (about 100 sq miles). As it is also, roughly, square – though a square orientated north-west to south-east so that it appears diamond-shaped on a conventional map – and is never more than a few miles to an edge, or to the main road that bisects it. Altogether a more user-friendly moor.

Bodmin Moor is, as with Dartmoor, a moor of antiquities, although here the sites tend to be on the moor edges rather than the centre. Just off the moor are Trethevy Quoit, one of Cornwall's best cromlechs (just south of Walk 23) and King Doniert's Stone, an inscribed stone commemorating the death (by drowning in the nearby River Fowey) of one of the last Cornish Celtic Kings in 875 or thereabouts, as well as the stone circles of the Hurlers which lie on the route of Walk 23.

Bodmin is also, like Dartmoor, a place of legend. Dozmary Pool, close to the Jamaica Inn at the start of Walk 24, is another stretch of water into which, it is claimed, Bedivere threw Excalibur after Arthur's last battle. The pool is also claimed to be bottomless, though it can be comfortably waded – though quite why anyone should want to bother is another matter. Most interestingly, the pool is associated with John Tregeagle, a legendary Cornish landlord's agent who was the scourge of his master's tenants. For his considerable sins Tregeagle's spirit is required to bail Dozmary with a holed limpet shell. As he carries out his task he is plagued by devils and eventually runs screaming across the moor to reach the sanctuary of the curious Roche Rock chapel.

Perhaps that noise was not, after all, the wind . . .

Walk 23 The Cheesewring and Kilmar Tor

On its southern side Bodmin Moor is divided into two unequal 'halves' by the Fowey River. To the west of the river is a low-lying marshy area out of the centre of which rises Brown Gelly. To the east of the river the moor is higher and more airy. Nowhere is this truer then on the extreme eastern edge where a series of high tors forms a final bastion before the land falls away into the Lynhor valley. This walk takes that ridge, visiting beautifully sculpted tors from which the views are magnificent and interesting historical and prehistorical sites on their flanks.

Walk category : Difficult (3½ hours)

Length : 13 km (8 miles)

Ascent : 250 m (820 ft)

Maps : Landranger Sheet 20, Pathfinder Sheet 1339 (SX 27/37)

Starting and finishing point : The unofficial but much frequented car-park at 260 711, just to the south of the tiny village of Minions

Note: In its northern section this route crosses sections of trackless and rough moor. It should not be attempted in limited visibility, and can be boggy if there has been heavy rain over a long period.

The southern section of the route, to Stowe's Hill, is much friendlier.

From the car-park go north-west on the obvious track towards the stone circles of the Hurlers (see (1) the Hurlers) crouching at the edge of the moor. From the circles go north-east on a series of vague paths between obvious tracks, heading for Rillaton Barrow, the obvious large mound. The mound, a Bronze Age burial mound, was excavated in 1837 when the famous Rillaton Cup was found. This 9-cm (3½-inches) cup can be seen at the British Museum, though a replica is on display at Truro Museum. Beyond the barrow is the rock pile of the Cheesewring. The best approach to the Cheesewring is by way of the western edge of the quarry below it (see (2) Cheesewring Quarry). The Cheesewring itself stands on top of Stowe's Hill. Go north over the hill past Stowe's Pound (see (3) Stowe's Pound) and descend gently over rough moor to reach a farm track. Go left along it towards North Wardbrook Farm. Before the farm gate is reached, go right to a gate beyond which is an old railway track that once served the quarries on Kilmar and Beerah Tors. Follow the track as it contours around Langstone Downs. Kilmar Tor soon comes into view, and can be climbed at any convenient point after the last gate is passed. Best, however, is to stay with the track until it splits, and to take the left fork towards the tor – the right fork goes towards Bearah Tor. Leave the track anywhere now and go up to the summit of Kilmar Tor which has a trig point and a ridge-long display of tors (see (4) Kilmar Tor and Twelve Men's Moor).

  To the north now are the long ridge of Trewortha Tor (north-west) and the more defined top of Hawk's Tor (just east of north). Our target is the former: descend from Kilmar Tor, cross the farm lane into Trewortha Farm, Bodmin Moor's most remote farm, and head for the wall ahead. Follow it around to the left, then go up to the Trewortha ridge. Go west along the ridge, crossing a fence at the point it reaches the western tors. Go along the tors to reach King Arthur's Bed (see (5) Trewortha Tor and King Arthur's Bed).

  Reverse the route to Kilmar Tor and study the view to the

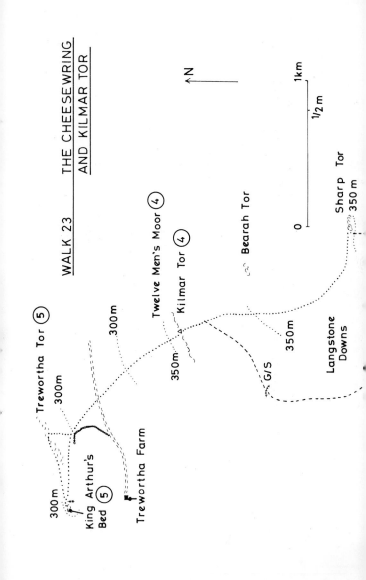

WALK 23   THE CHEESEWRING
          AND KILMAR TOR

N

0   ¹/₂ m   1km

Treworth Tor ⑤

Twelve Men's Moor ④

Kilmar Tor ④

Bearah Tor

Sharp Tor
350 m

Langstone
Downs

G/S

350m

350m

300m

300m

300 m

King Arthur's
Bed ⑤

300 m

Trewortha Farm

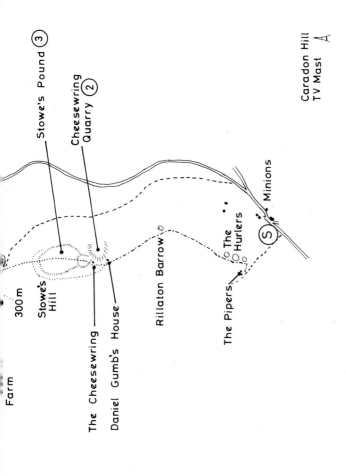

Farm

300 m

Stowe's Hill

The Cheesewring

Daniel Gumb's House

Rillaton Barrow

The Pipers

The Hurlers

Minions

Stowe's Pound ③

Cheesewring Quarry ②

Caradon Hill
TV Mast

S

south. To the left is Bearah Tor, then Sharp Tor with, to its right, the top of the Caradon Hill TV mast. Our walk heads for the latter, though Bearah Tor can easily be visited. The reason for heading for the mast, not Sharp Tor, is that there is a valley running away between Bearah and Sharp Tors, and it is necessary to go west in order to contour around its head. Climb Sharp Tor, an excellent peak, and look south. The final part of the route can be clearly seen from here: it goes down the field ahead, entered through the obvious small gate in the wall at the foot of the tor, and takes the walled 'lane' to the right at the bottom to reach the outward route at the track to North Wardbrook Farm. Then it takes the clearly defined old railway track that circles the base of Stowe's Hill.

   To accomplish that route go south of the tor – there is a poorly defined path but it is hardly needed – to the gate. At the end of the 'lane' reached to the right at the bottom of the field is a gate. Go through and up to the farm track. Now go left a little to the farm gate and go to the right of the fence to reach the railway. At first the railway is not that well defined but within a few yards it is and is comfortably followed all the way back to Minions (see (6) Minions).

(1) *The Hurlers*

The Hurlers is a complex monument consisting of three stone circles on a north-east to south-west axis. The central circle is the largest, being 41 m (135 ft) in diameter. The circle to the north is 35 m (110 ft) in diameter, the southern circle being the smallest, with a diameter of 32 m (105 ft). It is conjectured that each of the circles originally had about 25 stones, though now the numbers are 13 (north), 17 (centre) and 9 (south). The builders went to great trouble to bury the stones so that all the tops were level and had partially paved the centre circle, which also had a central stone in its earliest form. The name of the complex derives from a legend that the stones are men turned to stone for daring to play the Cornish game of hurling – still played on Shrove Tuesday in St Columb Major – on a Sunday. The nearby pair of standing stones, to the west, are called the Pipers, probably from the same legend, though music was not necessary to the playing of the game.

A study of the alignments of the circles suggests one with the star of Arcturus which, rising in August, might have signalled the time of harvest. I have to confess incredulity – did an agrarian society really need to put in this much effort in order to identify a star-rise to tell them when to harvest their crops? Longest day, shortest day, even the time to plant, I can believe but even non-farmers can tell when things are ripe for cutting. Undoubtedly some circles had astronomical significance: that does not mean they all had.

In the late 19th century someone made a study of the Hurlers and other Bodmin circles and found that they had been laid out according to the length of the Royal Persian Cubit. I don't believe that either.

(2) *Cheesewring Quarry*

Near the western end of the quarry, and on our route, are the remains of Daniel Gumb's house. Gumb was a stone-cutter from Linkinhorne who, in the early 18th century – that is before the quarry started, the hut having been built originally on the flank of Stowe's Hill – constructed a hut and lived in it with his wife and family. He seems to have been what we might now term a hippy, a self-taught mathematician who was interested in astronomy (notice the visualized Theorem of Pythagoras, with Euclidian overtones, carved on the hut's capstone) and who retired from the normal course of human events. The hut was originally 30 ft long, 12 ft wide and had a chimney and stone benches. On one stone of the hut the initials D.G. and the date 1735 can still be made out. Gumb also cut gutter channels in the roof slab to collect rainwater. Sadly the hut was destroyed by quarrying and what we see are the remains, moved about 100 m from their original position. In the way of such folk, Gumb had a belief in a universal wholeness and a poor opinion of the established church. One gravestone he carved for the Linkinhorne churchyard had an epitaph that ran:

Here I lie by the churchyard door,
Here I lie because I'm poor,
The further in, the more you pay,
But here I lie as warm as they.

At his funeral in the same church the, perhaps understandably, jaundiced vicar is said to have told the congregation that it was not for him to judge the stone-cutter and even if it were he could not because 'he has not been inside the church door for the last thirty years'.

The quarry that moved Daniel Gumb's cave-house supplied fine granite for building. The Cheesewring which gives the quarry its name stands above the quarry's north end. It pre-dated the quarry, being a natural feature rather than a quarried or manufactured one. Despite granite being an igneous rock, the flows from which it evolved were not always homogenous and the rock was then formed with a series of horizontal and vertical sub-beds which allowed a degree of weathering even when the rectangular blocks between the beds remained solid. The result is that some tors – the exposed granite lumps – have weathered into forms like piles of giant doughnuts. Of these the Cheesewring is one of the best, and certainly the best known (chiefly, it must be said, due to its accessibility – our walk passes one that is almost as good on Kilmar Tor but that one is rarely visited). Elsewhere on Stowe's Hill, on which the Cheesewring stands, there are other fine tor shapes – some with fancy names, the worst of which is the Devil's Armchair. The Elizabethan write Norden writing of the Cheeswring described it as 'a heape of stones, admirablye depending, wherein nature hath done more at adventure (if a man so speak) than arte or force can doe by greateste deliberation'.

The name derives not from anything to do with cheese-making, as the sensible visitor might expect, but from cider-making. The rocks look like an apple press, with *in situ* layers of apples and sack, the name 'cheese' being the West Country word for the dry, remnant apple husk.

The Cheesewring

(3) *Stowe's Pound*

The name Stowe's Pound is Saxon though the enclosure here is
much older, being the remains of an Iron Age hillfort. The Celtic
defenders of this hill top site used the local granite boulders to
create a drystone wall defence that knitted itself cleverly into the
natural rock outcrops. It seems a bleak place to want to defend,
though it is thought the climate was better two thousand years ago,
but the view is breathtaking, the tiny village of Henwood merely
enhancing the panorama. Sharp Tor, to the north, has been called
the Cornish Matterhorn, though it is necessary to go to Henwood
and to suspend belief to see why.

(4) *Kilmar Tor and Twelve Men's Moor*

It is a personal opinion but I think that only Rough Tor comes
close to being as impressive a Bodmin tor as Kilmar, though it has
to be said that the walker must work hard to get the best view as
Kilmar is at its best from the north. The long summit ridge is
littered with 'Cheesewring-like' rock clusters and the walker is
usually alone to potter around these. Kilmar is Bodmin Moor's
third hill, though the general uplift of the area means that this
hardly amounts to much, the tor rising barely 100 m (325 ft) above
the surrounding valleys. Twelve Men's Moor, from which Kilmar
Tor rises, is named from an agreement made in the 13th century
between the Prior of Launceston Priory and the twelve farmers of
named farms – of which Trewortha was one. Under the agreement
the boundaries on the eastern edge of Bodmin farms were defined.

(5) *Trewortha Tor and King Arthur's Bed*

Trewortha Tor is littered with rocks, two of which, at least, are
logans, though very small logans. See Note (2) of Walk 25 for a
definition of logans.

   King Arthur's Bed at the western end of the long ridge of
Trewortha Tor is a rock basin. Such basins are often found in
horizontal, flat slabs of granite and are formed by chemical erosion
due to standing water, rain water being lightly acidic, and by the
swirling action of mica granules during rain and winds. The basins
here – there are three – are etched into a roughly rectangular slab

4 m (13 ft) by 3 m (10 ft). Two of the basins are circular but the other is a crudely human shape, a shape which gives the rock its name.

To the west of the Bed is a monstrous Forestry Commision plantation on Smallacombe Downs. The plantation is chiefly of Sitka spruce and Lodgepole pine and has few redeeming features. The only one that springs to mind is the fact that redpolls have been attracted to the area.

(6) *Minions*

This tiny hamlet is the highest in Cornwall, standing just below the 1000-ft – or, less romantically, the 305-m – contour. Despite that, the shelter offered by Stowe's Hill and Caradon Hill, topped by a TV mast that is a waymark all across the eastern side of Bodmin Moor, keep it free from nature's more rigorous excesses. The hamlet grew up in the 19th century when the local area was extensively mined for copper. At its southern end our route is surrounded by the ruined engine houses of the Phoenix mines (East, West and United), of Wheal Jenkin, Marke Valley and Gonamena, while its northern end has the remains of granite quarries. Phoenix United was the biggest tin producer in eastern Cornwall, producing over 15,000 tons in its 50-year life – which almost exactly coincided with the last half of the 19th century. In addition the mine yielded over 80,000 tons of copper. Each of the mines, and the quarries, were serviced by sections of the Liskeard-Caradon railway, a section of which can still be followed on the north side of Caradon Hill. The railway was interesting for having been wholly gravity powered from the mines, and Cheesewring Quarry, to Moorswater near Liskeard. There stone and ore were transferred to the Liskeard and Looe Union Canal for shipment to the sea at Looe. Empty rail wagons were hauled back to the moor by horses. The railway continued to operate as far as Cheesewring Quarry until 1917.

Walk 24 Brown Willy

Though it rises only a few tens of metres from the surrounding

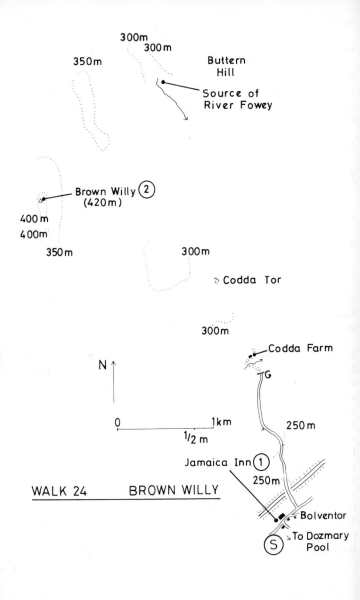

300m

300m

Buttern
Hill

350m

Source of
River Fowey

Brown Willy ②
(420m)

400 m
400m

350m

300m

Codda Tor

300m

Codda Farm

G

N ↑

250 m

0   1km

½ m

Jamaica Inn ①

250m

WALK 24   BROWN WILLY

Bolventor

S   →To Dozmary
Pool

moorland, Brown Willy is still a desirable top for the peak-bagger – the highest peak in Cornwall. The route starts from Jamaica Inn, for many a place of literary pilgrimage, in the tiny hamlet of Bolventor, set right in the centre of the moor, a position which sounds a little inaccessible, but which the A30 trunk road makes almost embarrassingly easy to reach.

Walk category : Intermediate/Difficult (3½ hours)

Length : 10 km (6¼ miles). An extension of 4 km (2½ miles) is possible.

Ascent : 250 m (820 ft)

Maps : Landranger Sheet 201, Pathfinder Sheet 1338 (SX 07/17)

Starting and finishing point : At 183 767 the Jamaica Inn

Note: In its final section this route crosses a section of trackless, barren moorland. It should not be attempted in limited visibility unless you are experienced in the use of map and compass.

Before the decision to drive a dual carriageway behind the Jamaica Inn (see (1) Jamaica Inn) public footpaths led from the car-park on to the moor at the foot of Brown Willy. At present the road carving has destroyed these footpaths and there is, strictly, no best walk to the top. However, everyone now uses a route from Codda Farm (at 180 784), a deserted farm due north of the inn. This route is not on a Right of Way but is permissive in the sense of being accepted. That could change tomorrow, so I do not intend to offer instructions on how to trespass. Suffice to say that the walker who goes left out of the Inn car-park and takes the first turning left – signed for Bolventor church – can follow the lane to the gate at its end. Beyond, take the mucky lane down towards Codda Farm. There is a stream that needs fording but 50 m before you reach it there is a well-hidden bridge on the right from which a slab path leads to the farm. Go through the farmyard and go north to the summit of Codda Tor. Now go north of west to Brown Willy (see (2) Brown Willy). Return along a similar route.

From the summit a worthwhile extension to the walk – adding about 4 km (2½ miles) of rough moor to the route and certainly pushing it into the Difficult category – is to go north-east from the summit across High Moor to reach the source of the River Fowey among the bogs at (172 809) (which is on Pathfinder Sheet SX18). The source was once marked by a chapel to St Peter but nothing of that remains and the visitor must hunt about among the bog pools.

(1) *Jamaica Inn*

Two-hundred and fifty years ago Bolventor was a tiny, remote hamlet set astride a track across Bodmin Moor, almost at the centre of the Moor. The moor sat across the mouth of Cornwall and there was a need to cross it if trade was to be carried on between the county and the outside world. So, in 1742, posts were set up every quarter mile right the way across. This did have the advantage of preventing people from getting lost in the wilderness but it was not until 1769 when a Turnpike Act was passed that the route through the hamlet was made finally secure and truly passable. As an aside, it was in the same year that the nearby, and comparably sized, village of Temple was destroyed overnight when its entire male population (both of them) were hanged for sheep stealing. Within a decade the Jamaica Inn had been built, though parts of the building are older, as one of the coaching inns on the route from Truro to Launceston (and on to London). In the 50-mile section between the two towns horses were changed six times, the Jamaica Inn coming after Ladock, Indian Queens, Roche and Bodmin, and being followed by Five Lanes. Many years later, in the mid 19th century, the inn was noted as offering 'comfortable though somewhat rude accomodation'. Today, the inn is still frequented by travellers – even occasionally coach-travellers! – many coming on a pilgrimage to the place that forms the backdrop for one of the better known books by Daphne du Maurier, perhaps Cornwall's most famous author. In her foreword to the

The Jamaica Inn, Bolventor

book, first published in 1936, the author pointed out that her book portrayed the inn as it might have looked around 1800 (not many years after it had started as a Turnpike Inn), though many visitors seem to believe the book is factual rather than fictional, a belief encouraged by the inn owners. It is quite probable that the inn did indeed see smuggling action – why not? Just about everywhere else did. It is also rumoured to be haunted by the ghost of a man murdered many years ago in what may have been a smuggling-related killing. It is said that the man was called out of the inn half-way through a drink and found dead the next morning. The ghost is thought to be looking for the half empty glass.

The inn's name may derive from smuggled spirits: some say it derives from Jamaican rum but there is a strong school of thought that sees the name deriving from the original owners' (the Rodd family) strong ties with the Caribbean island.

At the inn the visitor can visit Potter's Museum of Curiosity, a grotesque collection of malformed animals – a chick with four legs and so on – and tableaux created from stuffed rabbits, kittens, etc.

(2) *Brown Willy*

If there was a committee for the protection of mountains they would change its name. The name derives from the Cornish *bron ewhella*, which means highest hill. Indeed, all Bodmin's peaks have Cornish names, except Rough Tor which has a scruffy English one. In good weather the view from Brown Willy is surprisingly good for a peak that rises so little from its surroundings and takes in most of the high tors of the moor. Indeed there is no better spot from which to examine Bodmin Moor. There are also few better spots to feel the magic of the moor. I was once alone here with mist swirling around the summit area rock castles. I hunted for the trig point and when I found it there was a riderless white horse standing beside it. As I cautiously approached, it turned and disappeared into the mist. I am not suggesting anything supernatural: it was an ordinary, if unusual, encounter in extraordinary circumstances.

The local moors are a good place to see some of the rarer Cornish birds. Both ring ousel and whinchat breed on the moors and nowhere else. In the valleys around the hill the botanist will also be kept busy seeking out marsh violet, bog asphodel and several species of insect-eating plant.

Walk 25 Rough Tor

The second highest point on Bodmin Moor, and in Cornwall, lies to the north-west of Brown Willy and was given, along with many acres of surrounding moorland, to the National Trust in 1951 by Sir Richard Onslow as a perpetual memorial to the men of the 43rd (Wessex) Division who died in the 1939–45 War.

Walk category : Difficult (3 hours)

Length : 11 km (7 miles)

Ascent : 150 m (500 ft)

Maps : Landranger Sheet 200, Pathfinder Sheets 1325 (SX 08/18) and 1338 (SX 07/17)

Starting and finishing point : The car-park at 138 819 at the end of the road past Roughtor Farm

Note: This route covers trackless, barren moor and should not be attempted in poor visibility, or by those not experienced in the use of map and compass.

Go down the track from the car-park to the bridge over a tributary of the infant River Camel and go right to visit the memorial stone (see (1) Charlotte Dymonde Memorial). Now go south-east and up to reach Showery Tor, the extreme northern end of the long ridge of Rough Tor. From the top go southward along the ridge over Little Rough Tor and on to Rough Tor itself (see (2) Rough Tor). In this section between the 'little' tor and and the main tor look out for the remnants of drystone walling from an Iron Age hill fort. Our next objective is Middlemoor Cross at 1250 7925 which

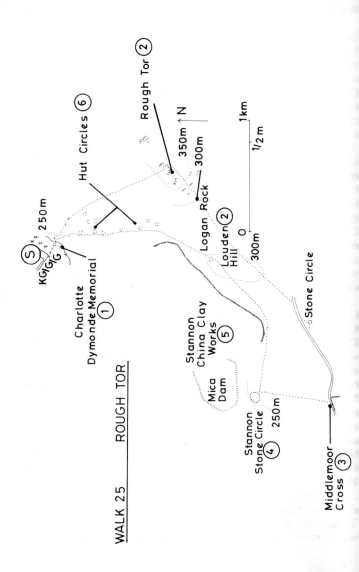

WALK 25   ROUGH TOR

Rough Tor ②

Hut Circles ⑥

N

350m

300m

250m

Logan Rock

Louden Hill ②

300m

1km

1/2 m

0

300m

Charlotte Dymonde Memorial ①

KG/G/G

Ⓢ

Stannon China Clay Works ⑤

Mica Dam

Stannon Stone Circle ④

250m

Stone Circle

Middlemoor Cross ③

lies on a bearing of 235° from the summit of the tor. The easy way to reach it is to go down off the summit, and to contour around the east side of Louden Hill, tending to the east to reach an unsurfaced road that can be followed all the way to the cross (see (3) Middlemoor Cross), which lies a few tens of metres along the northern edge of a wall that the track reaches. On the way a stone circle is passed (at 1325 7958, about 50 m to the east – left – of the road).

From the cross go 5° east of north to reach the Stannon Stone Circle, (see (4) Stannon Stone Circle) which is soon visible on the moor plateau's edge. If in doubt, head for the extreme left edge of the mica dam of the china clay works. This dam is stepped but its liquid pool edge acts as a convenient waymarker. From the circle go east, picking up and following the wall above the Stannon China Clay Works (see (5) China Clay) and follow it along the northern flank of Louden Hill (see also Note (2)). Where the wall elbows left, go due north for the car-park, losing height as you walk initially over difficult, boggy ground, and then past ancient cairns and hut circles (see (6) Bronze Age Village).

(1) *Charlotte Dymonde Memorial*

On Sunday 14 April 1844 a young serving girl, Charlotte Dymonde, set off to visit friends, heading towards the river ford where the bridge now stands. Nine days later she was found in the river close to where the memorial now stands. Her throat had been cut. Suspicion fell on a fellow servant, a crippled boy called Matthew Weekes. Weekes admitted having seen Charlotte on the moor but claimed that she had been heading for a secret rendezvous with a man named Tom Prout. Then Weekes ran away only to be traced to Plymouth from where he voluntarily gave himself up to Cornish police. The murder caused a local sensation. In the early summer 10,000 people gathered on the lower flanks of Rough Tor. A local paper notes 'long lines of carriages and carts . . . groups of booths and marquees where coffee and more solid refreshments were sold'. The meeting had been organized by Temperance groups (hence the coffee) but, the paper adds, there was no want of 'spots where other beverages than those used by teetotallers might be procurred'. A hat was passed round and enough money was raised to erect this granite memorial to the poor victim. The memorial is now a little away from the river: it was originally erected at the very spot of the murder, as far as was known, but the water undermined it. Charlotte's ghost is said to haunt the moor close to the memorial.

Matthew Weekes was charged with Charlotte's murder, found guilty and sentenced to death. He was executed publicly outside Bodmin Gaol in front of a crowd of 20,000, double the number that turned up at Rough Tor.

(2) *Rough Tor*

From the west Rough Tor is a beautiful mountain, the tors on the summit ridge giving it an elegance it loses from almost every other viewpoint. Though Stowe's Hill and Kilmar Tor on Walk 23 are excellent – the latter especially so, Kilmar being the only hill that competes with Rough Tor for title of Bodmin's finest tor – the tors here are quite superb. Norden, the Elizabethan writer, wrote one of the most delightful of all descriptions of tors, and it is worth quoting it here. He wrote that the 'inlands mountayns are so crowned with mightie rocks, as he that passeth through the Countrye beholdinge some of theis Rockes afar off, may suppose them to be great Cyties planted on the hills . . . ther appeareth the resemblance of towres, howses, chimnies and such like.' Norden was convinced that the tors had been created by the flood – the 'Universal Inundation' as he had it – 'whose force searching the verie foundations of the yielding earth, carried with violence heapes therof togeather'.

Close to Rough Tor's summit is a logan rock. Occasionally, blocks of granite weather free of their underlying supporting rock mass but remain balanced on it. So perfect is the balance of a logan that the boulder rocks gently when pushed. Legend has it that the rocking foretold the future to anyone who could ask the right questions and 'read' the answering vibrations. On nearby Louden Hill there is said to be one of the best of all local logans. It

The logan rock on Louden Hill

certainly looks very good but I have to confess to having been unable, ever, to make it rock.

(3) *Middlemoor Cross*

There are almost 400 granite crosses in Cornwall and though many are set in churchyards there are also many that stand in apparently open land. These mark old tracks, the crosses having been set up for the benefit of travellers. Some were erected at passes – so-called 'Thank God' crosses at which the traveller would pause and give grateful thanks for having completed a climb – while others might be erected by a traveller as a thanksgiving for having escaped the real threat of thieves and murderers, or the real/imagined threats of ghosts and demons.

   Middlemoor Cross is the most remote of all Bodmin's crosses (despite being only 200 m from a farm) set on an old track that crossed the moor's north-west corner. The cross is poorly hewn and inelegantly inscribed but it is not thought that these features indicate a great age; most scholars believe that Middlemoor is medieval.

(4) *Stannon Stone Circle*

Stannon is an extraordinary circle, 50 m (160 ft) in diameter, poorly defined as a circle, and comprising around 70 stones of irregular size, though it is likely that more existed when the circle was first formed. The circle is large by Cornish standards and has almost double the usual number of stones. The reason for the difference is not known. Does the apparent lack of planning – the poor shape and poor stone quality – imply a very early construction, a time before the builders had come to terms with the requirements of circle-making? Or does it imply a civilization in decline, with people who knew what had been done before but no longer had the skills to do it and who thought that using more stones might compensate for poor design? The only certainty is that we will never know for certain.

(5) *China Clay*

From the Stannon stone circle the mess that is the Stannon China

Clay Works can be seen. Granite is an igneous rock formed from molten magma oozing or bursting out from deep in the earth. The cooling conditions of the liquid rock defines the size of the constituent crystals of quartz, feldspar and mica. If the cooling was rapid because, for instance, the magma came into contact with overlying sedimentary rocks, then the crystals are small and the granite is fine-grained. If the cooling was more slow then the crystals are much larger, the granite coarse-grained. In general Cornish granites are coarser than those of, say, nearby Dartmoor.

Coarser grains also means the existence of jointing in the rock, and such joints allow water to seep in. The water attacks the feldspar crystals, decomposing them into hydrous silicates of aluminium and potassium. The further down the water goes the more complete the decomposition because of the additional action of an uprising gaseous 'chemical soup' which aids the process. In its finest form the decomposed powder is known as kaolin, the name deriving from a mountain in China – *Kao Lin* – where the powdered clay was first worked and used to form delicate porcelain.

In the mid 18th century William Cookworthy, a Quaker from Kingsbridge in Devon, visited Hensbarrow in Cornwall – to the south-east of Bodmin – and recognised the potential of the local kaolin deposits. The local tin industry was in decline and there was plenty of local labour to help Cookworthy extract the clay. In 1768 he produced the first genuine English porcelain in his factory in Plymouth.

Today the industry is still one of the mainstays of the Cornish economy. Water is used to produce a solution of kaolin, together with a mix of quartz and mica particles. The latter are separated by 'lavation' (a washing process), the kaolin solution going into drying rooms, the waste going to produce the huge white pyramids that are such a feature of the north Cornish scenery. The kaolin formed when the 'mud' has dried is used in various processes: in paper-making (the chief use), in the textile industry, in cosmetics and in the making of china and porcelain. Today only about a tenth of Cornish china clay is used for making china.

(6) *Bronze Age Village*

The 'village' on the side of Rough Tor is one of the few collections of huts that have been full excavated – as a result of a proposed extension of the Stannon clay works. The excavation revealed that the huts were circular, their diameters varying from 6 to 10 m (19 to 33 ft) but with walls consistently 1¼ m (about 4 ft) high. Other evidence of secondary supports suggests the huts had conical roofs supported on a wooden beam structure. It is conjectured that the roofs were thatch or turf. The huts were orientated so that their doors, many of which can still be recognized by the walker, were away from the prevailing winds. Some huts had entrance porches, many were paved internally, and paving slabs also covered drains and sumps. Other evidence suggested wooden furnishings, perhaps beds and cupboards, while frequently the walls had inlet niches for storage. Outside, the village had been drained by way of ditches going downhill, one ditch still showing clean spade cuts. In addition to the huts there were walls which are assumed to have been field walls. There were two types: one was crudely formed of various boulders. The fields these formed were narrow and ran downhill facing south-east. It is thought this was ploughed land, the walls being casually formed from ploughed up rocks. The second type of walls were more carefully constructed, with small-sized boulders between laterally placed slabs – a form of rubble wall with 'stretchers' not dissimilar in form to some modern drystone walls. It is likely that the enclosures with these walls were used for stock animals.

Excavations of the ground revealed some pottery shards and flint fragments. Dating suggests two phases of habitation, the first around 2000–1500 BC, the second around 1000 BC. Why the site was abandoned the first time is not known; the second abandoning was probably because the local climate had become colder and wetter. Also found were some quorn stones so it is likely that cereals were grown locally. However, the cultivated area was small which suggests that animal-rearing was the chief reason for the village's existence.

Cornwall

We have already walked in Cornwall, for the whole of Bodmin Moor lies within the county. However, since the moor is a self-contained area it seems appropriate to introduce the remaining walks by looking briefly at the history of Cornwall.

As with the areas we have visited previously, Cornwall was settled by Mesolithic (Middle Stone Age) peoples who have left remains, discernible only to the trained eye near, for instance, Dozmary Pool. The remains of Neolithic (New Stone Age) folk need no such discerning eye and are crowded on to the Penwith Moors, to the west of the Hayle River and visited by Walks 34 and 35, and the edges of Bodmin Moor. These concentrations do not necessarily imply that the folk preferred upland moor to the valleys, rather that the moors were less afforested than the valleys. Since the woods of the time were home to wolves and wild boar, as well as being thick enough to discourage travel, the moors were the easier option. The coming of the Bronze Age brought with it the real megalithic culture, with standing stones and circles, probably erected for ritual purposes, but perhaps having astronomical significance. Walks 34 and 36 visit important megalithic sites, the former including the remarkable and enigmatic Men-an-Tol.

Ultimately, the Bronze Age gave way to the Iron Age, the new fold being characterized by the hill forts they constructed to defend themselves. The best Cornish hill fort is Castell-an-Dinas but Walk 35 passes through the fine Chun Castle, while Walk 30 visits the best of Cornish cliff castles – a particular form of hill fort – on Pentire Point. The Iron Age folk of Britain were Celts, a name now synonymous with Wales and Cornwall. They were a fierce but sophisticated people who have received a bad press from the first of their conquerors, the Romans. The Romans did not conquer Cornwall in the same way that they did other areas of Britain, finding the Cornish Celts less hostile than their Welsh brothers and allowing them great freedom. There are few Roman remains in Cornwall, the rulers seemingly content to rule their (relatively) docile subjects from Exeter, though they did build roads into the country, probably to exploit Cornwall's mineral

wealth, most especially its tin. When the Romans left, the Celts
continued with their lives much as before. Unfortunately, much as
before meant tribal squabbling and petty intrigues, a social system
that was totally inadequate when faced with a determined invader.
When the Saxons arrived in eastern England the Celts, though a
match for the invaders in particular battles, lacked cohesiveness
and were never able to sustain an initiative. When King Arthur – if
he existed he was a 5th- or 6th-century Celtic leader – halted the
Saxon's westward advance for a decade or two, the invaders bided
their time. No attempt appears to have been made to force a
Saxon retreat, so that when Arthur had gone the Saxons were able
to pick up their swords again and continue their westward march.

In 577 the Saxons won the battle of Dyrham (near Bath) cutting
off the Celts of Wales from those of the West Country. The latter
they drove back into their final stronghold, Cornwall. From there
many emigrated to found a new Celtic Kingdom in a part of
France they called Little Britain, *Bretagne*, or Britanny as we
know it. The Saxons did not wholly conquer or displace the
Cornish Celts, and neither did the Normans who followed them,
even though they had subdued the county by 1072. The Normans
built four great castles: Trematon, Restormel, Launceston and
Tintagel. The latter is on Walk 29 and is a fascinating site, not only
for its Norman castle remains but for its place in Arthurian legends
and its links with the Celtic saints who were so influential in
spreading Christianity to the county.

Cornwall was staunchly in favour of the Latin mass in the time
of Henry VIII, but supported his daughter just as steadfastly when
the Spanish Armada came and were equally enthusiastic
supporters of the Crown at the time of the Civil War. So great was
their support that the King thanked them in a special address. The
King's defeat was a blow; the Cornish felt the desecration of their
churches by the Puritans keenly and stayed away from worship in
thousands. The healing balm was, as is usually the case, money.
Cornwall's mineral wealth, at first tin, then copper and finally
china clay, was added to the wealth from the sea, chiefly pilchard
fishing, to create a new level of prosperity. Several walks go close
to old mining sites – the engine house chimney would do well as a

symbol of Cornwall, particularly its western half – while Walks 31 and 32 visit fine old fishing ports. Yet despite it all, Cornwall managed to hang on to its identity: only in the last century did the Cornish language finally die. Ultimately both mining and fishing failed, each, in its own way, over-exploited. With china clay being an industry in decline and agriculture no longer labour-intensive, Cornwall is facing economic hardship again. Tourism is the only growth industry, but as with all industries it brings both benefits and curses. The adantages are obvious, the curses less so, apart from the traffic snarls, being more to do with the psyche of a folk reduced to advertising pasties and pixies as a way of life. Nevertheless, for the interested visitor Cornwall has much to offer, not least its coastline – mile after surprisingly endless mile of rugged cliff, with every step an adventure into salty air.

Walks 26 and 27 Truro and Idless Wood

Though these short walks can be completed as two distinct, easy outings they are best completed together. (See p. 241 for a combination of these walks.) Truro, the county town of Cornwall, is a fine city, encapsulating much of the history of the county, the better items from which are exhibited in the County Museum. In complete contrast Idless Wood is a Forestry Commission plantation, an unlikely place, it would seem, in which to gain useful information about the county or even the area. In fact the wood is a naturalist's delight and is an excellent place to get close to some of Cornwall's wildlife.

Walk 26 Truro

Walk category : Easy (1 hour)

Length : 3 km (2 miles)

Ascent : 50 m (165 ft)

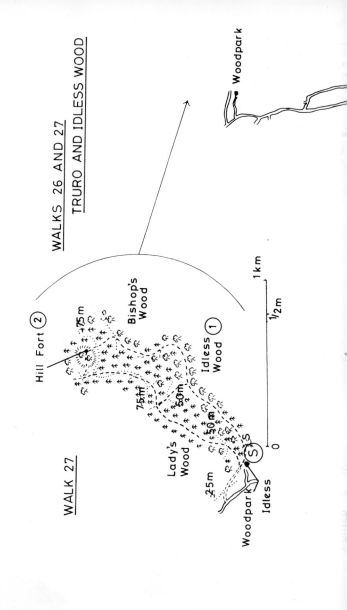

WALKS 26 AND 27
TRURO AND IDLESS WOOD

WALK 27

Hill Fort ②

75 m

Bishop's Wood

Lady's Wood

75m

50m

Idless Wood ①

50m

S

25m

Woodpark

Idless

0   ½m   1km

Woodpark

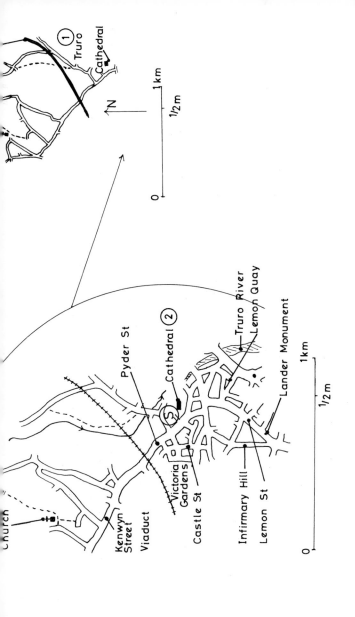

① Truro
Cathedral

N

0   ½m   1 km

② Cathedral
Pyder St
Truro River
Lemon Quay
Lander Monument
Infirmary Hill
Lemon St
Castle St
Victoria Gardens
Viaduct
Kenwyn Street
Church

0   ½m   1 km

Maps : Landranger Sheet 204, Pathfinder Sheet 1360 (SW74/84)
*though no maps are needed unless the walker is continuing
to Idless Wood*

Starting and finishing point : Truro is well supplied with car-parks.
The description below assumes a start
is made from the cathedral. The
closest car-park to the cathedral is the
multi-storey in St Clement Street.
From it a walkway leads to Union
Place, a delightful little street
dominated by the Victorian library
(paid for by a local man who made a
fortune from journalism in London)
and the fine neo-classical Methodist
Church of St Mary Clement.

From the end of Union Place, go left into Pydar Street (see (1) the
City of Truro) to reach Truro Cathedral. From the cathedral (see
(2) Truro Cathedral) go across High Cross to reach King Street.
At the T-junction go left into Boscawen Street.

   The square outside the cathedral's west end is High Cross, site
of Truro's monthly market, the city's commercial centre. An old
cross that, it is believed, once stood in the square – and which gave
it its name – has recently been re-erected on a granite plinth. The
cross, which may be as much as 1000 years old, was found in an
old sewage trench and after retrieval leaned against the cathedral
for many years. History does not record whether this was because
no one had the courage to handle it until it had aired for a few
decades. History does, however, record that after the local farmers
were ordered to set up their cattle market on Castle Hill in 1840 to
avoid the aggravation of regular herds of cattle in the city centre,
they frequently prayed *en masse* in the cathedral for a change of
heart by the city fathers. On the north side of the square are the
Assembly Rooms, built in fine style in the late 18th century. The
busts are of Shakespeare and either Garrick (most likely) or
Handel, depending upon your persuasion.

The highly ornate building, now occupied by Barclays Bank, on the corner of Boscawen Street was once the Miners' Bank. The street is named for Admiral Edward Boscawen, born at Tregothnan in 1711. The Admiral was a colourful character who was known as Old Dreadnought after a successful campaign as captain of HMS *Dreadnought*. This ended in 1744 when he came ashore to raise an army of Cornishmen to counter the Jacobite uprising of Bonnie Prince Charlie. It is said that Boscawen so enjoyed a fight that when one started against a French man-of-war he ran out of his cabin in his nightshirt and finished the battle before he changed. It is also said that once he helped save a ship in which he was serving from sinking by ramming his wig into a leaking hole.

Boscawen Street is as wide as it is because it was once divided by a row of shops and houses called Middle Row, now long demolished.

At the end of Boscawen Street bear right into Princes Street.

Look out for Boscawen House, a fine 17th-century building, and for Prince's House and Mansion House, both dating from the mid 18th century. Prince's House was built for William Lemon, a Cornish mining entrepreneur. The frontage of Mansion House is of Bath Stone.

At the bottom go right into Morlaix Avenue, named for Truro's French twin-town in Celtic Brittany.

Across the road here is Truro River. In its earliest days Truro was an important port, its apparently inconvenient position some 16 km (10 miles) from the sea being off-set by the protection from sea-borne pirates the position offered. Ultimately, as times became more lawful and ships bigger, Truro began to lose its importance, being unable to compete with Falmouth, set on its superb natural harbour.

Go right into Lemon Quay and follow this to Lemon Street.

William Lemon was born near Helston in 1696 and joined a mining company at Penzance. He rose to a position of some prominence by the age of 24 and at that time he made the inspired decision to bring Thomas Newcomen to the Wheal Fortune Mine to set up a steam engine pump. This one phenomenally successful decision set him up for life and he dominated Truro society until his death. In 1742 the 'Great Mr Lemon' as he was known with a combination of awe and derision, was made Sheriff of Cornwall. Look out for the Royal Hotel, a 19th-century coaching inn. The *Quicksilver* left Falmouth at breakfast time, stopped here at Truro and was in Launceston, about 110 km (about 70 miles) away, in time for the passengers to have an evening meal at the end of Day One of the trip to London.

Go up Lemon Street to the Lander Monument on the corner of Strangeways Terrace.

Richard Lander (1804–1834) and John Lander (1807–1839) were born at the Fighting Cocks Inn – on the corner of Green Street and Quay Street, no longer extant but marked by a plaque. Richard was an explorer from an early age, engaging on a merchant ship for the West Indies at eleven and rounding the Cape of Good Hope before he was twenty. In 1830 Richard and his brother were sent to explore the mouth of the River Niger by the British government. In all three journeys were made but Richard died at Fernando Po (now Macias Ngeumo) of wounds received from an African after completing his survey. Because of the brothers' involvement there is a Truro Island set in the River Niger and a hill on it called Cornwall Mountain. The monument shows Richard, the elder brother. Strangways Terrace is a row of excellent Georgian buildings.

Go sharp right down Infirmary Hill, crossing to and continuing along Calenick Street to Victoria Square.

Victoria Square is new, having been burned down in the mid 19th century largely as a result of the failure of city's fire brigade – said to have travelled at a 'snail's gallop' – to reach it in time. Walsingham Place off the square has a superb Georgian terrace.

Cross the square into River Street where the County Museum and Gallery is sited.

The museum holds an outstanding collection of Cornish minerals together with fine collections on the county's ancient past and natural history. The gallery has work by internationally famous artists, as well as paintings by Cornish artists.

River Street leads to Castle Street. Go right to reach, also to the right, the Leats.

The names here refer to the River Kenwyn, to the left, and to little tributary streams and cut ditches – leats – that were formed from the river and used as open drains and sewers in the older part of the city. Castle Street leads to Castle Hill, site of the city's Norman castle, a building that was ruinous by the mid 15th century and had disappeared altogether a couple of centuries later. Only in the last century was its site finally re-discovered.

A left turn into Union Street from Castle Street leads to Victoria Gardens.

This fine city park is dominated by the superb GWR viaduct on its granite legs. The viaduct was the work of Isambard Kingdom Brunel whose original plan conceived of a solid stone viaduct 300 m (100 ft) long and 25 m (over 80 ft) high. Money ran out, however, and the top (now gone) section was of wood. The park bandstand was built for Queen Victoria's Golden Jubilee in 1898.

Return to Castle Street from the park and go into the Leats, from where several narrow alleyways lead back to Pydar Street.

(1) *The City of Truro*
Though in a clearly advantageous position there is no firm evidence of any settlement at Truro before Norman times. The name is from the Norman French for 'three streets' – though one school of thought sees an older influence, perhaps deriving from the Celtic 'castle by water' – and the Normans certainly had a presence here as excavations on Castle Hill have shown. Later Truro was a stannary town, that is a town where tin was required to be taken for taxing and sale, and a major West Country port. Only with the rise of Falmouth did the latter importance decline. That decline followed the Civil War when staunchly Royalist Truro was a centre for the Royal Mint. Only in 1646 did the town's governor, Sir Ralph Hopton, surrender to Sir Thomas Fairfax. Despite the loss of its port Truro remained important and following the building of the cathedral in the 19th century it was granted city status (in 1877) by Queen Victoria. The city's coat of arms are a reflection of its history: a shield with a three-masted sailing ship above fish, being supported by a Cornish miner, complete with pick and hat-mounted candle, and a fisherman.

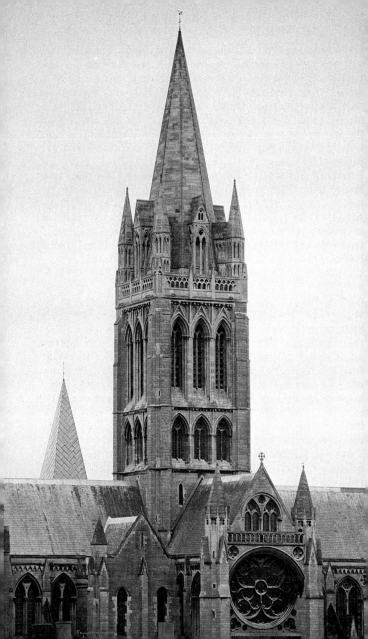

(2) *Truro Cathedral*

Truro's cathedral with its three elegant spires totally dominates the city. To such an extent is this true, the city seemingly nestling around the building, that it comes as a complete surprise that the cathedral is only 100 years old. In fact it was the first cathedral to have been built in Britain since St Paul's. It is also claimed to be the first on a new site since Salisbury in the 13th century, but that is a slight exaggeration as an aisle of an earlier church is included in the fabric. The architect for the work was John Loughborough Pearson who chose a Gothic style, the soaring lines making a nice link with the 'Celtic' cathedrals of Brittany (Treguier comes readily to mind) – though this has as much to do with the cramped site as with homage. A statue of the architect adorns a niche near the south porch. The main building was completed in 30 years though full completion has not yet been achieved. The chapter house on the north side was added only in 1967. Inside, the cathedral is modern, light and airy, though it does have work that pre-dates its construction. In the south aisle is a superb 14th-century stone *Pietà*, brought from Brittany, and close to this is a standard of the RNLI, the staff made from timbers of the Penlee lifeboat lost in 1981. The remarkably detailed terracotta relief of the Via Crucis in the North choir aisle is by George Tinworth and acknowledges the safe return of the sons of Mr F. Walter Bond from the Boer War. Much newer is the canvas 'Cornubia – Land of Saints' unveiled by the Prince of Wales (the Duke of Cornwall) in 1980. The painting shows Cornwall in evening light, with Celtic saints bringing the Light of God and Truro Cathedral itself illuminated by a shaft of light from the procession. The crosses represent the parish churches of the county.

Pride of place, however, must go to Pearson's baptistery, widely believed to be his masterpiece. The baptistery roof is supported by pillars of Bath Stone, the font being of Italian red marble.

Truro Cathedral

Walk 27 Idless Wood

Walk category : Easy (1 hour)

Length : 4 km (2½ miles)

Ascent : 60 m (200 ft)

Maps : Landranger Sheet 204, Pathfinder Sheet 1360/SW74/84)

Starting and finishing point : At 824 476, a Forestry Commission car-park signed and reached from the minor road that links Kenwyn, a northern 'suburb' of Truro to Idless and on to the B3284.

From the car-park take the obvious track beside – but separated from by a bank – a stream that goes north-eastward into the wood (see (1) Idless Wood). Ignore three turnings to the left, continuing on the track as it becomes increasingly stony and starts to rise. When the top of the up-slope is reached take the (fourth) turn left, following the path on to the top of a hill-fort now embedded in woodland (see (2) Hillfort). The path goes through the fort to reach an obvious track at a T-junction. Go left on this track, ignoring all minor turns to left and right. After about 500 m (550 yds) a path leads off left down steep log steps. This path leads back to the outward route and is a (relatively) short cut. The walk continues on the main track until this reaches another track coming in from the left. Take this to rejoin the outward route very close to the car-park. Go left, to regain the start.

(1) *Idless Wood*
Though Idless is the name of the Forestry Commission's plantation, the site incorporates Bishop's Wood, named for the Bishop of Exeter who owned the local manor. The wood is an excellent mix of conifer and native broad-leaved, the former including redwood as well as the more usual larches, the latter

including two species of oak (pedunculate and sessile), birch, holly, hazel and some willow. The wood is famous for its grasses and sedges but is equally good for ferns with male, lady and hard ferns being particularly noticeable. There are few flowers in the well-shaded areas but numerous species of fungi including an excellent crop of the evil-smelling and aptly named stinkhorn. In summer the butterflies are elusive but worth searching out, while most visitors will see squirrels, sadly only of the grey variety. Badgers also inhabit the woods.

(2) *Hillfort*
The fort definitely (obviously!) pre-dates the wood, probably being Iron Age. It is difficult to grasp its form now but would appear to have been circular and to have comprised a single rampart and ditch. That places it early in the development of hillforts, the invention of the sling-shot requiring the use of greater numbers of ditches and ramparts to keep an enemy out of sling-shot range.

Walk 26/27 Truro and Idless Wood

Walks 26 and 27 can be combined to form one fine, long walk.

Walk category : Intermediate (3½ hours)

Length : 14 km (9 miles)

Ascent : 150 m (500 ft)

Maps : Landranger Sheet 204, Pathfinder Sheet 1360 (SW74/84)

Starting and finishing point : Truro Cathedral

Having completed the Truro walk, go north-westward along Pydar Street, going over at the roundabout (the road is still Pydar Street) and under the railway (where the road changes to Kenwyn Road). Go right into Chainwalk Drive and left into Lychgate Drive. Along this, on the right, is a path for Kenwyn church, a fine church with 13th-century origins but largely rebuilt in the 19th century after severe lightning damage. Go through the delightful churchyard to where the path bears right. There, go left down steps to a lane. Go right to a minor road and left along it. The road leads through Idless to the turn for the Idless Wood car-park (see starting information for Walk 27.) Complete Walk 27.

Retrace your steps down the road but now, south of Idless, go left (just beyond the Mill) over the River Allen and follow the road. After about 1½ km (1 miles), at 825 458, go right on a footpath signed 'Maresk Road'. Cross a bridge near another millrace – for Maresk Mill, a flour mill – and go over Daubuz's Moor, named for the gardens planted by Charles Daubuz, a local man of the late 18th/early 19th centuries. The land was given to Truro to celebrate the Queen's Silver Jubilee in 1979 for the use of city folk 'for all time'. Go under the railway viaduct, where more of Brunel's piers can be seen, to reach Moresk Road. Go right to St Clement Street and right again for Pydar Street and the cathedral.

Walk 28 The Bude Canal

Close to where Cornwall meets Devon sits Bude, a town with a reputation for holidays on sandy beaches. It is true that the cliffs are lower and less imposing here than those further south – or, indeed, the Devon cliffs to the north – but those south of the town are impressive enough and the Coastal Path along them is taken for half of our walk. The other half takes the towpath of the Bude Canal, one of the wonders of Britain's canal age.

Walk category : Intermediate (3 hours)

Length : 13 km (8 miles)

Ascent : 100 m (330 ft)

Maps : Landranger Sheet 190, Pathfinder Sheet 1292 (SO 20/30)

Starting and finishing point : At 208 062, the car-park at Bude
                                   Tourist Information Centre

From the car-park the canal towpath (see (1) Bude Canal) is easily
reached. Go left along it for 1½ km (1 mile) to Rodd's Bridge.
Cross the bridge and continue on the towpath which is now on the
right side of the canal. As with many British canals that have fallen
from continuous use but remain filled, the waterway here is a
haven for wildlife. The bird-life is by no means exceptional –
ducks, swans, moorhens with, occasionally, other waders, wagtails
and smaller birds – but is none the less pleasing. Continue to the
main road bridge at Helebridge. To reach the Marhamchurch
incline, cross the road and continue on the towpath (now on the
left bank again). After visiting the incline return to the main road.
Go south on the road (go right if arriving from Bude, left if
arriving from Marhamchurch) for about 100 metres to reach a
concrete farm track on the right. Take this. After 100 metres go
left through a signed gate and cross the field diagonally. Cross the
next field by climbing to the ridge top. Follow the left edge in the
next field, and go down to the bottom left-hand corner of the next.
The final field is crossed close to the right fence to reach a road.
    Cross the road and take the signed Coastal Path near the
Salthouse (see (2) Salthouse). The Path cuts off Lower Longbeak
but a trip to its point is worthwhile. Beyond, the Path edges its
way between the cliff top and the (unfenced) road. The cliffs here
are very far from being the sheer and rugged granite cliffs of the
popular vision of Cornwall, being of interleaved beds of shale and
sandstone, the folding of the originally horizontal strata being a
geology lesson in earth movements. The shale is easily eroded by
wave action, the undermined sandstone collapsing on to the beach
at regular intervals. This makes the cliff edge a precarious place
and the beach below uninviting. At Upton the Path reaches the
road briefly, soon going left behind the houses on to the cliff line
again. Continue over Efford Down, passing a trig point from
where the view north is dominated by wok-like satellite receiving
dishes. Bear right beyond the trig to reach a gate through the last
hedge. Ahead now is the Storm Tower (see (3) Storm Tower) at

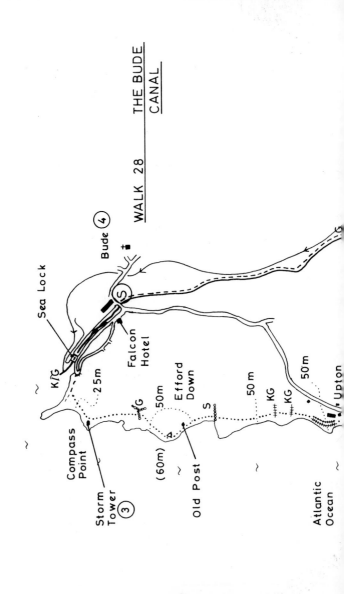

WALK 28   THE BUDE
                  CANAL

Bude ④

Sea Lock

K/G

Sea Lock

Falcon
Hotel

25m

Compass
Point

Storm
Tower
③

(60m)

Old Post

50m

Efford
Down

KG

50 m

KG

KG

50m

Upton

Atlantic
Ocean

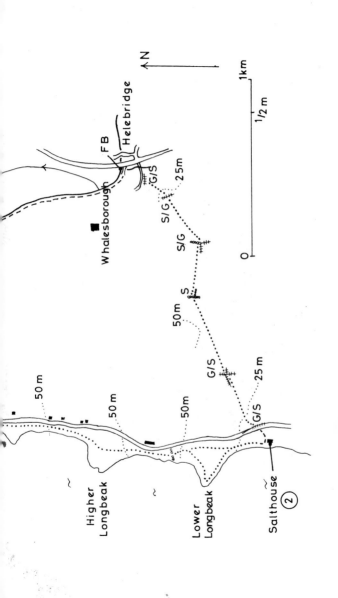

Compass Point. At the Point bear right to reach a made-up path
and go right along it to a kissing-gate. The road beyond is followed
to the Bude sea lock, reached by steps to the left. Cross the lock
and follow the far canal side to a road, the other side of which is
the car-park, from where a tour of Bude (see (4) Bude) can be
made.

(1) *Bude Canal*
The construction of Bude Canal began – as with all other
waterways – with the Act of Parliament enabling a company to be
set up for preparing and operating it. The first cut was made in
1819, with the Canal Company's intention being to prepare a route
through to Launceston. As with all other canals, Bude was hand-
dug by 'navigators' (men who dug 'navigations') – a name that has
come down to us as 'navvies'. Now it is usually used in a
derogatory sense but in the early 19th century there was no
alternative to such manual labour. The chosen route was fraught
with difficulties. For a start the terminal point was way above the
start point, too far above to rise by locks, and in addition there
were several deep valleys that had to be crossed, requiring long,
high aqueducts. To get over the former difficulty a series of
inclines were built with the idea of hauling the canal barges uphill
for refloating in new sections of the waterway. But so big were the
inclines that the barges had to be hauled on rails – they were
wheeled tub-boats that also floated. The best description of the
system I have yet seen is 'amphibious railway'. The Marhamchurch
incline – on the walk, or, rather, on a short detour from it – was
255 m (836 ft) long and rose 36½ m (120 ft). The motive power
for the towing was a huge iron bucket set in a 120-ft well. The
bucket was filled with water and as it descended the well the tub-
boat was hauled up the incline. As a back-up system there was a
steam engine. The canal's biggest incline was at Thurlibear at
244 047, some 2¼ km (1½ miles) east and a little north of
Marhamchurch, which can be visited but lies on private land. This
had a rise of 68½ m (225 ft) and required buckets in a 225-foot

Bude Canal

well. This method of tub-hauling, with the water being emptied at the bottom of the well and the bucket being hauled back up by a 15-m (50-ft) waterwheel, was inefficient in the sense that it required 3 times the weight of water to the weight of tub but cost-effective in that the water was free! A major drawback was that the towing systems available at the times – ropes or cast iron chains – were inadequate and frequently snapped. The tubs were hauled with the crews on board and they would need to jump off sharply as the 5-ton boat hurtled down the railed incline to smash itself, and everything in its path, to bits at the bottom. But for all its inefficiency and eccentricity the inclines were marvellous feats of enginering and a tub in motion must have been a great sight.

It seems a shame when faced with such a splendid scheme to have to report that it was an economic disaster. The plan had been to haul sand from Bude Beach to middle Cornwall for agricultural purposes, the sand being lime rich. The sand was horse-hauled to the Bude Wharf. In addition, there was (and still is) a sea-lock so that ships could dock at Bude and transfer coal and timber, taking on farm produce for their return journeys. Sadly, the venture was never a raving success and within 30 years of opening the canal was in serious financial trouble. It limped on until 1891 by which time the railways had completed what poor economics had begun. By 1912 the canal had closed as a waterway and today only the section covered by our walk is filled.

Those interested in the canal's history and engineering can see various exhibits, including models of the inclines, at the Bude Folk and Historical Exhibition on the Lower Wharf (beside the route) and in the old wharf building at Helebridge. The Bude centre is housed in the canal's old blacksmith's shop and includes other items on the local area – shipwrecks, local history, etc.

(2) *Salthouse*
This 18th-century, though much restored and modified, building was originally a salt store for local fisherman. The fisherman used both beach cast and boat cast nets and brought the fish here for rendering to oil and for salting as a means of preservation in the days before refrigeration. In Edwardian times the building was a

famous local tea-shop for walkers taking the air on the breezy cliff top walks.

(3) *Storm Tower*

The curious hollow octagonal building on Compass Point is the Storm Tower, sometimes known as the Temple of Winds, built by Sir Thomas Acland in the early years of the 19th century. From the Tower gale cones were hoisted to warn local shipping of strong winds at the headland – though I confess to being slightly surprised that such winds could be so local that any ship able to see the cone could not already feel the gale. At a later stage the building served as a coastguard look-out. Though original, the building is not in its original place, cliff collapse having forced a dismantling and a move inland. At present the tower is in danger yet again of disappearing as a result of coastal erosion. Compass Point is named for the marking of the eight compass directions on the tower's eight sides.

The same Sir Thomas Acland who was responsible for the tower also built Bude's first swimming pool. It is at the end of the Breakwater and, in pre-feminist 1840s, was for men only.

(4) *Bude*

Though Bude has a long history as a harbour, the coast near the town was actually notoriously dangerous for shipping and many ships came to grief on Compass Point and Upton Cliffs to the south. Such was the rate of disaster that Bude became the first and only port to have been presented with a lifeboat by the Crown: William IV gave 100 guineas for a boat to be built in the last year of his reign (and life) in 1837. Strangely, the number of shipwrecks declined sharply after the boat was installed. Today Bude has an inshore rescue boat.

Modern day Bude is very much a tourist resort, reminding visitors that Sir John Betjeman called it the 'least rowdy' (is that really a compliment?) of Cornwall's resorts. Within the town there is little to see, though Sir Goldsworthy Gurney's castle, built in the first half of the 19th century and now housing the Town Council's offices, is an exception. Sir Goldsworthy was an amateur scientist

who invented an improved lighthouse light system and is credited
with being the first man to make a significant journey in a non-
animal drawn vehicle – he travelled from London to Bath and
back in a steam carriage. The Falcon Hotel, close to the car-park
start of the walk, is also worth a look.

Walk 29 Tintagel

Our second walk on the north Cornwall coast takes us to Tintagel,
the most famous of all the British sites that legend attaches to King
Arthur. But Tintagel has more to offer than tales of chivalry: the
Coastal Path section north of the castle site is among the best on
the peninsula, while inland St Nectan's Glen is superb country
with a legendary tale all of its own.

Walk category : Intermediate (2¾ hours)

Length : 12 km (7½ miles)

Ascent : 150 m (500 ft)

Maps : Landranger Sheet 200, Pathfinder Sheet 1325 (SX 08/18)

Starting and finishing point :   At 055 885, the car-park at the
                                    western end of Tintagel's main street
                                    reached by a lane of 'interesting'
                                    narrowness. Tintagel has other car-
                                    parks if needed.

Take the signed track to the castle entrance (see (1) Tintagel
Castle). After visiting the castle go to the end of the track and
cross the footbridge. Left here is a fine viewpoint but the Coastal
Path goes up the stepped path to the right. Beyond a zig-zag
section the small headland of Barras Nose is reached, a point
offering what is probably the best view of Tintagel Castle. From
the Nose follow the cliff-edge Path that skirts Smith's Cliff to reach
the anvil-shaped headland of Willapark. Again the Coastal Path

cuts off the head, turning sharply right and going steeply down to reach a footbridge over a stream into Bossiney Haven. Willapark is worth the walk, however; its headland offers superb views, both along the coast, of the rocky island of the Sisters below and of semi-detached Lye Rock, home to nesting colonies of auks, shags and fulmars and a breeding-ground for seals. Willapark itself was once defended by a rampart and ditch, the sea cliffs forming the other defences of this Iron Age cliff castle.

Beyond the footbridge over the stream is a steep section of path before more level cliff top above Bossiney Haven. Then another steeply descending section reaches a footbridge over the stream flowing out of Rocky Valley. Do not cross the stream but go inland along the path through the delightful valley, the last known nesting-place of the Cornish chough. The path crosses a footbridge to the ruins of an old mill. On the rock face behind the building to the left there are two carved mazes (see (2) Rock Carvings). From the ruins a path as rocky as the valley's name leads to another footbridge. The house, formerly Trevillet Mill, on the far side is placarded with 'Private' signs and menus (?!) and from it a lane leads up to the B3263.

Go left and with great care around a hairpin bend to reach the Rocky Valley Hotel and go right beyond it to reach the Pottery, St Piran's Well and church (see (3) St Piran). Take the signed path beside the church – the one running south-east that is a continuation of the lane, not the one going south-west signed for St Nectan's Glen – and follow it around a right-angled bend, to the right, and on to a sharp leftward bend. Here stay left to avoid going along a house drive. The lane ends, and a path to the right reaches the Hermitage where the visitor must pay to see St Nectan's Kieve (see (4) St Nectan's Glen).

The glen itself is reached by going right. After about 400 m a footbridge is crossed, followed by two more in quick succession. From the end of the third go up to a kissing gate and cross a field to a road. Go left and take a stile to the right after about 200 m. Go over a field and stile to emerge on a road between houses. Go right and after 200 m bear left on a short lane that ends at a stile and gate. Cross a field to another stile and gate – beyond which a

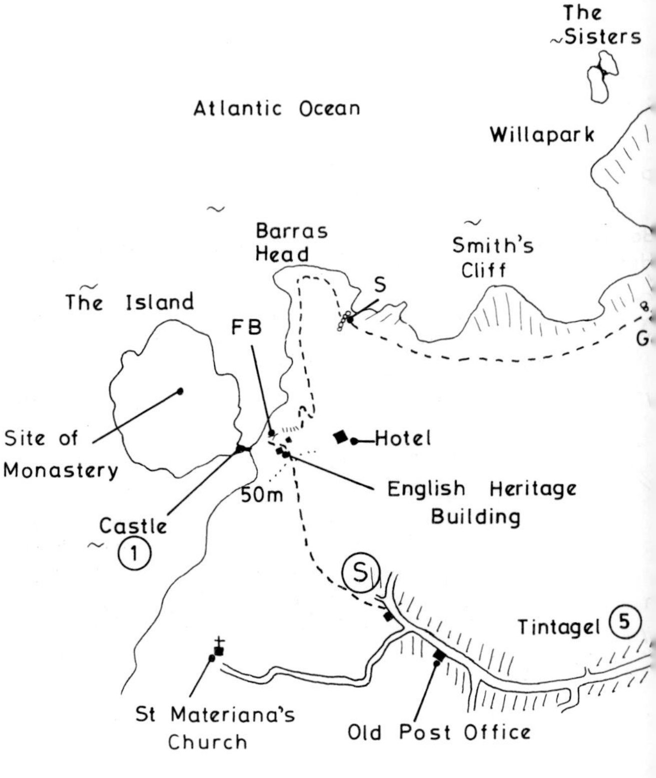

The ~Sisters

Atlantic Ocean

Willapark

~

Barras
Head

S

~
Smith's
Cliff

The~ Island

FB

Site of
Monastery

Hotel

English Heritage
Building

G

Castle
~
(1)

50m

(S)

Tintagel (5)

St Materiana's
Church

Old Post Office

WALK 29   TINTAGEL

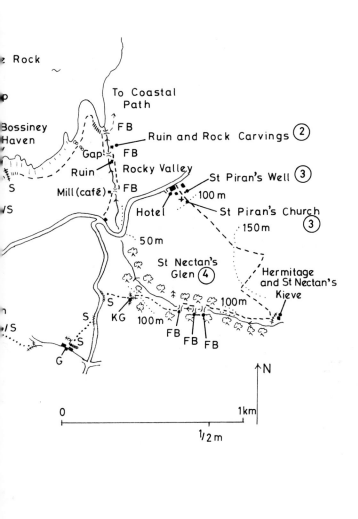

Rock

Bossiney
Haven

To Coastal
Path

FB

Ruin and Rock Carvings ②

FB

Gap

Ruin Rocky Valley

Mill (café) FB

St Piran's Well ③

100 m

Hotel St Piran's Church

150 m ③

50 m

St Nectan's
Glen ④

Hermitage
and St Nectan's
Kieve

S

S KG 100 m 100 m

S FB FB FB

G

↑N

0 1km

½ m

stream lies underground for a few metres, so be careful. Go
diagonally across the field to a stile, and diagonally across the last
one to another stile. Go left to reach the Tintagel village. The
mound seen to the right on this final field section is all that remain
of the Norman motte and bailey castle of Bossiney. Legend has it
that King Arthur's Round Table lies beneath it. Go through
Tintagel (see (5) Tintagel) back towards the starting car-park but
before reaching it take the lane to the left to visit the village
church (see (6) St Materiana's church). Return to the start along
the same lane.

(1) *Tintagel Castle*
In 1538 John Leland, the Elizabethan traveller, came to Tintagel.
He visited the castle site which, he found, 'hath bene a marvelus
strange and notable fortress and almost *situ loi inexpugnabile*
especially for the donjon that is on this great highe and terribil
cragge protected by the se, but having a drawbridge from the
residu of the castell reaching on to it. Shepe now fede within the
donjon grounde and rabbits abound'. The 'donjon' to which
Leland refers is the keep, but the French root of the word gives us
our word 'dungeon' for the prison of a castle. By Leland's time,
then, the castle was already ruinous. By then too it was already a
very ancient site, for though most people come here to see the
castle ruins, and to commune with the spirit of Arthur, the much
older monastic remains of the Celts are the more historically
important.
   It is probable that there was a hermitage cell on the 'island' of
rock that supports part of the castle ruins as early as the 5th
century as the site is associated with St Juliot, a very early Cornish
saint. Juliot is known to have been active in the area in the late 5th
and early 6th centuries, and it is likely that the earliest monastic
house on the site dates from the 6th century, making it one of the
first, if not the first, British monastery. The remoteness of the site
and the later defensive buildings that prevented easy access, has
also led to significant remains so that Tintagel is also the most
informative of British Celtic monasteries. Excavations have shown
that the monastery was sited behind a ditch and bank that

defended the narrow ridge linking the island with the mainland and comprised a guest-house, a treasury, an array of cells for the monks, an oratory and certain domestic buildings (library, refectory, etc.) including a kiln for corn-drying. The oratory contained a shrine, probably for the remains of St Juliot. The remains are spread over the entire plateau area of the 'island' giving the impression of a thriving and vibrant community, and it is likely that the monastery survived for several centuries.

When the first purely defensive structure was built is not known, though the name Tintagel could derive from *din-tagell*, Cornish Celtic for 'fort of the neck', in which case there may have been a very early fortress. This does not mean a pre-Saxon fort, Cornish being the local language long after the Saxons had been replaced by the Normans. However, it is possible that the name is from the Norman French *Tente d'Agel*, 'castle of the Devil', which is known to be the root of the name for the Channel Island sea stack of Tintageau. If the latter name is correct it is contemporary with the first known castle, built in the mid 12th century by Reginald, Earl of Cornwall, said to have been an illegitimate son of Henry I. Later in 1337, when Edward III made his eldest son, also Edward, Duke of Cornwall the Prince inherited the castle site. The young Edward, who, with his black chain-mail suit has entered history as the Black Prince, improved the castle, installing a drawbridge between the sections on the island and the mainland. Today, after centuries of weather have reduced the neck of land between the two to almost nothing, the visitor sometimes longs for a drawbridge rather than having to conform to Norden's idea that he must have eyes that will scale Tyntagell'.

The castle ruins are evocative rather than elegant or informative, though it is easy to see why it was maintained that three men could hold the site against an army. But good though the castle was, the affairs of state rarely included this far-flung fortress and it soon decayed away. Were it not for King Arthur few might come here.

There is little evidence for the existence of a real King Arthur but what little there is – from the Anglo-Saxon Chronicles and the works of Gildas and Nennius – suggests that he was an early 6th-century leader of the British Celts against the Saxons. The texts imply that he fought and won several battles before winning a decisive battle at Mount Badon (claimed by just about every mountain in Wales and Cornwall, as well as elsewhere, but most probably sited near the Ridgeway in Wiltshire) but was killed in a civil war battle with Mordred near Camlann (equally often claimed, one site being nearby on the River Camel). Around the time Reginald's castle was being built Geoffrey of Monmouth started the legend of King Arthur and he chose to set Arthur in Tintagel, probably not because he genuinely believed it to be true but because Arthur was a Celtic, therefore Cornish, hero – he could not be Welsh Celtic at a time when Wales had yet to be subdued. Geoffrey's suggestion was picked up by Mallory when he wrote *Morte d'Arthur* in the 15th century. Mallory's work was the start of many of the romantic legends about Arthur: the Round Table, the chivalrous knights and so on. Then, in the 19th century Tennyson's poem *Idylls of the King* put the final gloss on the story By then Dozmary Pool had become the water into which Bedivere threw Excalibur after the final battle at Slaughterbridge, and Tintagel was established as Camelot.

Interestingly, one version of the Arthurian legends has Tintagel occupied by Mark, King of Cornwall, a leading character in the tragic love story of Tristram and Iseult.

Today Arthur is big business at Tintagel, with King Arthur's Hall in the town, Merlin's cave in the bay below the castle – a really excellent place that offers a way through the headland – and an endless spin-off of Arthurian tea-shops and nick-nacks. But the story is a wonderful one, the more so for having an enigmatic half-truth buried in it somewhere. So ignore those buying their Merlin-burgers or whatever, and do not be too disdainful of the Arthur/Earth Magic seekers. For all the facts, Tintagel with its remote beauty and its mystery *feels* right. After all, independent of the Arthurian legend, the castle is supposed to disappear twice each year.

(2) *Rock Carvings*

The carvings are two small (23-cm/9-inch) mazes carved on a

vertical rock face at the back of a ruined mill building. The mazes are of Cretan form and many, particularly followers of Earth Magic, have speculated on their age and meaning. It has been suggested that the carvings are Bronze Age and that the maze is the same as the fabled Glastonbury Tor labrynth. It is, however, equally likely that they are the work of bored weavers from the nearby mill.

(3) *St Piran*

St Piran is another Celtic saint who was miraculously transported to Cornwall from Ireland. In Piran's case the journey was even more astounding than usual, the saint having been chained to a mill-stone and thrown from a cliff into the sea by the ungrateful Irish after he had performed several miracles on their behalf. The day was dreadful, the sea raging, but when the saint was rolled off the cliff the sun shone on him and the sea became calm. The stone floated and Piran calmly set out the journey to Cornwall. Piran is the patron saint of Cornwall; his black and white flag is also that of Free Cornwall and flies on 5 March. On the walk is St Piran's Well, a pleasant stone beehive topped by a rusting cross. Do not look inside if you have no wish to spoil the illusion; the well is full of old pipes and bits.

Close by is St Piran's church, first mentioned in the mid 15th century, though the present building was part of a farm until it was reconsecrated in 1942. The stained glass window above the altar shows the saint in St Nectan's Glen, the ground at his feet covered with spring flowers. One of the nicest parts of this delightful small chapel is the garden outside, a landscaped garden prepared with the help of a local nursery.

(4) *St Nectan's Glen*

The Glen is named for the saint to whom the church in Stoke (on Walk 19) is dedicated, the final resting-place of Nectan's remains being disputed between here and Hartland. When the saint lived here there was a small chapel in which hung a silver bell. When local fishermen heard the bell they fell to their knees on their boats, knowing that the saint was praying for them. Legend has it that St Nectan lived here with two of his sisters and that when he died they placed him in an oak chest along with his sacremental vessels and other treasures. They then diverted the waterfall and buried the chest under a rock slab in the rock basin into which the fall drops. The fall was then allowed to follow its old course. One of the treasures buried with St Nectan was his bell; one story suggests that if bad weather is approaching the Tintagel area the bell can be heard from beneath the fall, while another says that the bell rings continuously, but can only be heard by true believers. In the 18th century a group of miners tried to recover the bell using dynamite and crowbars after having diverted the waterfall. As they worked a voice told them that the child was not born who would be able to retrieve the treasure. Not surprisingly the miners beat a retreat. It is an odd story, with overtones of the Sword in the Stone, and begs the question of what really happened.

After Nectan's death his sisters are said to have continued to live in the glen, existing on a diet of berries, fish and snails. So oddly did they behave that the locals eventually decided that they were from the devil and possessed the Evil Eye. They were doubtless glad when the sisters died. The first one to depart was buried by the remaining sister under a rock slab in the glen. The second sister died of a broken heart. The sisters are said to haunt the glen, as are a group of grey-shrouded monks. Much later the tale of the sisters of the glen became a piece of romantic Victoriana when it was written-up as part of *The Echoes of Old Cornwall*, a collection of verse by the Revd Robert Stephen Hawker, vicar of Morwenstow, an eccentric practical joker and much more interesting than his tale.

At around the same time the painter Daniel McLise had a dream in London of an angel standing beside a waterfall. Eventually he found St Nectan's Kieve and painted 'The Nymph of the Waterfall' which now hangs in the V. & A. McLise's model for the work was Charles Dickens's sister-in-law, The Kieve, as the waterfall is known, is a pleasant fall, about 15 m (50 feet) high.

The Glen itself is narrow and deep, receiving less light than the surrounding country as a result and being, therefore, a haven for damp-loving plants. The ferns here are spectacular and include

broad buckler, lady and mole. The mosses and liverworts are
equally good. The Glen's stream is a favourite haunt of dippers.

(5) *Tintagel*

The village is correctly called Trevena (it is the parish that is called
Tintagel) though it is doubtful whether many of the villagers – and
especially those making a living from tourists – would welcome a
change to the real name. The village is a real tourist honey-pot,
from which the Old Post Office shines like a beacon. This
delightful National Trust property (the NT describe it as
'characterful' – a novel piece of word creation) is a small
Plantagenet manor-house from the mid 14th century that served as
the village post office in Victorian times and has been carefully
restored in that fashion. Much of the interest lies not in this
restoration but in the building itself, its smoke-blackened exposed
timbers, higgledy-piggledy roof and the assortment of gables,
chimney and add-on bits. Across from the Post Office, and a little
to the right, is another fine old building, wearing its date on the
outside like an old soldier's medal.

(6) *St Materiana's Church*

This superb early Norman church – started around the end of the
11th century or, perhaps, in the first years of the 12th – is almost
intact, a wonderful find for the lover of church architecture. The
dedication is to a Celtic saint, a princess of Gwent who landed in
this area around AD 500. The north porch doorway is definitely
late 11th-century and even shows a Saxon influence. It is very
likely that there was a Saxon building here (and probably a Celtic
one before that) and some experts claim that much of the north
wall is Saxon. Inside, the church is a treasure house. There are two
fonts, an early Norman work and a fine font bowl (by the south
wall) brought here from St Joliot's Chapel at the Castle – after
serving time as a pig trough; the statue of Christ the King is by
Faust Long and was presented in 1948; the rood screen is late
15th-century and the early English, triple lancet window above the
north transept altar has a beautiful and original stained glass
representation of St Symphorian (a saint with no special

attachment to Tintagel but perhaps significant to the artist).

In the south transept is a Roman inscribed stone – once used as a coffin rest and billhook sharpener – the inscription being to one of the contestants for the Emperor-ship in the early 4th century AD. It is thought that the stone was a milestone. In the same area is a brass to Joana Kelly, mother of an early 15th-century Tintagel vicar. The brass is dated to about 1430. Elsewhere there is a memorial stone to an earlier vicar. The inscribed cross suggests a late 13th-century date.

Outside, in the churchyard, notice how some of the headstones have been buttressed against Atlantic gales. One of the tombs is to the very young ship's boy (Domenico Catanese) of the *Iota* wrecked on Lye Rock in 1893.

Walk 30 Pentire Point and Port Isaac

South of Tintagel the headland of Pentire Point is one of Cornwall's best viewpoints and is the site of one of the county's best cliff forts, as well as being a good spot to watch birds and butterflies. Our walk follows the Coastal Path over Pentire and around Port Quin Bay beyond to reach Port Isaac, an exquisite fishing port, the north coast's rival to Polperro as the perfect Cornish villages.

Walk category : Difficult (4½ hours) for a single traverse

Length : 17 km (10½ miles) for a single traverse

Ascent : 410 m (1350 ft) for a single traverse

Maps : Landranger Sheet 200, Pathfinder Sheet 1337 (SW87/97)

Starting and finishing point : This is a straight line walk, starting at New Polzeath (935 796) and finishing at Port Isaac. Prout Brothers run a

The Old Post Office, Tintagel

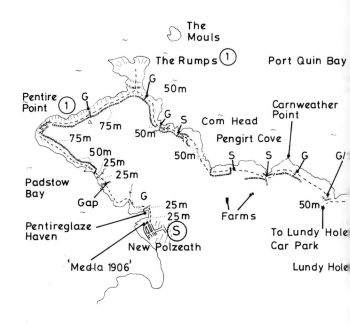

The Mouls

The Rumps ①

Port Quin Bay

Pentire
Point ①

G   50m

G

G S   Com Head

50m   Pengirt Cove

Carnweather
Point

75m
75m
50m
25m
25m

50m

50m

S   S   G   G/

Padstow
Bay

Gap

G   25m
25m

50m

Farms

Pentireglaze
Haven

Ⓢ

New Polzeath

To Lundy Hole
Car Park

'Medla 1906'

Lundy Hole

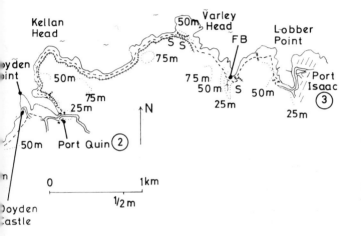

Kellan
Head

Varley
Head

50m

S S

75m

Lobber
Point

FB

Port
Isaac

③

oyden
oint

50m

75m

25m

75m

50m S

25m

50m

25m

N

50m

Port Quin ②

0   1km

½m

Doyden
Castle

Stepping Stones

WALK 30   PENTIRE POINT AND
                        PORT ISAAC

bus service between the two villages
with about five buses travelling each
way daily. Ring Bodmin 880 208 for
exact details of the service.

The Coastal Path leaves New Polzeath at its extreme north-
western corner going down to the sand of Pentireglaze Haven by
way of an enclosed lane beyond the house marked 'Medla 1906'.
From the far side of the sand the Path rises continuously to Pentire
Point, following a wall, on your right, for most of the journey.
Easy walking continues around the square headland with its sheer,
intimidating cliffs to reach the cliff castle of the Rumps (see (1)
Pentire). The Rumps are not on the route but are easily reached.
After an investigation continue along the Coastal Path, passing
some magnificent cliff scenery as it rounds Com Head and Pengirt
Cove. The cliffs above the Cove are very steep and very close: be
careful. Better is to come, a stile above Downhedge Cove being
placed in such a position that the walker receives full benefit from
the drop. Ahead now is Carnweather Point, beyond which the
Path drops into Lundy Hole, a fine bay with a sandy beach worthy
of a later visit.

Stepping-stones help cross a stream into Epphaven Cove, east of
Lundy Hole and then the Path continues in fine style passing, near
Gilson's Cove, the old shafts of an antimony mine, before reaching
a track to Doyden Castle, a 19th-century folly now in the hands of
the National Trust. Follow the track towards the castle to get the
best from the view from Doyden Point. A short cut path leads to
the road in Port Quin (see (2) Port Quin).

Leaving Port Quin between houses, the Path soon becomes
hedged with gorse, and then runs between the cliff, left, and a
wooden fence, right. At Varley Head a curious stile and gated
arrangement gives access to the final section of our walk. The Path
descends to cross a stream into Pine Haven, rising again for one
last cliff section before descending into Port Isaac (see (3) Port
Isaac) and the end of a quite superb cliff walk.

The harbour, Port Isaac

(1) *Pentire*

The name of this headland derives from *pen tyr* – head land –
which must be something of a rarity for its complete ordinariness.
The headland is dominated by the Rumps, the finest cliff castle in
Cornwall. By dating pottery found at the site it has been
concluded that the fort was constructed and occupied during the
century on either side of the birth of Christ – though lack of finds
does not, of course, preclude an earlier occupation. The fort was a
sophisticated piece of defensive architecture with the two mini-
headlands of Rumps Point and Sevensouls Rock being fortified on
either side of a sheltered, downland area. The whole was then
further defended by a triple ditch and rampart system that was
constructed right across the headland. Even today, after nearly
2,000 years of erosion and slippage, the central ditch is 5 m
(16½ ft) deep. The finds at the site have included not only 'local'
pottery but wine amphorae from the Mediterranean, suggesting a
trading network which comes as a complete surprise to some
visitors to the site.

From the fort the views eastward – along the walk – and of the
conical island of the Mouls offshore are excellent.

Pentire Point, at the other corner of the square headland, is
formed of a sweep of pillow lava which has created a sheer 80-m
(262-ft) cliff that is the reserve of more accomplished rock
climbers. From the Point the eye is drawn across Padstow Bay to
the Camel estuary protected by a sand bar called Doom Bar
reputedly created as the result of a curse placed on the town of
Padstow by a dying mermaid after she had been shot by a local. It
is likely, though, that the name reflects the opinion of local ships'
captains faced with having to navigate past the bar to reach the
river. On the Point side of the cliff, and particularly closer to
Pentireglaze Haven, are the scattered remains of ancient silver/
lead and antimony mines.

The cliff top both here and along the walk is alive with flowers
in spring and summer, with golden samphire, birdsfoot trefoil,
spring squill, sea pinks, thrift, sea campion and kidney vetch being
especially noticeable. At the right time, and with the on-shore
breeze at a minimum, the butterflies are also especially good.

2) *Port Quin*

'ort Quin is a curious place. It has been semi-restored by the
ational Trust so that delightful old cottages stand amid the ruins
f others, but it is the reason for the dereliction that is the
ystery. Little is known of the village's early history – indeed it
arely appears in the records at all until the 19th century, though
here are elusive traces way back to the 14th century. It was once a
easonably properous place, its menfolk working in the local silver/
ead and antimony mines, or fishing in the bay. The remains of the
illage's fish cellars – where the fish were rendered to oil or salted
imply that the local pilchard catch was a large one. But then,
lmost overnight, Port Quin ceased to exist. Local legend has it
hat the menfolk of the village were all out at sea when a sudden
nd violent storm sprang up, overturned all the boats in the fleet
nd drowned every living soul. Other versions recount that the
ncident occurred as retribution for the men having fished on
unday, or that they drowned trying to avoid the Revenue men
vhile running contraband. All stories have the womenfolk being
orced to leave the village as a result of the poverty that resulted.
he truth is hard to establish; the records do contain a hint of a
isaster with many men dying but it is likely that this was only part
perhaps the final part – of the story. The local mines had failed,
orcing some men to leave, and the pilchard fishing had also
uffered a series of disastrous years in the mid 19th century. For a
opulation never doing much better than subsistence living such
narvest' failures can be catastrophic. Today, Port Quin is a time
apsule.

3) *Port Isaac*

ike Port Quin, Port Isaac was a fishing village, though unlike the
maller port the men here fished for herring rather than for
ilchards. Port Isaac also had a small ship-building yard, which
llowed it to survive the fishing disasters of the mid 19th century
etter than its smaller neighbour. The village is a living thing,
herefore, and in many ways the better for so being. It is also a
rue delight, with pretty cottages huddling their way up steep hills,
ome built on land so steep that they have doors into the upstairs

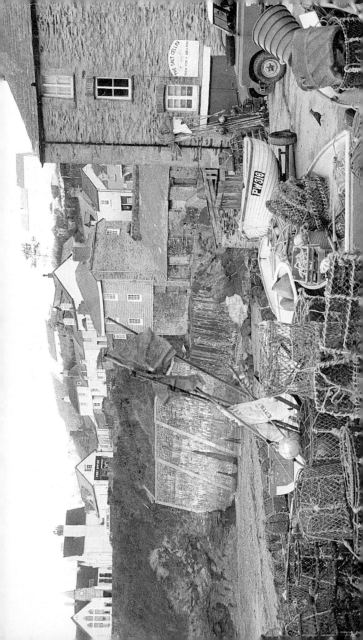

at the back and the downstairs at the front. We enter the village down Roscarrock Hill passing a house called 'Northcliffe', where, rumour has it, an anchor chain connects·the roof structure to the foundations to keep it on when the westerly gales are blowing. Close by is the best view of the village, the panorama taking in the harbour and stacked-up cottages, seen over the top of the old fish cellars.

Within the village the visitor is best left to wander at will but do find Temple Bar – go right at the left turn in Fore Street, approach the latter from Rosecarrock Hill – which has a section that is the world's narrowest thoroughfare. This 45-cm (18-inch) lane is known, not surprisingly perhaps, as Squeezie Belly Alley. Close by is Shuggy's Ope, another narrow *drang*, as such narrow alleys are termed locally. Elsewhere a house on three storeys called the Birdcage – in Margaret's Lane, off Rose Hill which is itself a turning off Fore Street – is a National Trust property. Sadly, this local skyscraper is not open to the public. Elsewhere, Wesley House is a link to John Wesley who visited the village fairly frequently. His first visit was inauspicious; one story has him stoned by the locals, and while this may be an exaggeration it is certainly true that the man who had invited him to Port Isaac barricaded himself in his house, having been told that if he allowed Wesley in, the house would be pulled down. Persistence, a trait that stood Wesley well, resulted eventually in the villagers embracing Wesleyan teachings enthusiastically.

Walk 31 Polperro

Of all the delightful small ports on Cornwall's southern coast the one that comes closest to most people's idea of perfection is Polperro. Many will consider it a bit twee, and indeed it is. But the alternative on too many occasions is a completely over-the-top honey-pot; on the whole Polperro has retained rather than sold its birthright. Indeed, out of season the village is a delight.

The quay at Port Isaac

Walk category : Easy (1¼ hours)

Length : 5 km (3 miles)

Ascent : 100 m (305 ft)

Maps : Landranger Sheet 201, Pathfinder Sheet 1355 (SX 25/35)

Starting and finishing point : At 205 515, the car-park at the top of
the hill into Polperro

Note: The walk starts from the car-park but there may be some
who will succumb to the use of a horse-drawn taxi to reach the
village itself. Perhaps you could walk down and ride back . . .

Go down towards the village. To the left is the 17th-century
Mermaid Inn, while the Land of Legend and Model Village (for all
village sites see (1) Polperro) is off to the right at the taxi turn-
round point. At Big Green, to the right and leading to Saxon
Bridge, the Smuggling Museum and House on Props are ahead –
as is the harbour. The walk bears left here, taking the sharp
Talland Hill. After about 800 m go right, passing the school to the
left. Go straight on where the lane bends right, but do not follow
the signed path to the Coastal Path at a gate/stile to the right
shortly, continuing instead to the lane's end, where it descends to
meet the Coastal Path directly. Just before this meeting a gravel
path, right, offers a barely worthwhile short cut.
   Either way go right, along the Coastal Path, soon going over a
stile and on to the cliff edge. A war memorial and a coastguard
lookout are passed to reach the fancifully named Reuben's Walk
and steps to the beach. Do not descend, continuing past another
memoral and 'the Watchers', some aptly named seats, to reach a
small pier close to the entrance to Polperro harbour. Beyond are
the pincer-like walls of the harbour itself. Ahead now is an
alleyway between fishermen's cottages (the Warren). Go through

Nearing Polperro on Walk 31

to reach the village near the House on Props and Smuggler's Museum. Reverse the outward walk – or taxi ride – to the carpark.

(1) *Polperro*

As might be expected of any self-respecting south Cornish port, Polperro has a long history of smuggling. It appears that many, but not all, of the locals were involved; there is even a story that the vicar of nearby Talland church was part of the local gang. Talland – named from *tal lan*, the holy place – is a small inland village set on the road our walk follows on its exit from Polperro. The vicar was a renowned local exorcist and many people from the area declined to go out at night for fear of meeting him driving evil spirits down the roads towards the sea. It is likely that this legend was invented and supported by the smugglers to keep potentially prying eyes in at night. Other stories are equally good: one involves the landlady of nearby Looe's Jolly Sailor inn, a large lady with a full skirt who once sat on a smuggled keg of brandy to stop the visiting Revenue men from spotting it.

One Polperro man, Zephaniah Job, was the local schoolmaster, a respected but poor man. Around 1770 he was approached by several of the local men who wanted him to concentrate on the teaching of arithmetic so that their sons could handle their smuggling accounts with the French, most particularly the conversion of sterling into francs and vice versa. Job decided instead to offer his services as the smugglers' accountant, operating on a 1% commission basis. In a remarkably short time Job made enough cash to buy all the Polperro quays and to set himself up as a local banker.

The boats the smugglers used were luggers built at Polperreo itself, low draft boats ideally suited to working in the local estuaries and shallow creeks. A good boat could cross the Channel to France in under eight hours.

It should not be thought, however, that smuggling was a Boy Scouts game played for fun by rival gangs of men. Talland church

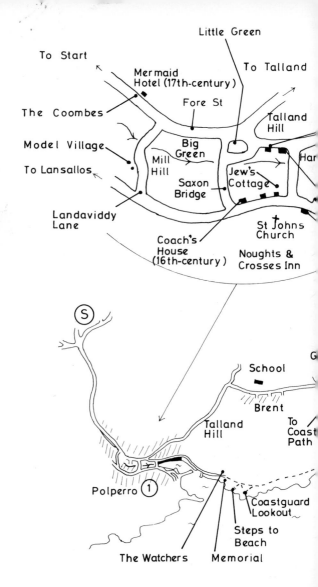

To Start

Mermaid
Hotel (17th-century)

Little Green

To Talland

The Coombes

Fore St

Talland
Hill

Model Village

Big
Green

Har

To Lansallos

Mill
Hill

Landaviddy
Lane

Saxon
Bridge

Jew's
Cottage

St Johns
Church

Coach's
House
(16th-century)

Noughts &
Crosses Inn

S

School

Brent

Talland
Hill

To
Coast
Path

Polperro

1

Coastguard
Lookout

Steps to
Beach

The Watchers

Memorial

WALK 31   POLPERRO

Smuggling Museum

The Warren

Island House (16th-century)

Walk 31 returns here

House on Props

Willy Wilcock's Cottage

Fishermen's Quay

Three Pilchard's Inn (17th-century)

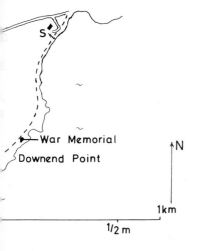

S

War Memorial

Downend Point

↑N

1km

1/2 m

holds the grave of Robert Mark, a Polperro lad shot during one sea chase, and another local, Tom Potter, was hanged after shooting a Revenue man when his party was surprised one night. Potter was betrayed by another local, Roger Toms, who became, instantly, the most hated man in the port.

Another local man became famous for quite a different reason. Robert Jeffery was a local youth who was press-ganged on to a Royal Navy ship which sailed for the Caribbean. There, found to have stolen and drunk a barrel of the captain's beer, he was put ashore on a tiny, uninhabited, treeless, waterless island and left to die. When the ship, the *Recruit*, made land in Barbados the Fleet Admiral, Sir Alexander Cochrane, was appalled and sent it back to the island to rescue Jeffery. Of the poor man there was no sign. The captain, Captain Lake, was court-martialled and dismissed from the Navy and all went quiet until, several years later, word arrived that Jeffery was alive and living in America. He had been picked up, close to death, nine days after being marooned and taken to America where he decided to stay, not knowing whether a return to England would mean a court martial for the beer theft. Amid great enthusiasm in the British press Jeffery was brought home and returned to Polperro. He made several tours in the manner of a freak circus, failing to come to terms with his fame and dying at a young age, probably from injudicious living.

Within the village there is much to interest the visitor: the harbour is delightful and at certain times in the summer the local Fishermen's Choir sings on its western edge. On the sea bed of the harbour mouth there is a submarine forest which some have fancifully taken as evidence for the legendary land of Lyonesse having lain off-shore here. Moving up Lansallos Street from the harbour's west side the visitor passes, beyond the end of the Roman Bridge, Jew's Cottage, a 16th-century house and the quaintly-named Noughts and Crosses Inn. To the left and above is the port's church, built in 1838. The House on Props, a 16th-century building with its stream side shored up by the props of the name is one of Polperro's better restaurants. The Smuggling Museum lies further along Talland Street. Closer to the top of the village the Model Village is a recreation of Polperro itself, while the Land of Legends is a miniaturized Cornwall, showing its history and stories.

Walk 32 Lizard Point

Though Land's End is better known, it is actually Lizard Point that is the most southerly point on the British mainland. Our walk rounds the Point and visits the delightful village of Cadgwith.

Walk category : Difficult (3½ hours)

Length : 14 km (8¾ miles)

Ascent : 300 m (1000 ft)

Maps : Landranger Sheets 203 and 204 (a very small part of the route is on the latter), Pathfinder Sheet 1372 (SW61/71)

Starting and finishing point : At 701 115, the small area used as a car-park near the most southerly point. There is also a car-park at Lizard lighthouse at 702 116.

After visiting the Most Southerly Gift Shop, Most Southerly This and Most Southerly That, go past the front of the Most Southerly Tea Shop on the Coastal Path. The Path goes down steps to reach what the National Trust sign calls Pistil Meadow but which most renderings have as Pistol Meadow (see (1) Lizard Point). The Path ahead is well-trodden, edging the cliffs above Crane Ledges, then using steps to descend to, and ascend from, Caerthillian Cove. Soon a building comes into view: the toilet block of the National Trust car-park above Kynance Cove – hardly one of the architectural delights of the route. From the car-park there are several ways. A signed path visits the cliff edge for one of the better views, while another descends to the cove: this is our route. Yet another way out of the car-park goes through the wall in the far right corner and offers a short cut to the inland section of the

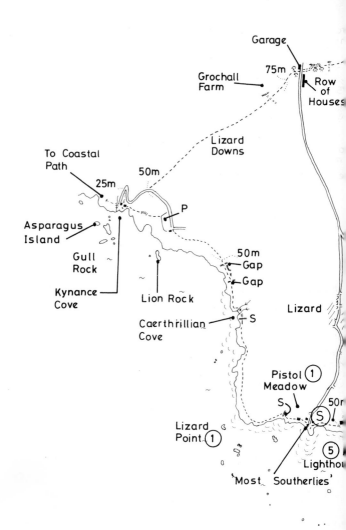

Garage

75m

Grochall Farm

Row of Houses

Lizard Downs

To Coastal Path

25m

50m

P

Asparagus Island

Gull Rock

Kynance Cove

Lion Rock

50m
Gap

Gap

Lizard

Caerthrillian Cove

S

Pistol Meadow (1)

S

50r

(S)

Lizard Point (1)

(5)

Lighthou

'Most Southerlies'

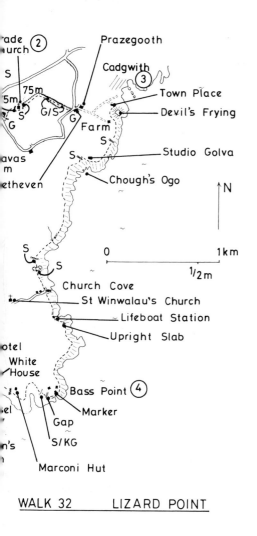

(2) rade urch

S

75m

5m

S G/S G

G

Farm

S

avas m

etheven

S

Prazegooth

Cadgwith (3)

Town Place

Devil's Frying

Studio Golva

Chough's Ogo

↑N

S

S

0   1 km

½m

Church Cove

St Winwalau's Church

Lifeboat Station

Upright Slab

otel

White House

Bass Point (4)

Marker

Gap

S/KG

el

n's

Marconi Hut

WALK 32   LIZARD POINT

walk. Descend to the hamlet of Kynance Cove. We have already passed Lion Rock, an offshore island, on the way to the cove. Offshore of the cove itself are several more: Asparagus Island is named for the wild asparagus that once grew there. On it is a blow-hole, the Devil's Bellows, that booms impressively and shoots up a fine spray when a high tide is running. Other islands include Gull Rock, Steeple Rock and the Bishop. Many of these islands, and the caves in their cliff bases, can be reached at low tide. If you are visiting be careful: the tides are fast and if you are cut-off rescue could be a long time coming. Kynance Cove achieved fame in 1846 when Prince Albert came ashore here with the young princes and princesses: at once the Cove was fashionable and it has been a favourite with artists and tourists ever since. It is backed by a pretty little hamlet.

The next cove touched by the Coastal Path is Rill Cove, reputed to be the place where the Spanish Armada was first sighted. The Path leaves Kynance Cove over a footbridge but we take the lane beside the stream which zig-zags back up towards the car-park. After the last zig-zag a wide, sandy, hoof-printed path heads off across Lizard Downs. Take this, ignoring a footpath sign pointing left, and head for a row of houses in the distance. Use these houses as a beacon all the way across the Down, ignoring all side tracks as you pick a way between the muddy bits. The heather on this section of salty moorland, Cornish Heath (*Erica Vagans*), is limited to the area around the Lizard. It is a short but robust heather with delicate lilac pink or whitish flowers which have prominent, protruding brown anthers.

The path exits the Down by way of a tree-shrouded avenue, arriving at a road next to a garage. Here a walker discovers that the row of houses he has been following are across the road. Take the track down their left side. A path soon leaves this track, going through short shrubs to reach a really good section of heathland. Grade church is now visible to the left: the church is the route's next landmark. Visible ahead are the satellite dishes on Goonhilly Down. At a road go right, bearing right at a road junction. Take the signed lane for Grade church (see (2) Grade). Go over the stile at the far (east) end of the churchyard and follow the wall, eft, to reach the bottom right corner of a field. From there a path eads to a road. Cross to the white house (Metheven) and follow he lane to the left of this – going between Metheven and Prazegooth, another house – signed 'South Coast Path (Frying Pan)'. Bear left on the lane at a farm entrance to reach a junction. Ahead now is Cadgwith (see (3) Cadgwith) a convenient half-way (more or less) point. If the village is visited you will need to return here.

We go right, past 'Townplace' to reach the Coastal Path again, close to the Devil's Frying Pan, a cauldron-like hole formed when a huge sea cave collapsed. In Cornish the feature is known as *Hugga Dridgee*. The wood to the north of the hole is of the unusual dwarf elm, much decimated by Dutch Elm Disease but staging a comeback. The undercover is escaped hydrangea. The Coastal Path ahead is straightforward now, passing Studio Golva where pictures are sold in the summer months. Beyond, at the base of the cliffs, there are several *ogos*, or caves. The word is interesting, the Welsh for a cave being *ogof*, a clear Celtic brother to the Cornish word. Chough's Ogo is named for the chough, now, sadly, a bird of memory on the Lizard. At Polbarrow note the natural rock arch. On again, adjacent to Whale Rock, there are a couple of stiles in the local serpentine rock, a very slippery rock.

The Path descends into Church Cove, where there is a National Trust sign commemorating the gift of land by the Caravan Club. In the 19th century there was a lifeboat station at the cove, but in 1885 it was abandoned when launches, always difficult, proved too unpopular. The church of the name can be seen inland beyond the thatched cottages. This is St Winwalaus' church, Landewednack, the most southerly church in England. Its low pinnacled tower is built of the local serpentine. The next cove, Kilcobben, houses a lifeboat, installed in 1961 to replace the Lizard and Cadgwith boats. Plaques record the lives saved by the two older boats: Cadgwith 400 and Lizard 600. The lifeboat upper house is reached by steps, and more steps lead down to where the boat can be viewed by those with the energy to go down (and up!).

The Coastal Path continues down steps away from the lifeboat station, passing a prominent leaning rock before reaching the Bass

Point House complex (see (4) Bass Point House). Go past the red and white marker (see also Note (4)) and continue to the cleft of Polledon, the house above which was used by Marconi during early experiments with radio. From the hut he transmitted messages to the Isle of Wight nearly 290 km (about 180 miles) away. A memorial plaque notes his servies to all seafarers. Ahead now is Housel Bay whose hotel can be visited by taking the path through the gate at the side of the Coastal Path. There is now one last descent and ascent, the latter up seemingly interminable steps, before the final headland of Bumble Rock is reached. Here is the Lion's Den, a fierce hole also created by the collapse of a sea cave Continue along the wall of Lizard Lighthouse (see (5) Lizard Lighthouse), with fingers crossed that those enormous foghorns will stay quiet, back to the start.

(1) *Lizard Point*

The name of the point is from 'headland court' and has nothing to do with reptiles, though there are those who suggest that it derives from the snakey-smooth texture of the local serpentine rock. In Cornish this is Predannack, the headland of Britain, both a more evocative and more accurate name.

Geologically the area is very interesting, not least for the local heathland, the soil of which is made of rendered serpentine and is magnesium-rich. This makes it a poor soil for plant life – apart from the extremely local Cornish Heath. In the village of Lizard behind the Point, a straggling place, the rock is turned to good purpose: the tourist shops sell items in the glossy green or white stone named for its snake-like red and black veins and soft enough to be worked with hand-held metal tools. As an ornamental stone it is also ideal in taking, and keeping, a shine.

Elsewhere in the area of the Point the plant life is surprisingly extensive, most visitors seeking out Lizard Plant, the salt-hardy red-flowered mesembryanthemum, though there are also red campion, yellow vetch, milkwort and tormentil, and, in spring, bluebells and primroses.

Kilcobben lifeboat station

Off the Point are a large number of small islands with odd and interesting names. Man of War is named for the *Royal Anne*, a man-of-war that was wrecked on it in 1721. Only three of the crew of over 200 men survived, the dead being buried in Pistol Field. Though most shipwrecks are grim, one, at least, had its lighter moments. The crew of one ship wrecked at night hung on to offshore rocks until daybreak when the seas dropped and they could wade ashore. They arrived in Lizard, much to the astonishment of the locals, with a pig that had survived and was sold for the price of a ride to Falmouth, a barrel of rum that one man had clung to all night and which was promptly drunk dry (all 9 gallons of it) and the ship's cat which they gave to the Lizard inn's landlord.

(2) *Grade*

The church of the Holy Cross, or to St Grada, dates from the 13th century when a crusading knight, shipwrecked close by, gave thanks for his survival by changing the name to *Sante Crucis* from the dedication to an early Celtic saint. The church is pleasant for its remoteness – there is no electricity, services in winter being lit by oil lamps – but has little to seriously detain the visitor, apart from the fine 14th century tower in local serpentine.

(3) *Cadgwith*

Cadgwith's thatched cottages clustered around a small harbour make it a delightful spot. It is genuinely unspoilt, the chief reason for which is probably that it is undevelopable rather than any inherent desire to maintain it tourist-trap-free. Anciently it was a pilchard fishing port, the fish being loaded into salt-ladened fish cellars where over a four- or five-week period the oil was pressed out for use in the soap and leather industries. The pressed fish were exported in barrels. Today the fish cellars are holiday apartments and a tea room, and the village's remaining fishermen catch lobster and crab. The small black building on the harbour's north side is Huer's Hut, where a look-out was posted to watch for pilchard shoals, and to raise the hue and cry when he saw one. Elsewhere, look for the chained eaves of one thatched cottage, the chaining being a necessity if the roof was to survive winter's winds.

The port's first lifeboat was presented in 1867, a boat with the snappy name of *The Western Commerical Traveller*. Later, in 1940, the Girl Guides Association collected money for a new boat which promptly sailed to assist in the Dunkirk evacuation. This boat remained in service until 1963 when the station closed down.

(4) *Bass Point House*
The first signal house on this site was built in 1872 and was used to spot vessels in- and out-bound to southern English ports for Lloyds, the shipping agents and insurers. The present house was built in 1954 but ceased to be used as a signal house in 1969. In its earliest days messages were passed from ship to shore, or vice versa, by flags and there are several recorded incidents of ships having to come so close inshore to receive or give signals that they were wrecked on the nearby rocks. One boat that suffered the fate of being wrecked here, though not as result of flag messages, was a German trader, the *Mosel*, which, in 1882, steamed on to Bass Point at 14 knots in zero visibility fog. The crunch was heard by the coastguard who hurried down to see what had happened and was able to walk on to the *Mosel*'s deck.

The red and white marker slab we pass was used by ships at sea to fix the position of Vrogue Rock, a lump of unpleasantness that everyone wanted to avoid. Lining up the markers with those on the wall of the House gave one fix, the second fix being a white patch at Hot Point to the north and a beacon inland of Parn Voose Cove, also to the north.

(5) *Lizard lighthouse*
There has been a lighthouse at this spot since 1619. The first one was built and maintained by tolls on passing ships. The earliest light was coal-fired, the asymmetry of the building having been produced when one of the hexagonal chimneys was dismantled. The present lighthouse was built in 1751, though it was renovated in 1903, with an oil-fired light replacing the earliest beacon in 1812. Electricity was first used in 1878. The light installed in 1903 has the power of 15 million candles and can be seen 32 km

(20 miles) away. That distance is the horizon distance, i.e. the furthest spot at which the light itself is visible. In good viewing conditions the light can be seen by reflection off the sky at over 150 km (nearby 100 miles). The foghorn – first installed in 1840, but now upgraded – produces a double boom that can be heard for 22 km (14 miles). I wonder how much sleep the inhabitants of Lizard village get on foggy nights.

Walk 33 Zennor

On its western side Penwith drops steeply into the sea, producing several miles of uncompromising sea cliffs that offer unparalleled seascapes and fine, if rugged, walking. This walk follows a part of that cliffline, visiting a fine village – known locally as Churchtown to distinguish it from hamlets in the larger parish of Zennor – set on the short, flat shelf that stands between the high Penwith moor and the cliff edge.

Walk category : Intermediate (2½ hours)

Length : 9½ km (6 miles)

Ascent : 200 m (650 ft)

Maps : Landranger Sheet 203, Pathfinder Sheet 1364 (SW 33/43)

Starting and finishing point : At (454 384), the car-park in Zennor

From the car-park go firstly to the village museum (see (1) Wayside Museum), recognizable not only from its sign (!) but from the waterwheel set at the road's edge. If the wheel is turning, the museum is open.

Now go back towards the church, going to its left to reach a sign 'Farm Area Only'. There go left along a metalled lane signed 'No Cars, Footpath Only', which is followed to the coastguard building and a stile on to the Coastal Path. Go straight on to reach Zennor Head, a National Trust area. Look for the plaque on rocks above

Horseback Zawn from where the immediate view is of Pendour Cove (see (2) Pendour Cove). Beyond the Head, do not follow the track that goes right, apparently avoiding an unnecessary drop in height. This does visit a forlorn trig point – at 96 m (322 ft) – but from it there is no continuation to the Coastal Path.

So, take the continuous path that dips down toward the shore. The path is obvious but rugged, sometimes forcing its way between granite boulders, sometimes dropping steeply down to sea level and rising equally steeply. However, as compensation, the views – both forwards and backwards – are wonderful. Watch out for the Carracks, a collection of rocks a few hundred metres offshore, after Mussel Point has been rounded. Just as the Little Carracks, the second, smaller group is reached, the path ahead can be seen to drop down to cross the River Cove. Just before this drop, take an unsigned, but obvious, path that goes inland along the side of the cove valley. Care is needed on this path, especially in summer: the undergrowth of bracken and scrub is thick and conceals occasional leg-biting boulder ruckles. The path ends at a concrete strip lane. Go right to reach Boscubben Farmhouse and there go right to reach Wicca Farm. The way is signed here, a faded white arrow and sign 'Zennor' pointing our walk between house and barn over the first of many granite strip 'cattle grids' that we shall cross. Beyond, the way is indistinct and, frankly, confusing, so follow the line of the overhead power lines past Tregerthen (see (3) D.H. Lawrence) and on to Tremedda, leaving them only when they swing left near this latter farm. The walk here is on what is now called a part of the Tinners' Way, though the local name is Coffin Way, this being an old corpse road. Go over the Tremedda farm road and head off across fields on an indistinct but straightforward route: Zennor church comes into view as a waymark. Head to the right of it to emerge into the village through a gate set between church and barn. Go left to the church (see (4) Zennor Church) and village pub.

1) *Wayside Museum*
The tiny hamlet of Zennor would seem to be an extraordinary place for a museum. Do not let that persuade you into believing

WALK 33   ZENNOR

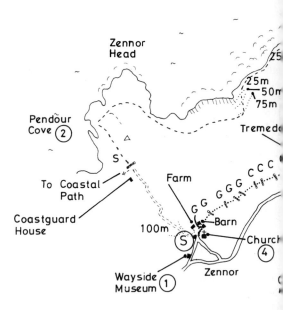

Muss•
Point

Atlantic
Ocean

Zennor
Head

25

25m
50m
75m

Pendour
Cove ②

Tremede

S

To Coastal
Path

Farm

Coastguard
House

C C C
G G G G
G G

Barn

100m

Ⓢ

Church
④

Wayside
Museum ①

Zennor

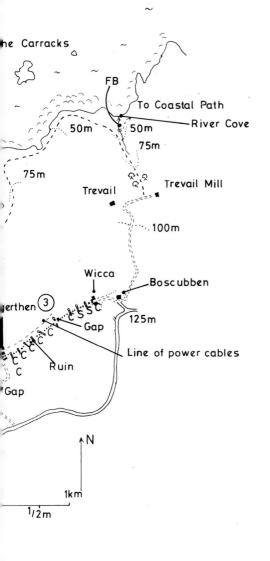

The Carracks

FB

To Coastal Path

River Cove

50m   50m

75m

75m

Trevail   Trevail Mill

100m

Wicca

Boscubben

erthen ③

Gap

125m

Line of power cables

Ruin

Gap

N

1km

1/2 m

that the Wayside will not be worth a visit: it has one of the most amazing and complete collections on an ancient way of life to be found anywhere. Primarily the museum is devoted to that period in history when the localfolk who were not involved in the tin industry were fishermen catching pilchards.

The scene is set by the 10-foot waterwheel at the gate, a wheel brought from Redruth where it powered a tin-ore crushing plant. Inside there are other, smaller wheels – and, soon, there will also be a big one – and a set of wooden tin stamps, astonishing for the crudeness of their construction. In huts in the garden of the museum, which is also the house of the curator, are a series of craft shops. The wheelwright's shop has the tools of not only the wheelmaker's trade but also of carpenters and shipwrights. Next door is a tyring shop with equipment for making cartwheel tyres and a photographic record of the process. Elsewhere there is a blacksmith's forge and a room devoted to the mining industry itself. The forge is interesting for the position of the door lintel – mind your head – and the fact that the hearth is blind. It would seem that the smith opened a window and hoped the wind was in the right direction.

The map room has items from the local pilchard industry, now long gone, as well as maps of the areas.

Finally, one part of the curator's house has been furnished in 19th-century style. The Cornish range, known locally as a slab, is the pride and joy of the kitchen. It apparently needed a hundredweight of coal daily to keep it going. Elsewhere there is a fine collection of flat irons and some interesting old advertisements.

(2) *Pendour Cove*
Centuries ago the Sunday congregation at Zennor church were enchanted by the singing of a beautiful young girl in a long flowing dress who appeared each week as if by magic and disappeared equally quickly at the end of the service. The girl was fascinated by Matthew Trewhella, the churchwarden's son, a handsome lad with

The Wayside Museum, Zennor

a voice almost as good as her own. One night she lured him to a
nearby stream. The pair slipped into the water and were taken
down to Pendour Cove and never seen again. Except once that is,
when a ship dropped anchor in the cove. The skipper was
astonished to be hailed from the water and loking down saw a
mermaid who told him that his anchor had blocked the entrance to
the cave she shared with Matthew and their children. Today the
cove is often called Mermaid's Cove and it is said that on calm
moonlight nights in summer the voices of Matthew and the
mermaid can still be heard from under the water. When you go to
Zennor church (see note (4) below) look for the Mermaid's Chair,
on the end of which is a carving showing the girl with comb and
mirror, long hair and fish's tail – the archetypal mermaid. The
carving is difficult to age but was probably completed 500–600
years ago, suggesting that the folk story is very ancient indeed.

(3) *D.H. Lawrence*

During the 1914–18 war Lawrence, together with his German-born
wife Frieda, Katherine Mansfield and her partner John Middleton
Murray, lived locally, at one time in a house at Tregerthen. The
footpath we follow from there to Zennor was followed by the
writer as he walked down to the Tinners' Arms for a drink. Sadly,
the villagers did not take to the newcomers. This was in part a
comment on writers (Lawrence was at the time working on
Women in Love) and partly due to suspicions about Frieda. At
night Lawrence would read in the bedroom, a lamp by the bed and
the windows open to allow the salt air to fill the room. This was
the final straw for the locals. To them the fluttering curtains across
the light looked like a signal and they became convinced that
Lawrence was a German spy passing messages to a submarine
surfaced off Zennor Head. The enraged locals made life so
unpleasant that Lawrence and Frieda were forced to leave.

(4) *Zennor Church*

The church is dedicated to Senara, a Celtic saint about whom
almost nothing is known with certainty. Legend has it that the
saint was Princess Asenora, a Breton princess married to King

Goello. Asenora was beautiful and virtuous, to such an extent that her stepmother hated her and persuaded Goello that she had been unfaithful. The saddened king condemned her to be burnt at the stake and delivered her to her executioners. When Asenora told them she was pregnant they decided they could not burn her and instead they put her in a barrel, nailed on the lid and threw the barrel into the sea. The story tells this decision was made because the executioners did not want to live with the guilt of killing an unborn child, though quite how their consciences were likely to be assuaged by the barrel sentence is not clear to me.

However, things did turn out well as an angel provided food for the princess and after her son, Budoc, was born in the barrel, the pair were washed up in Ireland. Goello, hearing of their miraculous escape and having realized Asenora was innocent, asked the pair to return. Their return to Brittany was by way of Cornwall where Asenora founded a church at Zennor and named a parish near Falmouth after her son.

It is likely that the first church at Zennor was built in the 7th century, though today's building is 12th-century with significant 15th-century additions. Inside, the eye is drawn to the superb barrel-vaulted ceiling. It is usually said that these ceilings were shaped this way because the carpenters who built them were shipwrights and this was the shape of ship keels, but it would be nice to believe that it was a reminder of Asenora. Elsewhere, be sure to see the Mermaid's Chair, mentioned in Note (2) above. The chair is made from two bench ends and stands in the side chapel, where there is also a small and ancient stone saint. The schooner near the organ is a memorial to W.A. Procter who was lost in the Pacific during a single-handed attempt to sail round the world. Look too for the memorial stone to Will Champen in the tower. Part of it reads:

Hope, fear, false joy and trouble,
Are those four winds which daily toss this buble [sic]
His breath's a vapour and his life's a span
'Tis glorious misery to be born a man.

Oh dear!

More cheerfully, though not much in reality, is a plaque on the outside of the church to the memory of John Davey, a local man claimed to have been the last man to have spoken Cornish. Davey died in 1891 which is a century after Dolly Pentreath of Mousehole who is more usually said to be the last person to have spoken Cornish as a first language. It is likely that Davey was not fluent, and that his Cornish was second to his English, but that he was indeed the last person to have spoken the language in anything like a real way. Lately there has been a revival of spoken Cornish

Also in the churchyard there are a number of Cornish crosses. These originally marked the Coffin Way our walk took across the fields from the River Cove. The best one stands near the main churchyard entrance, with two others guarding the grave of Admiral Borlase near the side entrance.

Walks 34 and 35 Men-an-Tol and Chun Castle

Penwith District is the real Cornwall, the land west of Hayle River. The district is named for Penwith itself, the other Cornish moorland, insignificant when compared to Bodmin, barely hauling its way past the 250-metre contour and being criss-crossed by minor roads that break it up into manageable portions. Yet it seems big enough to any holidaymaker lost among its lanes as he searches for a way to the tourist traps of Penzance or Land's End. And it is not altogether manageable if the mist plays havoc with route-finding on Amalveor Downs which lies only 6 km, as the seagull flies, west of St Ives.

Penwith is usually termed 'an ancient landscape' in the half-sentence descriptions of the tourist guides that sprout in profusion from the shop racks in Penzance and St Ives. But for all its glibness, the description is true – provided, of course, it is applied to man in the landscape rather than the country itself – because Penwith has one of the highest concentrations of excellent ancient sites. Neolithic, Bronze Age and Iron Age, in Britain. The following two walks will visit many of these together with the ruin of the Ding Dong mine, a relic from a much later age. They are

isted as a pair, but the real walk is a combination of the two, a
ine figure-of-eight route.

Walk 34 Men-an-Tol

Walk category : Easy (1¾ hours)

Length : 6½ km (4 miles)

Ascent : 70 m (230 ft)

Maps : Landranger Sheet 203, Pathfinder Sheet 1364 (SW33/43)

Starting and finishing point :   At 419 345, a small car-park/lay-by
on the minor road from Penzance to
Zennor. Leave Penzance on the
Madron road and continue through
that village towards Morvah and
Zennor. Look for the sign for Lanyon
Quoit (passed on the walk) to the
right, and then for the Men-an-Tol
Studio on the left. Park near here.
Do not attempt to drive up the lane
that forms the first part of the walk –
access is not permitted and you will
be a real hazard to any walkers you
meet.

Go up the walled lane opposite the Studio. The lane, as with the
rest of the walk, is a riot of colour from early spring to late
summer, with flowers being gradually replaced by heather and
gorse. After a few hundred metres there is a huddle of ruined
buildings to the left. Soon after, look for the stone stile to the right
which gives access to a heathway path. Follow this to Men-an-Tol
(see (1) Men-an-Tol).

    After viewing the site, return to the lane and continue along it
to reach, in a field to the left, Men Scryfa (see (2) Men Scryfa).

Continue along the lane, first passing a track and then a ruin to the left, to reach the Parish Stone (see (3) Parish Stone), recognized by the incised cross. The cross-track here goes to the coast at Bosigran, left, and the Ding Dong mine, right. Go ahead on a narrow, distinct path that climbs a ridge to reach a round barrow and the Nine Maidens stone circle (see (4) Nine Maidens Circle).

From the circle continue along the narrow pathway to reach a wider track towards the Ding Dong mine engine house (see (5) Ding Dong Mine). The track you arrived on continues to Madron but our route leaves it by going east below the house and over a stile by a rusty gate. Head westward on a wide green track to reach another stile. Go over. To the left here, about 100 m away among the bracken, is Bosiliack Barrow (see (6) Bosiliack Barrow). Continue along the rutted green track to reach the road. Go left along the road to reach Lanyon Quoit (see (7) Lanyon Quoit). From the cromlech, reverse the last section of the walk and continue along the road to the start point.

(1) *Men-an-Tol*

The name means 'stone-with-hole', a name that seems to sum up the central stone perfectly, being at once an excellent description and, at the same time, offering absolutely no clues about the reasoning behind the stone's form and existence. Since facts are at such a premium here we should begin with a few, a very few. The monument consists of three stones, two short uprights about 1¼ m (4 ft) high, each about 2½ m (8 ft) away from the crudely circular flat slab of rock, about 1 m (3 ft) in diameter at the centre. A fourth stone, lying as a slab behind the south-western upright is believed to have formed part of the group at some time. It is possible that the relative orientation of the stones has been altered over the years; a ground plan from 1754, but one drawn by a local doctor who is known to have made mistakes elsewhere, shows the central stone to be clearly offset from the line between the uprights. Since it is known that both Lanyon Quoit and Men Scryfa of local monuments were disrupted by people digging for treasure believed to lie below them, it is speculated that here too there may have been disturbance. Those, in large part, are the

facts. The academic assumptions are that the stones are early
Bronze Age, making them about 4,000 years old, and that they
were connected with a fertility rite. Their shape makes the latter
suggestion plausible – indeed it makes any other suggestion
somewhat difficult to support – but no useful information can be
gained about possible alignments of the hole and/or uprights with
sun risings or settings because of the likelihood of disturbances. It
is not known with certainty how the hole was cut; bear in mind
that this is granite and very, very hard.

Until quite recently, if indeed it has ever stopped, babies and
young children were passed naked through the hole three times
against the sun to ensure their health. Adults could also make use
of the supposed protective qualities of the stone, being expected to
pass through nine times for greatest benefit. In addition,
engagements 'sanctified' by holding hands through the hole,
especially at New Year, were likely to lead to long and fruitful
marriages and the stones could also help with childlessness, ease
the difficulties of oncoming labour and help farmers by promoting
better health in their stock and better yield in their crops.

Old women with the knowledge of Earth Magic could divine the
future by placing brass pins on the holed stone and then lifting
them above it on thread. Movement of the pins pointed the way
ahead or gave answers to specific questions.

All these tales are dismissed instantly and out-of-hand by the
pragmatist, and there is certainly no scientific credence for any of
the claimed properties of such stones as centres of magnetic or
electrical power. Yet for all that, such sites do have a profound
presence. The enigmatic quality of the stones, oddly carved,
curiously set up, strangely sited among ground shrubs, is real
enough. Perhaps theories based on 'alternative' science are
derived to allow those carrying out the derivations to rationalize
their own desires, or their understandable ignorance of the original
motives, a modern day equivalent of worshipping lightning as the
sparks from Thor's hammer before the science of the discharge of
static electricity was understood. Whether it is that or a genuine
awareness of some hidden (but if hidden, then who is doing the
hiding and why?) truth, it is certainly true that Men-an-Tol is an
unsettling place.

   Last time I came, as the last of a summer's sun was giving even greater colour-depth to the yellow gorse and purple ling, the holed stone had several coins on its top surface, most of them topped by a blackberry. A curious ritual performed by a long-gone soul offering bronze, silver and fruit. The blackberries were well past their best: they had clearly been there some time. Just a piece of nonsense really but no one had taken the coins, even though there were very few people about. And I didn't either.

(2) *Men Scryfa*

The name is Cornish for Stone of Writing, an inscription on the northern face, barely legible and, in part disappearing below ground level, reading *Rialobrani*, *Cunovali Fili*. The language is Latin, though the names are distinctly Celtic, implying a date around the 5th or 6th century AD. No unambiguous, authoritive translation exists because of the difficulty of distinguishing some Celtic names from their symbolism. *Rialobrani* is 'royal raven' but is that the name of a man or a poetic reference to a battlefield? The Celts often referred to a battle as a feeding of ravens, the raven, a carrion feeder, being their symbol of death. *Cunovali* could be a name but could equally be famous warrior or leader. Of *Fili*, there is no doubt; it means 'son of'.

   One legend of the stone has a local leader being ousted by sea-borne invaders, his son leading an army to recover his father's lands and being killed in the subsequent battle. The battle was successful and the stone was erected over the dead son's grave. It would seem odd that the famous warrior/leader should lose his lands in the first place but it is certainly the case that the stone is a menhir (from the Celtic *maen hir*, long stone) and so pre-dates any supposed battle by two or three millennia. It is possible that the stone was standing close to the battle site and so was utilized, but overall both stone and inscription are enigmas.

   An alternative story that links the writing with the legendary Cornish giant Holiburn – who lived on nearby Carn Galver and is said to have died of grief after accidentally killing a boy – sheds little useful light on the stone. What is known is that for several years in the early 19th century Men Scryfa lay on its side, having fallen over when it was undermined by a local digging for the gold that reputedly lay beneath it. The prospector found no gold, or anything else, and was very lucky not to have been killed by the toppling stone. In 1824 the stone was re-erected by Captain Giddy and Lieutenant Goldsmith of the Royal Navy. Goldsmith is infamous as the man who tipped over the most famous of all Cornish logan rocks, at Treen. This is a digression but worthwhile. Logans are geological erratics, boulders left in positions by ice or weathering such that they are perfectly balanced and can be rocked without tipping (see Note (2) of Walk 25). In the early 19th century the Treen locals made money from their logan, showing it to tourists. Lieutenant Goldsmith was determined to prove the locals wrong when they said it could never be tipped. By using the crew of his custom's cutter and various levering devices he succeeded in rolling it over. There was much merriment and Goldsmith was pleased with himself. The locals were not, and such was the outcry that an embarrassed officialdom ordered Goldsmith to restore the rock – at his own expense. This he did, though it has never rocked again.

It is widely reported that the expense of restoring the logan ruined Goldsmith but that suggestion is not born out by the officer's subsequent decision to tour the area re-erecting megaliths toppled over by weather and treasure-seekers. When his party re-erected Men Scryfa they buried several extra feet into the ground for good measure, reducing a very impressive 3-m (10-ft) menhir to a less, but still, impressive 2-m (6½-ft) one.

(3) *Parish Stone*

The flat slab of stone to the right here marks the point at which the parishes of Zennor, Madron, Morvah and Gulval meet. Look for the incised cross on the end, the 'official' boundary mark. The track which crosses here is an old ridgeway path that is now followed by the semi-official Tinner's Way path. It may also lie on a far older track, as those who believe in ley lines may already know. Ley lines were discovered (invented?) by Alfred Watkins earlier this century when he noticed that many ancient places, cromlechs (quoits in Cornwall), standing stones, stone circles, etc.

WALKS 34 AND 35
MEN-AN-TOL AND CHUN CASTLE

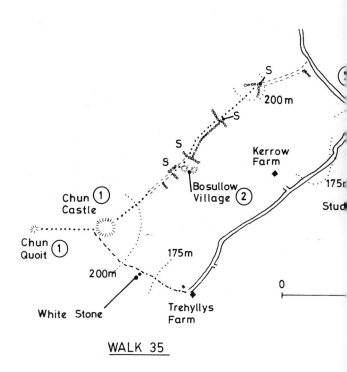

WALK 35

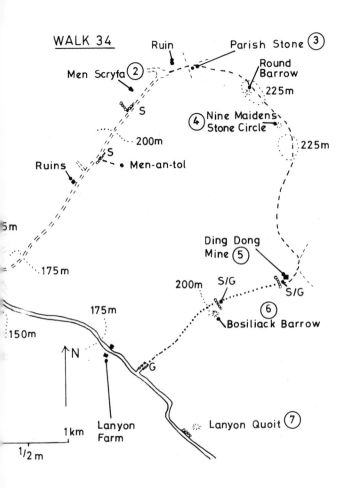

WALK 34

Ruin

Parish Stone ③

Men Scryfa ②

Round Barrow
225m

S

④ Nine Maidens
Stone Circle

200m

225m

S • Men-an-tol

Ruins

5m

175m

Ding Dong
Mine ⑤

200m   S/G

S/G

⑥ Bosiliack Barrow

150m

175m

↑N

G

1 km

Lanyon
Farm

Lanyon Quoit ⑦

½ m

were aligned along straight lines that also pointed at obvious horizon features, a notch in a hill, a pass and so on. He conjectured that Neolithic and Bronze Age merchants and travellers – and these are known to have existed – moved about the country on paths surveyed between prominent features and that, in time, sacred sites or settlements grew up along those track so defining them for all time. In one sense, given that the paths existed, the sites lying on them is no surprise – we too usually build beside the road. Watkins also pointed out that many churches lie on these ley lines, as later religions used the sites of earlier seats in order to benefit from their holiness or to ensure a successful obliteration of the old style. With a little imagination, one such ley line links Castell-an-Dinas, a hillfort to the east, the Chysauster Iron Age village, Mulfra Quoit, the Nine Maidens, and the stone here. The alignment is not perfect but allowance must always have been made for local features such as the ridge above the stone.

(4) *Nine Maidens Circles*

As with Men-an-Tol, it is easier to state the facts of the circle than to offer an explanation of its purpose. Despite the name there are only seven standing stones – and some of those are leaning – with several more lying concealed in the shrubbery. Two centuries ago a survey stated that there were thirteen stones, the circle having been plundered at various times since its erection. If other local sites are considered as indicative it is likely that there were originally about twenty stones varying from 1–2 m (3–6½ ft) high in a circle about 21 m (70 ft) across. The stones had their flatter sides facing inwards. The 18th-century survey mentioned above states that there was a single menhir about 40 m (130 ft) to the north-west, though only a short stone is visible there now. Following the suggestion that Stonehenge was an astronomical calendar someone pointed out that this stone, when viewed from an edge of the circle, indicated the position of the setting of the midsummer sun. The sceptic would say that viewed from somewhere the menhir was bound to do that but in the face of the now overwhelming evidence that such solar alignments exist at some (but not, apparently, all) sites, it is likely that this alignment is other than pure chance. Interestingly, the use of 'nine' in the names of such circles is too frequent to be explained by miscounting or some obscure mysticism about the number. The best suggestion seems to be that it is derived from 'noon', a clear solar reference and one that ties in with the legend heard about many of the sites – though not, as far as I am aware, at Nine Maidens – that the stones bowed to the sun at noon.

The round barrow at the southern edge of the circle is Bronze Age, dating from about 1000 BC. Excavations revealed evidence of a cremation.

5) *Ding Dong Mine*

The engine-house is more accurately termed Greenburrow and formed part of an entensive local tin mine. The engine-house was home to the whim engine that raised ore or to a pump that drained the workings. Ding Dong's great days were in the 60 years around 1840 though there were attempts to revive it in 1912 and again in 1928. Today it has been partially restored – perhaps stabilized would be a better word – and gated off to make it less of a death-trap. The name is said to derive from the church bell at Madron which could be heard from the site. Equally close, however, is Morvah church. The original church in this village became ruinous in the early 19th century and one day a cow wandered into the belfry and chewed on the bellrope. The bells began to ring and frightened the villagers witless. Only when the braver of the local miners came back to investigate was the truth discovered.

To the side of the ruin there is a slight rise. Stand on this for the best view of the walk. To the east are St Michael's Mount and Lizard Point, while to the west is Chun Castle. Southward is Lanyon Quoit, another stop on our journey.

6) *Bosiliack Barrow*

Bosiliack is one of the few local barrows that was excavated before it was plundered, though even here there was damage, probably by miners. Other local sites date from the Bronze Age though the barrow plan does have significant Neolithic (long barrow) features.

The passage to the central chamber appears to have been aligned to the mid-winter sunrise, a clear 're-birth' symbol, a view reinforced by the inclusion of turf in the mound, a symbol of the earth's fertility.

(7) *Lanyon Quoit*

In Neolithic (New Stone Age) times (about 6,000 years ago) man made his first tangible impact on the landscape with the erection of long barrow burial chambers. These were created from stone pillar uprights supporting a flat capstone, the bodies of the tribal chiefs being interred inside. Usually the chamber would be earthed over to form the barrow. In England the usual term for the exposed chambers is dolmen or cromlech, a Welsh name. In Cornwall such chambers are known as quoits.

In the 18th century Lanyon must have been an impressive site. A local doctor, Dr Borlase, describing it in 1754 maintains that a man on a horse could ride under the capstone. Unfortunately the whole thing collapsed in a gale on 19 October 1815, though it is likely that previous undermining by treasure hunters had weakened it. It lay on the ground until 1824 when Lieutenant Goldsmith (see Note (2) above) re-erected it. Sadly here, as with Men Scryfa, he planted the uprights deeper than they had been, presumably to improve stability. In addition, a piece that had been broken off the capstone meant that the original form – known from a drawing by Dr Borlose – could not be reformed.

For all that the quoit is impressive. The capstone is 3 × 5½ m (10 ft × 18 ft) and weighs over 13 tons. Presently it is about 2 m (6½ ft) above the ground. Imagine it several feet higher and wonder at how men without metal managed to raise it into position.

Ding Dong Mine

Walk 35 Chun Castle

Walk category : Easy (1½ hours)

Length   : 5½ km (3½ miles)

Ascent : 90 m (300 ft)

Maps : Landranger Sheet 203, Pathfinder Sheet 1364 (SW33/43)

Starting and finishing point : As for Walk 34

Now take the lane that runs west from the far side of the Studio, and the far side of the road – signed by the telephone box for Chun Castle – and follow it to Trehyllys Farm. At the farm go right and head for the white boulder that defines the start of a narrow path up through bracken to the castle. Before visiting the castle, however, go left for a few hundred metres to visit Chun Quoit (see (1) Chun Castle and Quoit). Return to the castle (see also Note (1)).

   The remainder of our walk is on a permissive path, not a right of way, so you should be prepared, if necessary, to reverse the route through the farm.

   From the castle's eastern 'side' take the path signed by a yellow arrow across the hillside to reach a walled lane. Follow this to a stile and a break in the right wall through which the site of Bosullow village can be reached (see (2) Bosullow Village). Continue along the lane to reach another stile and a path section where the left wall is missing, the right wall being complete. At the end of this is another stile. Cross the moor ahead – there are yellow marks on strategic stones – to a stile to a walled lane. Go down this to the road. Turn right to the Studio and start point.

(1) *Chun Castle and Quoit*
Chun Castle is a small but remarkably well-defended hill fort

Lanyon Quoit

sitting on top of a small outcrop that itself defends a ridge of the Penwith moors. It is assumed, though without absolute proof, that the fort site was used to defend a ridgeway route in Bronze Age or earlier times but the massive construction that now sits among the scrub is Iron Age, from the 3rd century BC.

By the standards of hill forts elsewhere, Chun, at 85 m (280 ft) in diameter, is tiny but the defences were formidable. The walls were probably 4 m (13 ft) high when completed – and are still 2½ m (8 ft) high now in places – and there were both inner and outer walls. A cunning design of the entrance, on the south-west side, ensured that any attacker who breached the outer gate had to turn his undefended right side to the inner wall when making for the inner gate. Inside the walls the visitor with time and patience to pick through the scrub will find the circular remains of Iron Age huts. A more expert eye is required to see the shape of rectangular huts said to overlie the early huts. These are likely to be from an occupation by 6th-century AD copper and tin miners. In contrast, even the most undiscerning eye can pick out the old well on the northern side of the castle interior.

Chun Quoit, about 250 m (300 yards) west of the castle, is a classic 'Penwith' chamber tomb. These tombs, Neolithic cromlechs, are so-called because they are almost unique to this area of Cornwall – though, as we have seen at Lanyon, they are not the only Neolithic form – and consist of square chambers with closed or very narrow entrances, originally set beneath round mounds. Chun is a fine example, its capstone weighing around 8 tons, but the best example for the interested visitor to view is Zennor Quoit, situated at 469 380 on the flank of Zennor Hill above Walk 33.

The curious structure on the hill to the south of Chun Castle is part of Britain's air traffic control system.

(2) *Bosullow Village*
Summer's bracken growth usually obscures the Celtic village that lies here in the defensive shadow of Chun Castle but when the

Chun Castle

scrub dies back the old walls of houses similar to those at the nearby and vastly more famous village of Chysauster (at 473 350) come into view. Bosullow has not been systematicaly excavated, so its date is not so well-established but it is certainly a contemporary of the castle – that is around 2000 years old.

Walk 34/35 Ancient Penwith

This is the best walk around Penwith's historic sites: a figure-of-eight walk that follows Walk 34 and then Walk 35.

Walk category : Intermediate (2¾ hours)

Length : 12 km (7½ miles)

Ascent : 160 m (500 ft)

Maps : As Walks 34 and 35

Starting and finishing point : As Walks 34 and 35

Walk 36 Lamorna Cove

The extreme western tip of Cornwall, where the Penwith moors meet the sea is real tourist land; for the tourist attracted by Land's End – the most westerly point if not the most southerly – and the Treen logan rock. On this walk we go south of Land's End, to Lamorna Cove, linking a delightful stretch of the Coastal Path with a fine inland section past some ancient sites.

    Lamorna Cove is a beautiful spot. In summer it would be expected to be heaving with people but the limited parking space at the sea edge and the (relatively) long walk from the village usually limits the throng. It does make a cove start difficult, and those who wish to use this as a start would do better to come off-season. I started from there once in late September on a day with brilliant sunshine and a pleasant autumnal nip in the air. The cove was home to a group of scuba divers in bright wet (or, perhaps, dry) suits, young children in optimistic swimwear and grandparents in pessimistic overcoats. A typical English seaside scene.

Walk category : Easy/Intermediate (2¼ hours)

Length : 9½ km (6 miles)

Ascent : 150 m (500 ft)

Maps : Landranger Sheet 203, Pathfinder Sheet 1368 (SW32/42)

Starting and finishing point : At 450 241, the car-park at the quay, Lamorna Cove

From the car-park head west past the cafés and the quay on a metalled track that very rapidly downgrades to a standard footpath. The footpath then rapidly becomes typical granite Coastal Path, picking its way through a boulder ruckle. Follow the occasional yellow arrows and keep an eye to the left, especially if you are with children as some of the drops are very close, very steep and very dangerous. At one point an old cross is set above the sea close to a huge pulpit of rock (see (1) Shipwreck Cross). Beyond the path continue along Tregurnow Cliff to Carn Barges beyond which the view is dominated by the lighthouse of Tater Du (see (2) Tater Du Lighthouse) reached after a pleasant section of Path.

From the lighthouse the Coastal Path takes a lane past a white house that once, and may still, belong to the author John le Carré. Beyond the walled lane the Coastal Path crosses easier cliff top ground to Boscowen Point. It was off the Point that, in 1981, the *Union Star* foundered. The Penlee lifeboat, the *Solomon Browne*, went to her assistance but went down with the loss of all her crew of eight. It was one of the worst disasters suffered by the RNLI and cannot be considered without mounting admiration for the crews of all the Institute's boats.

Beyond the Point the ground is rougher again, before a final descent, which is not much easier, through an old cliff garden

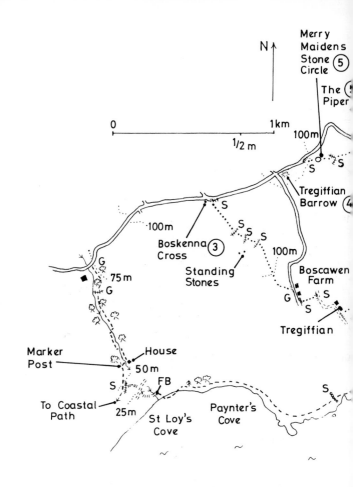

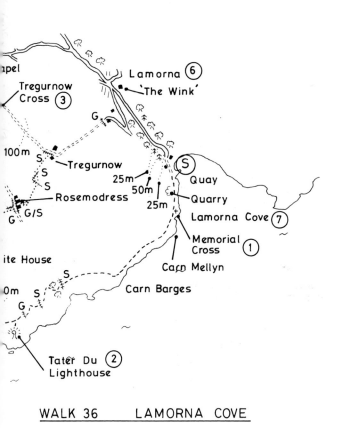

apel

Tregurnow
Cross ③

Lamorna ⑥
'The Wink'

G

100m
S
S
S
Tregurnow
25m
50m
25m
Rosemodress
G G/S

S ⓢ
Quay
Quarry
Lamorna Cove ⑦

Memorial
Cross ①
Carn Mellyn

ite House
S S
Carn Barges

0m
S
G

Tater Du ②
Lighthouse

WALK 36   LAMORNA COVE

leads to the beach at St Loy's Cove. St Loy's claims to be the warmest spot in England, a thought to savour as you cross a short section of beach littered with ankle-turning boulders. Once over, the Path is picked up again and followed as it crosses a small footbridge and starts to climb. Go over a driveway and steeply up – steps and tree roots help here – to reach a fence. Over this the Coastal Path goes left, but our walk goes right.

Watch now for a post with a yellow marker that points the way off the obvious track on to a narrower path that goes around a garden fence and then rises through a very pretty valley where hydrangeas grow in abundance. Go through a gate and soon reach another, entirely redundant one on to the B3315. Go right with caution, following the road to Boskenna Cross (see (3) Boskenna Cross). Here there is a choice.

The stile at the corner of the lay-by beside the cross can be used to reach an old field path that once took local farmers to church at St Buryan. Follow the right hedge, then go left to a stile. Cross to another, noting the 2-m (6½-ft) Boscawen-Ros menhirs in the centre of the field to the right. Beyond the third stile is a fourth. Cross the field beyond and follow the left hedge to Boscawen-Ros Farm, usually protected by a flock of hissing geese. The continuation is over one of Cornwall's finest stiles. On the last stone wall before a small garage, climb protruding stones. A stile ahead gives access to a track, right, to Tregiffian. There take a stile left and cross fields to Rosemodress where a gate and stile lead to a field. Cross more fields to reach Tregurnow (see also Note (3)) where the second alternative is rejoined.

The alternative, and better, way is to continue along the road, passing Tregiffian Barrow (see (4) Tregiffian Barrow) to reach the Merry Maidens stone circle (see (5) The Merry Maidens Circle). Cross the field beyond to a stile and cross to another back on to the B3315. To the left here; in two fields that are private land, are two fine menhirs (see also Note (5)). At a stile to the right, go over and head diagonally across the field, the left hedge of which follows a wavy course. Cross a stile in the far hedge and take the

Guard-dog geese on Walk 36

lane beside Borah Chapel, passing Tregurnow Cross (see also Note (3)) to reach Tregurnow (see also Note (3)).

Bear left along the lane towards Lamorna, going through a gate, swinging right and then going sharply left to reach the village (see (6) Lamorna). Follow the road back to the cove (see (7) Lamorna Cove).

(1) *Shipwreck Cross*

It is said that this Celtic cross bears the inscription 'Emma, March 13, 1873' though I must confess that I have never seen anything remotely similar. The story is that Emma was one of a group of eight children who died, along with eight other passengers, when the *Garonne* was lost here in 1868. That seems fair enough but there is another local story that suggests that the cross was erected as a memorial to a student of Jesus College, Cambridge who fell from the spot in 1873 and was killed. The date ties in better but 'Emma' – if it is real – certainly does not.

Close by is the Mermaid's Rock, named for a mermaid who once used it as chair while she combed her hair in time-honoured fashion. It is said that her singing can still be heard but that if young men swim towards her voice they are never seen again.

(2) *Tater Du Lighthouse*

The lighthouse, which must be one of Britain's most picturesque, was built in 1965, making it one of the newest. It was also the first fully automatic light. The light can be seen for over 25 km (16 miles) and the noise from the foghorn, a honeycombed array of 72 speakers, is awesome.

(3) *Boskenna Cross*

The cross has had a chequered history since it was first erected, and even that date is not known with any great precision. The figure on the cross is a representation of Christ, but not Christ crucified as might be expected. This form, with out-turned feet and outstretched arms, was popular in the 8th to 12th centuries. Then

The memorial cross near Lamorna Cove

the cross would have marked a wayside shrine, or a popular place of pilgrimage due to a miraculous event.

It remained hidden for centuries until 1869 when it was accidentally uncovered during road widening. The cross (only the last 0.8 m (2½ ft) is original) was set up at the centre of the local road junction, but was knocked over so often it was moved to the lay-by. The base is a motley collection of stones including, it would seem, a grindstone and one from a cider press.

Tregurnow Cross, at 439 244, and only visible by climbing the roadside bank, is an upright 1½-km (4½-ft) slab of granite with an incised cross.

(4) *Tregiffian Barrow*

The barrow has been much disturbed and it is by no means clear whether it is in its original form, or whether what we see is the survival after road-widening and slab-stealing. From a burial urn and cremated remains found inside it is likely that the chamber is early Bronze Age, so was probably originally a stone-built, roofed chamber with a round mound of earth, possibly with a revetment wall. This would mean that the present roof slab is original, though many have speculated that it is, in fact, a repositioned menhir, such is its shape. The most interesting part of the monument, though, is the edge-on-slab away from the road which is covered with indentations known as cup marks. There are twenty-five of these, twelve ovals and thirteen circles. Many have pointed out that these figures correspond to the number of moons – full and new – in a year, a fact that is most unlikely to be accidental. The stone itself is actually a cast replica of the original which is held at the County Musuem in Truro.

(5) *The Merry Maidens Circle*

The two menhirs across the road from the stone circle stand near a farm called Boleigh which is said to mean 'place of blood', legend having it that here Athelstan the Saxon defeated the Cornish in the 10th century and that the stones were set up to commemorate the battle. In reality they are almost certainly older, late Neolithic or early Bronze Age, and are probably in some way associated with the circle. In legend, the menhirs are the Pipers, stones which occasionally came to life to play their pipes when the moon was full and the air still. One night nineteen young maidens from Lamorna were drawn to the music. Next day there was consternation in the village when it was realized that none of the girls had returned home. A search revealed nineteen stones in a circle beside the now-silent Pipers. The legend goes on to suggest that even now, at times when the moon is full, the Pipers play, and then the Maidens come alive again and dance. It is only a story of course, but perhaps it would be a good idea not to go near the area then . . .

Merry Maidens – once themselves called the Nine Maidens, recalling the name of the circle on Walk 34 – is considered the best of Cornwall's stone circles and is believed to be complete. Several stones have been re-set but, allowing for changes in their position, studies have shown a very regular spacing of the stones with the heights ducking in an ordered way, the tallest stones being to the south-west, the shortest to the north-east. It has been suggested that this mimics the phases of the moon, though it would seem to be a reasonable model for all waxing and wanings, tides, sun, seasons, etc. What is very noticeable is that the regular spacing has been broken at the eastern side where there is a one stone gap. Excavations to see if this gap is real, or just the result of a missing stone, have not been possible because of continuous ploughing. It has been suggested that if the gap is real, then the circle is a good stone representation of a Bronze Age *torc*, a horseshoe-shaped ornament.

6) *Lamorna*

The name Lamorna means 'valley by the sea' which is entirely appropriate for this most delightful of villages. The village is famous as a haunt of artists who have visited and stayed in an attempt to capture the elusive light on sea, trees and granite. Sir Alfred Munnings and Dame Laura Knight both spent time here. Munnings lived at 'The Wink', as the village pub is called. The story is that the name derives from a time when good spirits were hard to come by but a regular could give the barman a wink and be served a glass of best brandy that had recently fallen off the back of a lugger.

(7) *Lamorna Cove*

The quarries at the cove supplied best granite for building, stone that was horse-hauled to Newlyn until the quay was functional. Much of the stone went to London where it was used to build the Embankment. The Lamorna quarries also supplied the 7-m (22-ft) obelisk for the Great Exhibition of 1851. This was hewn in one piece and lowered by special cranes on to a horse-drawn carriage that took it to a ship at Penzance. The obelisk weighed 21 tons, so the labour and care needed can only be marvelled at. Finally, one local story suggests that Bob Fitzsimmons, the only British-born boxer ever to hold the world heavyweight championship, once worked at the Lamorna quarries.

The Isles of Scilly

The Isles of Scilly represent the final granitic 'boss' in the great chain of igneous rock that stretches like a leg-bone through the South-West Peninsula. In former times it is likely that the islands were connected to the mainland, though that was aeons before man's arrival in either the Isles or Cornwall, so there is no chance of the mythical land of Lyonesse said to lie between the two being based on a folk memory. Until the last Ice Age it is likely that the Isles were one large island, the rise in sea level after the ice melted filling valleys to form the numerous small islands we now see. Historically, the early presence of man on the islands mirrored that on the mainland, there being evidence of Neolithic, Bronze and Iron Age cultures. The modern history of the group begins with the shipping of seaweed to Bristol for use in the glass and soap industries, and with the shipping of casks of illicit brandy, etc. to the mainland from France. With the eventual demise of smuggling as a trade the Isles took advantage of their position to become a flower farm, spring coming a little earlier here, the weather being rather warmer than the rest of the country. The early harvest is also taken full advantage of by potato farmers. For the visitor, the Isles offer peace and isolation, the latter not to be derided. It may only be a few minutes by helicopter to the mainland but once the machine has disappeared from view the isolation is real enough. It would appear at first sight that the walker would have little to detain him but such is not the case. Our walks circumnavigate one island – Tresco, the most 'natural' of the islands – and offer an evening stroll through history on the main Isle, St Mary's.

Walk 37/38 Isles of Scilly: Tresco and St Mary's

These two walks offer a brief exploration of the Scillies: the first a circumnavigation of Tresco, at 630 hectares (735 acres) the second largest of the Isles and one of its most interesting; the second a short walk around the Garrison on the main island of St Mary's.

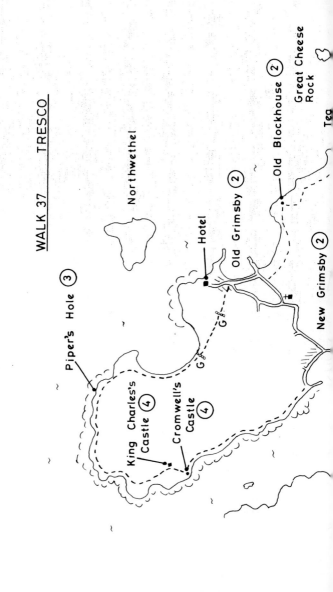

WALK 37   TRESCO

Northwethel

Piper's Hole ③

King Charles's Castle ④

Cromwell's Castle ④

Hotel

Old Grimsby ②

Old Blockhouse ②

Great Cheese Rock

New Grimsby ②

Tea

G
G

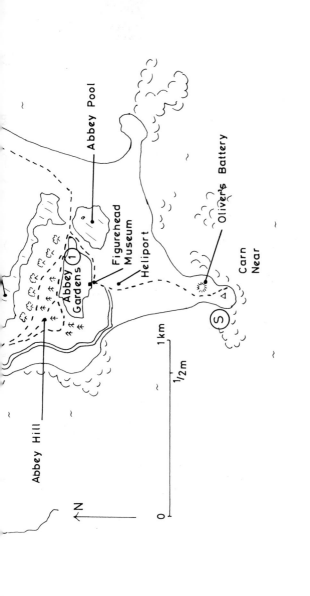

Abbey Pool

Abbey Hill

Abbey Gardens ①

Figurehead Museum

Heliport

Oliver's Battery

Carn Near

⑤

N

0   ½m   1km

Walk 37 Tresco

Walk category : Easy (2½ hours)

Length : 10 km (6¼ miles)

Ascent : 100 m (325 ft)

Maps : Landranger Sheet 203, Outdoor Leisure Sheet 25

Starting and finishing point : A little dependent on the tide! The route is described from, and to, Carn Near (Low) Quay but it also passes the New Grimsby (High) Quay.

From the Carn Near Quay take the concrete path that heads inland and to the left (west) of a small knoll topped by Oliver's Battery, a ruinous remnant of the Civil War. It was built after Tresco had been taken for Parliament – hence the name. The path goes past the perimeter of the heliport to reach Abbey Gardens (see (1) Abbey Gardens). From the gardens take the path signed for Pentle Bay, a path that meanders between the gardens and the Abbey Pool before heading due east to a bay of white sand and clear water. From the bay head north along the beach edge to Lizard Point with its fine views of Tea Ledge and Great Cheese Rock, and continue around to Rushy Point and the Old Blockhouse (see (2) The Old Blockhouse and the Grimsbys). A track continues now to Old Grimsby (see also Note (2)) – beware of the transfer train carrying hotel guests' luggage! – from where a signed path is taken towards Gimble Porth. The way is along the road at first, then left on a path through two gates – the only two on the island? From this path the lighthouse on Round Island dominates the seaward view.

    Follow the edge of Gimble Porth, then join a path on the bleaker, northern end of the island passing Piper's Hole (see (3) Piper's Hole), Kettle Point and Gimble Point to reach the remains of King Charles's and Cromwell's Castles (see (4) Tresco Castles).

From the castles the coastal path leads straightforwardly to New Grimsby and the High Quay (see also Note (2)).

A signed path from the quay leads past the Estate's Office and Abbey Farm to the base of Abbey Hill. From here there is a profusion of routes, one going left (north) of the hill directly to the Abbey, while others go over the flank or summit of the hill itself. To return to Carn Near from the Abbey reverse the outer route.

(1) *Abbey Gardens*

The Celtic saints who frequented the Cornish peninsula from the 5th century onwards also landed in the Scillies, most of the small islands having a hermitage from earliest times. The story is told that in the late 10th century a Viking raider, landing here with an army of men from over 100 ships, was converted to Christianity by St Elid and left in peace to spread the Gospel in Iceland and Norway. Tresco's Christian tradition dates back at least to the mid 10th century when a priory was dedicated to St Nicholas, though it was not until 1114 when Henry I gave the island to the Abbey of Tavistock, that the Benedictine Priory was built. The Priory was dissolved in 1539 and only a few ruined walls remained when, in 1834, Augustus Smith arrived here from Hertfordshire. Smith built a house close to the old site, called it Tresco Abbey, and started work on the Gardens that are now the chief attraction of the island. Smith obtained seed and plants from all over the world, persuading many ships' captains to obtain specimens on their journeys and to deliver them back here to Tresco. When Smith died, in 1872, he left behind an impressive Victorian garden set on terraces cut from the hillside and protected by belts of tall, thick trees. Smith also built 'Valhalla' to house the collection of ships' figureheads that visitors see soon after arriving at the Gardens. The collection is from ships wrecked on the Isles over a period of about 300 years and is now owned by the National Maritime Museum. Augustus Smith was succeeded by his nephew, Thomas Dorrien-Smith; the Dorrien-Smith family still own the property.

At the entrance visitors are greeted by a very new statue (1990) by David Wynne, entitled 'Tresco Children'. Beyond the statue – the Valhalla figureheads are to the left – the gardens are divided

into three terraces crossed by a number of named walks. The last remnants of the priory have been utilized at one point, a pair of old archways now assisting a variety of climbing plants to flourish. Near one of the arches is an old Roman grave-stone, from an earlier occupation. The gardens themselves are beyond reasonable short description, but the should-be-visited sections include the Mexico section with its huge succulents, the West Rockery where another Mexican plant, *Furcraea Longaeva*, flowers only every 10 or 20 years (but is almost worth the wait) and the collection of Aki-Aki from New Zealand. The gardens are also famous for their *Protea* collection which do not flower outside anywhere in Britain except at Tresco.

(2) *The Old Blockhouse and the Grimsbys*

When preparing plans for their Armada of 1588 the Spanish Commanders decided to use the Isles of Scilly as a rendezvous and forward command point for their invasion. The Armada failed but the Spanish did not lose all interest in their invasion and in 1590 they built a naval base in Brittany. The British responded by fortifying the Scillies. Star Castle was built on St Mary's to protect the Pool, and was completed in 1594, just in time to be used to see off a small force of Spaniards in four ships who landed in 1595. Tresco's Blockhouse was completed during the same phase of defensive architecture to protect the harbour of Old Grimsby, though it was on the site of an earlier fort, probably mid 15th-century, built as an outpost of Pendennis Castle.

A road across the centre of the island, all of about 600 m (650 yards) long, now joins Old and New Grimsby, Tresco's two villages. The road passes St Nicholas's church, named, as with the priory, for the paton saint of sailors and built in 1882, and the New Inn where the walker can stop at half-circuit. When the nearest policeman was on St Mary's, and the sea was rough, the inn had 'flexible' opening times. The Island Hotel at Old Grimsby was one of the first of the Isles' tourist ventures and has succeeded in integrating tourism with the island's looks, the building looking

Tresco Abbey gardens

more like a row of cottages then a luxury hotel. It is the transfer train of guests and luggage to the hotel that occasionally threatens to mow down the unexpecting walker.

The concrete slipways at New Grimsby were built for sea-planes at the time of the 1914–18 War.

(3) *Piper's Hole*
The hole is a sea-cut cave going back nearly 100 m (325 ft) into the island. From the entrance a low duck leads to a chamber almost 10 m (32 ft) high and some 20 m (66 ft) long which ends at a freshwater pool. This should be the limit of normal exploration – and even this requires a torch for a really worthwhile look – but until recent years one islander ran boat trips across the pool, on the far side of which another 50 m or so of cave can be explored.

(4) *Tresco Castles*
In the mid 16th century when Henry VIII had broken with the Pope and the church of Rome there was a real fear of a Franco-Spanish invasion, and to forestall the possibility of a landing in the Scillies a fort was built to protect the harbour of New Grimsby. The harbour was to be defended by the newest weapon of war, the cannon, and the castle's structure reflects this, with two tiers of gun-carrying embrasures. Sadly, the science of military architecture had not kept pace with the new technology and it was found that as far as the harbour was concerned the guns offered no protection at all. It is widely written that this discovery led to the building of the round tower and blockhouse below the first castle but, as we shall see, this is a disputed suggestion. As we have already seen – Note (2) above – the later defence of Tresco against a perceived Spanish threat concentrated on the Old Grimsby harbour. The names of the New Grimsby castles, King Charles's for Henry VIII's work and Cromwell's for the later, round tower are from the time of the Civil War.

In 1645, with the Civil War going badly for him, the King sent his son, the fifteen-year-old Prince Charles, to the West Country. Nominally the boy was commander of Royalist forces on the peninsula but in fact the move was to protect the young prince. By early 1646 even the far west had become hostile and Prince Charles and his advisors and protectors sailed from Sennen to the Scillies. It was 2 March, a cold miserable day, the sea running high enough to give all the prince's party sea-sickness and, to cap it all, the ship's crew stole most of their belongings. Nevertheless St Mary's welcomed the royal guest who installed himself in Star Castle. It was a short visit, however; by mid-April the party had moved on to Jersey, leaving the Isles to Parliament whose forces arrived in August.

The islanders and Roundheads got on badly. No one paid the former for billeting the latter, and the latter were not paid at all – a recipe for sourness all round. When the second Civil War broke out in 1648 the islanders threw out their unwelcome guests and Sir John Grenville took over the islands for the King. When Charles I was executed in 1649, Grenville declared the young prince Charles II and set about ravaging Parliamentarian shipping in the Channel. Soon, however, Grenville's men widened their net and started to attack anything that came within range. When Dutch shipping was attacked, retaliation was swift with a Dutch force under an Admiral Van Tromp arriving off the Isles. The Admiral came with an odd request, to take over the running of the Scillies for the new king. It is believed that Charles I may have 'sold' the Isles to Holland for £50,000 to continue his war effort which might explain Van Tromp's offer, or it might be that the Dutch admiral did not like the idea of a frontal assault. Grenville refused and Van Tromp sailed to Plymouth where he told bemused Parliament leaders that he had declared war on the Scillies and would help them capture the Royalists. The Parliamentarian leaders also refused – Grenville might be the enemy but he was English – and Van Tromp sailed into history.

Parliament was, though, sufficiently concerned by events to decide upon its own invasion and Admiral Blake set out with a force of men and ships. Deciding that St Mary's would be too difficult to take, Blake decided to land on Tresco. Aware of the blockhouse at Old Grimsby and the castle at New Grimsby he decided upon a northern landing and found a local pilot to take him that way. Due to one of those things that would be hilarious if war was not such a deadly game, Blake landed his men on Northwethel but soon found the right island and, attacking from the landward side, took the New Grimsby castle. The Royalists retreated – possibly blowing up Henry VIII's (King Charles's) Castle as they went – to St Mary's but as they were now completely encircled they surrendered after a few weeks.

Blake built the new battery at the south of Tresco – Oliver's Battery passed near the start of our walk – did nothing at the ruinous site of King Charles's Castle but worked on the lower (Cromwell's) castle. But what exactly did he do? Some contend that Cromwell's Castle is mid 16th-century, the problems over the lack of harbour protection offered by King Charles's Castle having been discovered very early. Blake would then merely have improved an existing fort. But – there is no lower castle on a seaman's chart reliably dated as drawn in 1585, and in 1600 there was an attempt to fortify Hangman's Island on Bryher because the guns of King Charles's Castle fired too high – why was this comment needed if Cromwell's Castle existed already? This has led to the suggestion that Blake built rather than improved Cromwell's Castle. Either way, it is a fine ruin, wooden and spiral stone stairs leading to a fine vantage point.

Walk 38 St Mary's

Walk category : Easy (1 hour)

Length : 3¼ km (2 miles)

Ascent : 50 m (165 ft)

Maps : Landranger Sheet 203, Outdoor Leisure Sheet 25

Starting and finishing point : At 901 108, Guard Gate, where the
Hugh Town road reaches the
Garrison

Gig racing at St Mary's

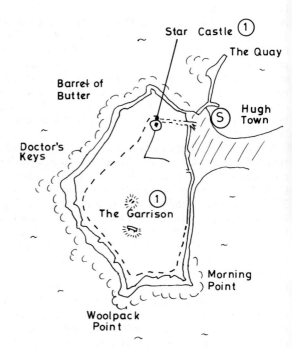

N

0   1km

¹/₂ m

Star Castle ①

The Quay

Barret of
Butter

Hugh
Town

Ⓢ

Doctor's
Keys

The Garrison ①

Morning
Point

Woolpack
Point

From the Gate it is possible to go left or right around the whole perimeter of the Garrison (see (1) The Garrison) or to walk directly up to Star Castle (see also Note (1)) and to continue along the crest of the Garrison Hill. The walk length assumes a complete trip around the perimeter and a visit to Star Castle.

This walk is best left for an evening when the dying sun picks out the island chain, or for when there is gig racing in the harbour (see also Note (1)). It is also a good walk for the birdwatcher.

(1) *The Garrison*

As stated in Note (2) of Walk 37 above, Star Castle was started in 1590 as a response to a threat of Spanish invasion, and completed in 1594. It is two storeys high and surrounded by a 5½-m (18-ft) granite rampart and dry moat. The original roof was thatch, which seems a little strange since it was a fire risk, but must have been a nice, if incongruous, touch. The remaining batteries on the hill date from the mid 18th century when the Guard Gate was also built. In all there were 18 gun batteries, built in response to the War of Jenkin's Ear.

Gigs are a specifically Cornish form of boat that in full sail version looks a little like a cut-down Viking long boat. The boats are about 9 m (29 ft) long and built with planking only 6 mm (¼ inch) thick, giving them a remarkably light weight (about 370 kgs/800 lbs). In addition to their two sails – a low lug foresail and sprit mizzen – gigs had six oars. More were possible but forbidden as with greater than six the smugglers' gig could easily outrun the Revenue men's cutter. The boats were used for ferrying pilots to and from ships, for inter-island travel and trade, to salvage wrecks and also as lifeboats. Today, their use is more recreational and they are raced in St Mary's Pool.

Many visitors to the Scillies come for the bird-life because of the number and variety of sea birds and also the frequency with which rare species turn up after an enforced, usually gale-driven, crossing of the Atlantic. Of the normal population there are mostly auks and gulls, together with storm petrels and fulmars, Manx shearwaters, terns (mostly common but including roseates), cormorants and shags. At the water's edge and inland there are numerous waders including sanderlings and purple sandpipers. Of the rareties the list is almost endless and completely useless, as they are here today and either here again or dead tomorrow. If you see a vast binoculared crowd suspect something interesting, and a little sad. For its species ask a friendly twitcher.

Finally, few will visit the Isles without taking a boat to Bishop's Rock. Though there are a few rocks to the west this is the agreed western outpost of Britain, the start and end of Blue Riband races across the Atlantic. The lighthouse is 51 m (167 ft) high and is permanently manned by three keepers. The light, thrown out by a 9 ton lens revolving in a vat of mercury, is visible for 30 km (over 18 miles).

Appendices

APPENDIX 1 THE DARTMOOR RANGES

Within the Dartmoor National Park there are three M.o.D. Ranges in which live firing occurs. The ranges are called Okehampton (parts of Walks 11 and 12 lie within this range), Merrivale (part of Walk 11 lies within this range) and Willsworthy (no walks lie within this range). The ranges are indicated on the map attached to this Appendix. On the ground the ranges are indicated by Range Posts in red and white, and by Range Notice Boards giving range information. When the ranges are in use red flags are flown from flagpoles erected on certain high points. If the firing is at night these show red lights. The positions of the poles are also shown on the Appendix map. Those points marked (Day) are *not* used to indicate night firing. When the flags or lights are showing, entry into the ranges is forbidden. It is also, of course, dangerous. In addition to live firing so-called dry training also takes place within the ranges. This involves pyrotechnics and blank ammunition which sound like live firing but are not. Access is permitted when such dry training is in progress.

When you are walking within the ranges *do not* pick up or disturb any metal objects. Such actions are potentially dangerous and are an offence under M.o.D. Range Bylaws. Any object discovered should be reported to the police or the Camp Commandant of Okehampton Camp.

Please note that the ranges butt on to each other. If, therefore, there is firing on two or three ranges simultaneously there is *no* safe corridor between the ranges.

Firing Times:
Information on Firing Times can be obtained in advance, to avoid red flags spoiling your trip, by reading the *Western Morning News* or *Express and Echo* on Fridays. The National Park Information offices and some local post offices and pubs also display the times.

Alternatively, phone one of the following numbers for a recorded message of times:

Exeter	(0392)70164
Okehampton	(0837)2939
Plymouth	(0752)701924
Torquay	(0803)294592

Non-firing Periods :
At the time of writing (winter 1991) live firing is not allowed during the following periods. This information may *not* apply for 1992 or later times.

Okehampton

Every Saturday and Sunday

Two weekdays each week during the lambing season from 1 April to 11 May

During the week commencing and including the Wednesday before Easter

During the week commencing and including the Wednesday before Spring Bank Holiday

15 July to 15 September inclusive

During Public Holidays

Willsworthy

Every Saturday and Sunday except for one weekend per month

During the month of August

During Public Holidays

A Dartmoor range notice board. This one is on Walk 12 near the junction of Methor Brook and Red-a-Ven Brook

DANGER

OKEHAMPTON RANGE
DO NOT PASS THE LINE
OF RED AND WHITE POSTS
WHILE A RED FLAG OR
LAMP IS FLYING FROM
THE HIGH GROUND TO THE
FRONT OF THIS BOARD
DO NOT TOUCH ANY
METAL OBJECT IT
MAY EXPLODE

THE DARTMOOR RANGES

St Michael's Bungalow

Watchet Hill

Halstock (Day)

Rowtor

Black Down (Day)

Yes Tor

OKEHAMPTON RANGE

Steeperton Tor

Hangingstone

Kitty Tor

E

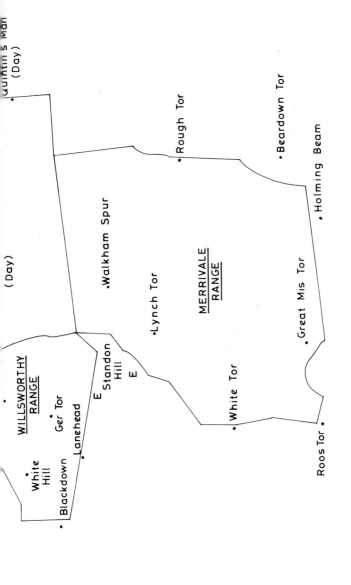

Merrivale

Every Saturday and Sunday

During the week commencing and including the Wednesday before Easter

During the month of August

During the Public Holidays

Cancellations:
If there are *no* warning flags or lights it is safe to enter the ranges. If firing has been advertised but no flags are flying by 0900 from April to September or by 1000 from October to March then there will be no firing during that day or the subsequent night. Dry training may still take place though, so you may still hear 'fireworks'. Will your heart stand it?!

Emergencies:
There are three emergency telephones for use during live firing. These are all *outside* the ranges and all on the western edge. They are indicated on the map.

APPENDIX 2 OTHER WALKS ON THE SOUTH-WEST PENINSULA

The Coastal Paths
Almost the whole coastline of the South-West Peninsula covered by this book is followed by officially designated long-distance footpaths. Technically there are four paths. The Dorset Coastal Path (no part of which lies within the area of this book) starts at Bournemouth – or, more pedantically, at Studland Point – and ends at Lyme Regis. There, the South Devon Coastal Path starts, continuing to Plymouth. From Plymouth the Cornish Coast Path goes right round Land's End, ending at Marsland Mouth where the North Devon and Somerset Coastal Path starts. This finishes at Minehead, though it is possible to continue on a non-official path to cover the whole of the Peninsula's coastline. The whole path is, at 880 km (550 miles), the longest official long-distance footpath in

Britain. The whole route is waymarked with the Countryside Commission's acorn symbol. Several of the walks in this book include sections of these superb routes.

The Two Moors Way
This fine route between Lynmouth and Ivybridge is described in Note 2 of Walk 8. Walk 8 follows a section – and an alternative section – of the route.

The Tarka Trail
A new initiative to create a 290-km (180-mile) waymarked footpath around the Land of the Two Rivers is described in Note 2 of Walk 20.

The Saint's Way
This fine walk – known also by its Cornish name of *Forth an Syns* – traces a route through mid-Cornwall, starting at the south door of Padstow church on the north coast and finishing at Fowey on the south coast. The name is not historically accurate as there is no evidence to suggest the existence of a single route followed by the Celtic saints. However, as a locally produced guide to the route points out, the name is not claimed as literally true. Rather it is an exploration of the country of those old Christian missionaries. The route goes south from Padstow to Little Petherick, then over St Breock Downs to Withiel. It continues to Lanvit and Helman Tor from where the walker has a choice. The western route goes towards Luxulyan, then down to St Blazey, east to Tywardreath, south to Tregaminion and hence to Fowey. The eastern route goes via Lanlivery and St Samsons direct to Fowey.

Other Short Walks
Both of the National Park Authorities organize short (day or ½ day) walks throughout the summer months. The Park Information Centres issue a programme. Several local areas of Cornwall (e.g. The North Cornwall Heritage Coast – a section from Constantine Bay to the Devon border) offer similar programmes. These can also be obtained from the local tourist offices.

Walks for the Disabled

Both the National Park Authorities and the National Trust are increasing the number of surfaced walks suitable for wheelchairs. The section of Walk 18 from the car-park to Baggy Point – but *not* the continuation to Woolacombe Bay or the return over the hill – has been gravel laid and is suitable for wheelchairs even though it has not been metalled. For a full list of suitable walks it is best to contact the relevant Information or Tourist offices as the number of such routes is constantly being updated.

APPENDIX 3 TRANSPORT AND WEATHER

Over such a wide area it is not possible to be definitive about the transport that is or will be available. The local information centres will have such information.

Weather Reports

A weather report for the Exmoor and Dartmoor National Parks is available by dialling 0898 141203.

A weather report for Cornwall and other areas of Devon is available by dialling 0898 500404.

A weather report for other areas of Somerset is available by dialling 0898 500405.

APPENDIX 4 USEFUL ADDRESSES

Dartmoor National Park

Dartmoor National Park Authority
Parke
Haytor Road
Bovey Tracey TQ13 9JQ
Tel: 0626 832093

Information Centres

Newbridge	Tel: (03643) 303
Okehampton	Tel: (0837) 53020
Postbridge	Tel: (0822) 88272
Princetown	Tel: (082289) 414
Steps Bridge	Tel: (0647) 52018
Tavistock	Tel: (0822) 612938

Exmoor National Park

Exmoor National Park Authority
Exmoor House
Dulverton
Somerset TA22 9HL
Tel: (0398) 23665

Information Centres

Coombe Martin	Tel: (027188) 33198
Countisbury	Tel: (05987) 321
Dulverton	Tel: (0398) 23841
Dunster	Tel: (0643) 821499
Lynmouth	Tel: (0598) 52509

Other Organizations

Council for National Parks
45 Shelton Street
London WC2H 9HJ
Tel: (071) 240 3603

West Country Tourist Board
Trinity Court
Southernhay East
Exeter EX1 1QS
Tel: (0392) 76351

Devon Tourist Board
Civic Centre
Paris Street
Exeter EX1 1JJ
Tel: (0392) 383260

Cornish Tourist Board
59 Lemon Street
Truro
Cornwall TR1 2SY
Tel: (0872) 74057

English Heritage
Keysign House
429 Oxford Street
London W1R 2HD
Tel: (071) 973 3000

English Heritage (local office)
Bridge House
Clifton
Bristol BS8 4XA
Tel: (0272) 734472

Countryside Commission
John Dower House
Cresent Place
Cheltenham GL50 3RA
Tel: (0242) 21381

Countryside Commission (South-West Regional Office)
Bridge House
Sion Place
Clifton
Bristol BS8 4AS
Tel: (0272) 739966

National Trust
36 Queen Anne's Gate
London SW1H 9AS
Tel: (071) 222 9251

National Trust (Wessex Regional Office)
Stourton
Warminster
Wiltshire BA12 6QD
Tel: (0747) 840224

Nature Conservancy Council
Northminster House
Northminster Road
Peterborough
Cambridgeshire PE1 1UA
Tel: (0733) 40345

Royal Society for the Protection of Birds
The Lodge
Sandy
Bedfordshire SG19 2DL
Tel: (0767) 680551

Index

Figures in *italics* refer to illustrations

Abbey River, 175, 176
Abbot's Way, 20, 125, 129, 133–4
Alfoxton, 33
Alfred's Road, 35, 40
Allen, River, 242
Aluric, 49
Amalveor Downs, 294
Arthur, King, 205, 230, 250, 254, 255–6
Ashburton, 99
Asparagus Island, 280
Avill, River, 45, 53

Badgworthy Water, 65, 70
Bagborough plantation, 41
Baggy Hole, 169
Baggy Leap, 170
Baggy Point, 18, 164, *168*, 169, 170, 171, 342
Barle, River, 82, 86, 87
Barnstaple, 144, 182
Barras Nose, 250
Bass Point House, 281–2, 285
Bat's Castle, 44, 45, 55
Bayards Cove, 185, 190, 191, 193
Beacon Hill, 32, 33, 41
Bearah Tor, 207, 210
Bearcove Castle, 191, 193
Becka Brook, 157
Becka Brook valley, 106
Becka Falls, 157
Beehive Hut, 107, 113, *114*
Beesands, 198, 203
Bicknoller, 28
Bicknoller Post, 28, 41
Bideford, 182
Bishop's Rock, 334
Bishop's Wood, 240
Black Ball, 45
Black Ball wood, 28
Black Gate/County Gate, 74
Black Ridge Brook, 110
Black Ridge pass, 110
Blackdown Copper Mine, 122
Blackmore, R. D., 63, 68–70, 80, 90
Blackmore Memorial Stone, 65
Blackpool Bridge, 77
Blackpool Sands, 195
Blackstone Point, 188
Blowing House, 137, 138

Bodmin, 218, 224
Bodmin Moor, 20, 25, 91, 205–28
Bolventor, 217, 218
Boscawen Point, 311
Boscawen-Ros menhirs, 315
Bosiliack Barrow, 296, 303, 305
Boskenna Cross, 315, 316, 318
Bossiney castle (remains), 254
Bossiney Haven, 251
Bosullow village, 307, 308, 310
Bovey, River, 156, 157
Bovey Tracey, 105, 106, 156
Bovey valley, 101 *see also* Lustleigh Cleave
Braddon Lake, 112
Brendon Common, 63, 65
Brendon Hills, 42
Bridge Pool, 77
Britannia Royal Naval College, 188, 189–90
Broad Down, 112
Broada Marsh, 107
Brown Willy, 20, 215, 217, 218, 220–1
Bryher, 330
Buckfast Abbey, 133, 138
Bude, 242, 243, 246, 248, 249–50
Bude Canal, 19, 242, 243, 246, *247*, 24
Bumble Rock, 282
burial sites, ancient, 62, 97, 129, 134, 207, 303, 305, 308, 318
Burrator Reservoir, 20, 125, 130
Butter Hill, 71, 75

Caddow Combe, 71
Cadgwith, 277, 281, 284–5
Caerthillian Cove, 277
Camel, River, 145, 221, 256
Camel estuary, 266
Caradon Hill, 210, 215
Caratacus stone, 89
Carn Barges, 311
Carn Galver, 298
Carn Near Quay, 324, 325
Carnweather Point, 264
Carracks, the, 287
Castell-an-Dinas, 229, 302
Castle Drogo, 152, 153–4, *155*
Cat's Scramble, 56, 59
Chagford, 113
Cheesewring, 20, 207, 212, *213*
Cheesewring Quarry, 207, 211–2, 215
Chew Magna, 39
Chiselcombe Bridge, 77
Chough's Ogo, 281
Chubhill Combe, 71

un Castle, 15, 229, 307–8, *309*
un Quoit, 307, 308
urch Cove, 281
urch houses, *38*, 39, 162
urchtown, 286
ysauster village, 302, 310
vil War, 49, 50, 57, 132, 153, 183, 184,
 193, 194, 230, 237, 324, 328–9
umbridge, 157
eeve Abbey, 49, 52
ovelly, 171
dda Tor, 218
ffin Way (Tinners' Way), 287, 294,
 299
m Head, 264
mbe Martin, 42
mbe Point, 188
mbestone Tor, 135, 138
mbwich, 32
mpass Cove, 188
mpass Point, 246, 249
ncrete Wall, 169
nygar Tower, 45, 48
ombe, 152, 153
rn Ridge, 121
rnish Coastal Path, 242, 243, 250,
 261, 264, 272, 277, 280, 281, 282, 286,
 287, 310, 311, 315, 340
rnubian Mountains, 91
rnwall, 15, 18, 19, 20, 25, 229–320,
 341 *see also* Bodmin Moor
untisbury, 43, 70, 71, 74, 75
church, 75
untisbury Cliffs, 19, 70–6
untisbury Hill, 71, 74–5, 80
untry Code, 23
anbrook Castle, 152, 153
ane Ledges, 277
anmere Pool, 21, 106, 110, 113, 115,
 116
omwell's Castle, 324, 328, 330
owcombe, 18, 34, 35, *38*, 39, 41
oyde, 164, 170, 171
oyde Bay, 169, 171
st Combe Water, 110, 112
st Hill, 112, 117

art, River, 149, 185, 188 *see also* East
 Dart River; West Dart River
art Valley, 90
artmeet, 15, 134, 135, 137–8, *139*
artmoor, 12, 15, 18, 19, 20, 21, 25, 87,
 89, 90, 91–162, 335–40
artmoor Military Ranges, 93, 107, 117,
 335–40

Dartmouth, 19, 149, 164, 185–94
 Bayards Cove, 185, 190
 Castle, 188, *192*, 193–4
 Museum, 185, 191
 St Petrox Church, 188, 193
Dead Woman's Ditch, 33
Deadman's Cove, 188
Deancombe, 130
Devil's Armchair, 212
Devil's Bellows, 280
Devil's Bridge, Wales, 87
Devil's Cauldron, 141, 149
Devil's Frying Pan, 281
Devon, 15, 18, 19, 25, 164–204 *see also*
 Dartmoor; Exmoor
Devonport Docks, 203
Dicky's Path, 59
Ding Dong Mine, 294, 296, 303, *304*
Dinger Tor, 120, 124
Doom Bar, 266
Doone, Lorna, 25, 69, 70
Doone Gate Lock, 65
Doone Valley, 19, 42, 44, 63–70
Dorset Coastal Path, 340
Down Tor, 130, *131*
Downhedge Cove, 264
Dowsborough, 32
Doyden Castle, 264
Doyden Point, 264
Dozmary Pool, 205–6, 229, 256
Dragon Line, 124
Drewsteignton, 89, 152, 154, 156
Drift Lane, 112
Drizzle Stream, 129
Drogo Castle, 152, 153–4, *155*
du Maurier, Daphne, 218
Dulverton, 42
Dunkery Beacon, 20, 42, 55–6, *57*, 58,
 62, 89
Dunster, 18, 42, 44–57
 Butter Cross, 45, 49
 Castle, 44, 45, 49–50, 52
 Conygar Tower, 45, 48
 Dovecote, 45, 48–9
 Gallox Bridge, 44, 45, 53, *56*, 57
 King's Hedge, 45, 57
 Mill, 45, 53
 Nunnery, 45, 52
 St George's Church, 45, 52–3
 Yarn Market, 45, 49, *51*
Dyer's Lookout, 172

East Dart River, 107, 110, 138
East Dart Waterfall, 107, 112
East India Company, 191

East Lyn River, 76, 77, 81, 89
Efford Down, 243
Emsworthy Rocks, 105
Epphaven Cove, 264
Erme Plain, 93, 125
Exe, River, 42
Exeter, 59, 144, 229
Exmoor, 12, 18, 19, 20, 25, 33, 42–90
Eylesbarrow Mine, 129, 133

Falmouth, 235, 236, 237
Fingle Bridge, 152, 153
Fisherman's Path, 153
Five Lanes, 218
Foggin Tor, 96, 100
Foreland Point, 70, 71
Forest Courts, 144
Fowey, 341
Fowey, River, 205, 206, 218
Foxworthy, 157
France Wood, 200
Fur Tor, 110, 115, 117

Gallant's Bower fort, 194
Gallox Bridge, 44, 45, 53, *54*, 55
Gallox Hill, 45, 55
Georgeham, 180
Giant's Basin, 129
Gilson's Cove, 264
Gimble Point, 324
Gimble Porth, 324
Glenthorne cliffs, 43, 71
Gommerock, 194
Gonamena, 215
Goonhilly Down, 280
Grabbist Hill, 45
Grade, 280, 284
Granny's Ride, 56, 59
Grant Hill, 35
Great Cheese Rock, 324
Great Hill, 35
Great Kneeset, 110
Great Road, 32
Great Torrington *see* Torrington
Great Western Railway, 101
Grey Wethers Stone Circle, 107, 113

Hallsands, 198, 203–4
Hamel Down, 89–90
Hangingstone Hill, 110, 113
Hangman's Island, 330
Hannicombe Wood, 152
Hartland Abbey, 172, 175, 177
Hartland Point, 171
Hartland Quay, 15, 172, *174*, 175–6

Harland Tor, 107
Harton Chest, 159
Hawk's Tor, 207
Hayle River, 229, 294
Haytor, 18, 101, 102, *104*, 105, 106
Haytor Quarry and Railway, 102, 105–
Helebridge, 243, 248
Helman Tor, 341
Hendon Moor, 171
Hensbarrow, 227
Henwood, 214
High Moor, 218
High Willhays, 21, 93, 117, 120, 124
Hingston Hill, 130, 134
Hisley Bridge, 157, *158*
Hoar Oak Bridge, 77
Hoar Oak Water, 77, 81, 89
Hoccombe Combe, 65
Hodder's Combe, 28, 33
Holne Cross, 138
Holne Moor, 133, 138
Holnicote Estate, 59
Holwell Quarry, 102, 105
Holwell Tor, 102
Horner, 56, 60–1
Horner Hill, 58
Horner Water, 42, 56, 58, 62
Horner Wood, 62
Horseback Zawn, 287
Horsham Steps, 157
Hot Point, 285
Hound Tor, 106
Housel Bay, 282
How cairns, 58, 62
Hunter's Path, 152, 153, 156
Hunter's Tor, 159
Hunt's Tor, 152
Hurlers, 205, 207, 210–1
hut circles, 97, 138, 223, 228

Idless Wood, 15, 19, 231, 240–1, 242
Ilfracombe, 164, 182
Ingra Tor, 101
Inner Froward Point, 188
Isles of Scilly, 15, 18, 25, 91, 321–34
Ivybridge, 90, 341

Jamaica Inn, 205, 217, 218, *219*, 220
Joey's Lane, 125

Kenwyn, 240, 241–2
Kenwyn, River, 237
Kettle Point, 324
Kilcobben Cove, 281, *283*
Kilmar Tor, 20, 207, 212, 214, 224

King Arthur's Bed, 207, 214–5
King Charles's Castle, 324, 328, 330
King Doniert's Stone, 205
King Way, 121
King's Hedge, 45, 55
King's Tor, 94, 96
Kingswear, 188, 190, 194
Kitty Tor, 120, 121
Knowstone, 89
Kynance Cove, 277, 280

Lade Hill Brook, 107
Ladock, 218
Lady's Edge, 28
Lamorna, 316, 319–20
Lamorna Cove, 18, 310, 311, 316, *317*,
    320
Land of the Two Rivers, 164, 177, 180,
    341
Landcross, 180
Land's End, 310
Langstone Downs, 207
Lank Combe, 65, 70
Lankcombe ford, 65
Lanlivery, 341
Lanvit, 341
Lanyon Quoit, 295, 296, 305, *306*
Launceston, 214, 218, 230, 236, 246
Linkinhorne, 211–2
Lints Tor, 120
Lion Rock, 280
Lion's Den, 282
Liskeard and Looe Union Canal, 215
Liskeard-Caradon railway, 215
Little Carracks, 287
Little Kneeset, 110
Little Petherick, 341
Little Quantock Combe, 35
Little Rough Tor, 221
Lizard Downs, 280
Lizard Lighthouse, 285–6
Lizard Point, Cornwall, 20, 277, 282, 284
Lizard Point, Tresco, 324
logan stones, 159, 214, 224, *225*, 299
London Bridge, 100, 101, 105
Long, Faust, 259
Long Ash Brook, 94
Long Rock Slabs, 169
Longstone Hill, 32, 33
Lorna Doone (Blackmore), 62, 63,
    68–70, 90
Louden Hill, 223, 224, *225*
Lower Longbeak, 243
Lundy Hole, 264
Lustleigh, 156, 157, 159, 162, *163*

Lustleigh Cleave, 19, 156–63
Luxulyan, 341
Lyd, River, 141, 144, 148
Lydeard Hill, 41
Lydford, 140, 141, 144–8
    Castle, 141, 144–5, *146*
    Church, 141, 145, 147–8
Lydford Gorge, 15, 140, 141, 148–9
Lye Rock, 251, 261
Lyme Regis, 340
Lyn Flood, 76, 81–2, 89
Lyndale Bridge, 77
Lynhor valley, 206
Lynmouth, 44, 70, 74, 75, 76, 77, 80–1,
    82, 89, 341
Lynton, 75, 80, 81, 182

Madron, 299, 303
Malmsmead, 63, 65, 68
Man of War island, 284
Mapstone Hill, 162
Marhamchurch incline, 243, 246
Marke Valley, 215
Marsh Hill Pass, 110
Marsland Mouth, 340
Marsland Water, 171
Meavy, River, 130
Meldon Pool, 120, 122
Meldon Quarry, 120, *122*
Meldon Reservoir, 117, 120, 121–2
Meldon viaduct, 122, *123*
Men-an-Tol, 15, 229, 295, 296–8
Men Scryfa, 295, 296, 298–9
Mermaid's Rock, 316
Merrivale, 18, 93, 94, 96, 98
Merrivale military range, 335, 340
Merry Maidens Circle, 315, 318–9
Mether Brook, 120
Middlemoor Cross, 221, 223, 226
Middleworth plantation, 130
Minehead, 42, 74, 340
Minions, 206, 210, 215
Moorswater, 215
Moreland Bishop, 89
Moretonhampstead, 112
Morte Point, 164
Morvah, 299, 303
Mosel, 285
Mousehole, 294
Mulfra Quoit, 302
Mussel Point, 287
Myrtleberry Cleave, 80

National Parks, 22, 26, 121 *see also*
    Dartmoor; Exmoor

National Trust, 43, 53, 58, 61, 71, 82, 140, 141, 149, 154, 221, 259, 264, 267, 269, 277, 281, 286, 342
Nether Stowey, 33
New Grimsby, 324, 325, 327, 328, 329, 330
New Polzeath, 261, 264
Newleycombe Lake, 125
Newlyn, 320
Nine Maidens Circle, 296, 302–3
Norden, 212, 224, 255
Norsworthy Bridge, 125
North Devon and Somerset Coastal Path, 70,71, 74, 164, 169, 170, 171, 172, 175, 340
North Devon Water Board, 121
North Hessary Tor, 96, 99, 112
North West Passage pass, 112
Nun's (or Siward's) Cross, *128*, 129, 133, 134
Nutcracker logan stone, 159

O Brook, 137, 138
Oare Church, 63, *64*, 65, 68, 69, 70
Okehampton, 120, 121, 182
Okehampton military range, 335, 336
Old Burrow Hill, 74, 76
Old Grimsby, 324, 327–8, 329
Overflow Pool, 77
Oxen Tor, 80

Padstow, 266, 341
Parish Stone, 296, 299, 302
Parn Voose Cove, 285
Pendour Cove, 287, 291–2
Pengirt Cove, 264
Pentire Point, 20, 229, 261, 264, 266
Pentireglaze Haven, 264, 267
Pentle Bay, 324
Penwith, 18, 25, 229, 286, 294, 308, 310
Pine Haven, 264
Pipers (at the Hurlers), 211
Pipers (at Merry Maidens Circle), 319
Piper's Hole, 324, 328
Pistol Meadow, 277, 284
Pixie Glen, 141, 148
Pixies' Cave, 130, 132
Plym Ford, 129
Plymouth, 99, 100, 130, 189, 203, 223, 227, 329, 340
Polbarrow, 281
Polperro, 15, 269–7
Ponsworthy, 89
Porlock, 58, 59, 75

Port Isaac, 20, 261, 264, *265*, 267, *269*, 271
Port Quin, 261, 264, 267
Postbridge, 21, 106, 107, 112–3
Prestonbury, 153
Princetown, 91, 99, 100, 101, 105, 112
Promontory Slab, 169
Pudleep Gurt, 71
Punchbowl, 62, 87

Quantocks, 18, 19, 25, 26–41
Quarm, River, 42
Quintin's Man, 110

Raven's Tor, 159
Red-a-ven Brook, 120, 122, 124
Restormel Castle, 230
Rill Cove, 280
Rillaton Barrow, 207
Rillaton Cup, 207
River Cove, 287, 294
Robber's Bridge, 70
Roche, 218
Roche Rock chapel, 206
Rocky Valley, 251
Rodd's Bridge, 243
Romans, 76, 89, 229
Rosemodress, 315
Rosemoor Garden, 184
Rough Tor, 20, 214, 220, 221, 223, 224, 228
Round Island, 324
Rowberrow, *57*, 58, 62
Rubble Heap, 102, 105
Rumps, the, 264, 266
Rushy Point, 324

St Blazey, 341
St Breock Downs, 341
St Buryan, 315
St Columb Major, 210
St Loy's Cove, 315
St Mary's, Isle of Scilly, 15, 321, 327, 329, 330–4
St Mary's Church, Oare, 63, *64*, 65, 68, 69, 70
St Materiana's Church, Tintagel, 259, 261
St Nectan's Church, Stoke, 172, 175, 176–7, 257
St Nectan's Glen, 176, 250, 251, 257–9
St Nectan's Kieve, 251, 258
St Petrox Church, Dartmouth, 193
St Piran's Church, 251, 257
St Piran's Well, 251, 257

St Samsons, 341
St Winwalaus' Church, Landewednack, 281
Saint's Way, 341
Salthouse, 243, 247–8
Sandy Hole Pass, 107, 113
Saunton Down, 171
Scarhill Stone Circle, 115
Scattling Zawn, 169
Scilly, Isles of, 15, 18, 25, 91, 321–34
Selworthy, 42
Sharp Tor (Bodmin Moor), 210, 214
Sharp Tor (Dartmoor), 152, 153
Sharpitor, 157, 159
Sheeps Tor, 125, 130, 132–3
Sheepstor, 125, 132–3
Shepherd's Bush Pool, 77
Sheppard's Combe, 28
Shipwreck Cross, 311, 316
Showery Tor, 221
Sir Robert's Chair, 74
Sisters, 251
Siward's Cross see Nun's (or Siward's) Cross
Slab Cove, 168, 169
Slapton, 198, 200, 201–3
    College, 201, 202, 203
Slapton Ley, 19, 195, 198, 200
Slapton Sands, 195, 198, 199, 200
Smallacombe Downs, 215
Smallacombe Rocks, 102, 106
Smith's Cliff, 250
Somerset, 25 see also Exmoor; Quantocks
Sourton Ice Factory, 121, 124
Sourton Tors, 121
South Devon Coastal Path, 185, 188, 198, 340
South Teign River, 110
Spanish Armada, 230, 280, 327
Stannary Courts, 144, 145
Stannon China Clay Works, 223, 226–7, 228
Stannon Stone Circle, 223, 226
Staple plantation, 28
Star Castle, 327, 329, 333
Start Bay, 195, 204
Start Point, 195, 198, 204
Statts House, 110
Stentaway Lane, 170
Stoke Church (St Nectan's), 172, 175, 176–7, 257
Stoke Fleming, 185, 188, 194–5
Stoke Pero, 56, 59, 62
Storm Tower, Compass Point, 243, 249

Stover, 105
Stowe's Hill, 207, 210, 211, 212, 215, 224
Stowe's Pound, 207, 214
Strete Gate, 195, 198
Swannet Combe, 71
Swell Tor, 94, 95, 96, 100, 101

Talland, 273
Tamar, River, 171
Tarka the Otter (Williamson), 164, 177, 180, 182
Tarka Trail, 182, 341
Tarr Steps, 19, 42, 82, 86-9, 137
Tater Du lighthouse, 311, 316
Tavistock, 99, 112, 121, 325
Taw, River, 177, 178
Taw Head, 110
Tea Ledge, 324
Teign, River, 105, 152, 153
Teign Valley, 15, 89, 149–56
Teignmouth, 106
Temple, 218
Thurlibear, 246
Tinners' Way (Coffin Way), 287, 294, 299
Tintagel, 19, 250, 256, 259–61
    Old Post Office, 259, 260
    St Materiana's Church, 259, 261
    see also Tintagel Castle
Tintagel Castle, 230, 250, 254–6
Torcross, 195, 198, 200, 203
Torridge, River, 164, 177, 178, 180, 182
Torrington, 15, 177–84
    Leper Hospital, 180, 182–3
    Waterloo Memorial, 178, 180
Totnes, 144, 200
Treen, 299, 310
Tregaminion, 341
Tregerthen, 287, 292
Tregiffian Barrow, 315, 318
Tregurnow, 315, 316
Tregurnow Cliff, 311
Tregurnow Cross, 316, 318
Trematon Castle, 230
Tresco, 18, 321, 324–30
    Abbey Gardens, 324, 325, 326, 327
    Castles, 324, 328–30
    Grimsbys, 324, 327–8
    Old Blockhouse, 324, 327
    Piper's Hole, 324, 328
Trevethy Quoit, 205
Trewortha Tor, 207, 214
Triscombe Stone, 35, 40
Truro, 15, 19, 207, 218, 231–9, 241, 242, 318

Cathedral, 234, *238*, 239
Tunnel Falls, 141, 148
Twelve Men's Moor, 207, 214
Two Moors Way, 86, 89–90, 341
Tyrwhitt, Thomas, 99, 100
Tywardreath, 341

Ugborough Moor, 90
Upton, 243
Upton Cliffs, 249

Varley Head, 264
Vellacott's Pool, 77
Vinny Combe, 32
Vrogue Rock, 285

Walford's Gibbet, 33
Walkham Valley, 94
Warren Cliff, 172
Warren Down, 172
Warren Tower, 172
Watchet, 68
Watersmeet, 18, 42, 76, 77, 82, *83*
Watersmeet House, 76, 77, 82
Weacombe, 28, *29*
Webber's Post, 58
Week Ford, 134, 135, 137, 138
West Anstey, 89
West Dart River, 135, 137, 138
West Dart valley, 112
West Hill, 35
West Lyn River, 81
West Okemont River, 120, 122
West Okemont valley, 121
West Quantoxhead, 28, 32, 33–4

West Water Stream, 86
Whale Rock, 281
Wheal Fortune Mine, 235
Wheal Jenkin, 215
Wheeler's (Willer's) Stone, 169, 170
Whitchurch Priory, 133
White Gate (County Gate), 74
White Lady Waterfall, 141, 149
Whitehorse Hill, 110
Widdicombe Ley, 198
Widecombe-in-the-Moor, 101
Willapark, 250, 251
Willer's (Wheeler's) Stone, 169, 170
Will's Neck, 35, 40, 41
Willsworthy military range, 335, 336
Wind Hill, 75, 76
Wingate Combe, 71, 74
Winney's Down, 110
Windsford Hill, 87
Witheridge, 89
Withiel, 341
Withypool, 82, 86, 90
Withypool Hill, 90
Woodside Bridge, 77
Woolacombe, 164, *165*, 169

Yar Tor, 135, 137
Yellowmead Down, 132
Yelverton, 101
Yes Tor, 120

Zennor, 20, 286–94, 299
    Church, 287, 292–4
    Wayside Museum, 286, 287, *290*, 291
Zennor Head, 286
Zennor Quoit, 308